T0274923

PUNCHING ABOVE OUR WEIGHT

PUNCHING ABOVE OUR WEIGHT

The Canadian Military at War Since 1867

DAVID A. BORYS

DUNDURN
PRESS

Publisher: Meghan Macdonald | Acquiring editor: Kathryn Lane | Editor: Michael Carroll
Cover designer: Karen Alexiou

Library and Archives Canada Cataloguing in Publication

Title: Punching above our weight : the Canadian military at war since 1867 / David A. Borys.
Other titles: Canadian military at war since 1867
Names: Borys, David A., 1981- author.
Description: Includes bibliographical references and index.
Identifiers: Canadiana (print) 20240378121 | Canadiana (ebook) 2024037813X | ISBN 9781459754126 (hardcover) | ISBN 9781459754133 (PDF) | ISBN 9781459754140 (EPUB)
Subjects: LCSH: Canada. Canadian Armed Forces—History. | LCSH: Canada—History, Military.
Classification: LCC FC226 .B67 2024 | DDC 355.00971—dc23

We acknowledge the support of the Canada Council for the Arts and the Ontario Arts Council for our publishing program. We also acknowledge the financial support of the Government of Ontario, through the Ontario Book Publishing Tax Credit and Ontario Creates, and the Government of Canada.

Printed and bound in Canada.

Dundurn Press
1382 Queen Street East
Toronto, Ontario, Canada M4L 1C9
dundurn.com, @dundurnpress

To Eileen and Robert: find solace in your family and adventure in the continual pursuit of knowledge. Love, Uncle.

CONTENTS

INTRODUCTION

Canada is not a nation of pacifists. It has never been a country that decried war as some unthinkable policy. Yet, for some reason, many Canadians are uncomfortable with the idea that we have been and can be a military people. Some find it surprising that Canada has gone to war many times. Some even find it distasteful that we still commemorate those wars. True, Canada has not participated in war as often as some of our strongest allies, especially our neighbour to the south, yet our history is rife with conflict. Despite that, common misconceptions exist within Canada's public and academic spheres. One of these is that this nation has no discernible military history to speak of. Another is that our military has had no significant impact on our development as a nation. A third is that our military history is easily defined by only a few key events or ideas from the 20th century — Vimy Ridge, the disasters at Hong Kong and Dieppe, the liberation of the Netherlands, peacekeeping, et cetera. And finally, that our military history is simply not important. The fact is that the record of Canada at war is an account of the country itself, and the social, political, and economic developments throughout our history cannot be easily, comfortably, or accurately separated from the military chronicle of this nation.

The history of conflict in the land that came to be known as Canada is, of course, much older than the nation itself. Before Europeans arrived, large

Indigenous confederacies dominated huge tracts of territory coast to coast, competing with one another for trade, resources, and power. When the first Europeans appeared along the east coast, they encountered the powerful Wabanaki Confederacy, which had been formed due to the threat posed by another mighty coalition to its west — the Five Nations Confederacy.

After the first Europeans disembarked on the St. Lawrence River, they found themselves in the middle of a desperate conflict as the Indigenous communities along that river attempted to hold back the growing strength of the Five Nations. For much of the 17th century, this confederacy posed the greatest threat to the French presence along the St. Lawrence. The Europeans who arrived in North America were co-opted into these long-standing conflicts, and the technology these newcomers brought with them was sought after to tip the scales.

As more and more Europeans arrived, the First Nations became caught up in the intruders' dynastic conflicts in North America. Despite the ravaging effects of disease in tipping the power balance toward the European colonizers, the First Nations continued to play a role in all the major clashes on the continent, even as their powerful confederacies declined.

During the 18th century there were six conflicts in the part of North America that would become Canada: three major European dynastic wars (the War of the Spanish Succession, the War of the Austrian Succession, and the Seven Years' War) as well as two localized ones and a war for independence. Battles erupted on land and at sea in the regions that today make up central and eastern Canada. With the end of the War of the Spanish Succession in 1713 and the Treaty of Utrecht, the British gained a foothold in French-controlled Acadia and established the colony of Nova Scotia. Tension persisted in this region as the Acadian population and the powerful Wabanaki Confederacy, led by the Mi'kmaq, resisted British expansion, and brutal frontier violence erupted regularly over the next several decades. The mistrust the British placed in the Acadian population and their perceived menace to British hegemony led to the British deporting them en masse in the early years of the French and Indian War. This event marked a significant moment in the developing Acadian identity as well as in the history of Nova Scotia (and eventually New Brunswick). With the Acadians out of the way by the early 1760s, the British began settling Nova Scotia with English-speaking Protestants, though in the ensuing decades thousands of Acadians returned to the Maritimes.

Along the St. Lawrence River, in the colony of Quebec, the French and Indian War proved equally decisive in altering the human geography of what became Canada. The British were able to inflict a significant defeat upon the French at the Battle of the Plains of Abraham and thus capture the stronghold of Quebec. Despite the French returning the next year and decisively defeating the British in the Battle of St. Foy, Quebec remained in British hands and the Royal Navy ensured it was protected. The British had thus secured their hold on the St. Lawrence River, and when the French and Indian War ended in 1763 (as part of the global Seven Years' War), the French were forced to recognize British suzerainty over almost the entirety of their former North American possessions. Now the British colony of Quebec consisted of a large French-speaking Catholic population governed by a small number of English-speaking Protestants representing the world's most powerful empire.

Yet that formidable empire soon faced a serious reshaping of the North American map when in 1776 American colonials along the eastern seaboard rose in defiance of their British political masters and declared independence. The American Revolution threw the continent once again into war, and the colonies of Quebec, Nova Scotia, Prince Edward Island, and Newfoundland chose the Crown over this new republic. In 1783, the war concluded, and the United States of America was born. War had fashioned the United States, but it also created a new British North America. At first this included the four British colonies along with the vast expanse of territory known as Rupert's Land, but in the aftermath of the American Revolution, thousands of British loyalists fled from the new republic northward. They settled in such large numbers on the east coast that a new colony had to be formed: New Brunswick. By the end of that century, the arrival of so many English-speaking Protestants also led to the splitting of the colony of Quebec into a French-speaking Lower Canada and a new English-speaking Upper Canada. The Canada of 1867 was now taking shape.

In the decades leading up to Canada's formation, warfare remained a reality of North American life. The War of 1812 saw British, First Nations, and both English- and French-speaking colonists defend against repeated invasion attempts by the United States. The successful defence of British North America contributed to an emerging sense of colonial identity in the disparate British colonies as people began to refer to themselves as Nova Scotians,

New Brunswickers, and Canadians. Among the French-speaking *Canadien* population of Lower Canada, some of the key battles of the war proved significant in contributing further to a unique identity that had already been shaped so dramatically by the French colonial experience.

Identity played a key role in the rebellions of 1837 and 1838, particularly in Lower Canada where many, though certainly not all, French Canadians rose against a colonial government ignoring their demands for greater political rights. Conflict and violence ensued in both Canadas. In the years following the rebellions, greater political rights were slowly granted. At the same time, London sought to free itself from much of the financial baggage of governing the domestic affairs of its colonies, and by the mid-19th century, more and more leading colonial figures, backed by Whitehall, debated the possibility of a confederation of the British North American colonies into a single country. While this was certainly a top-down process, meaning one with very little public participation, military conflict played a role in its ultimate result. Beginning in 1866 and into the early 1870s, a radical Irish Republican organization known as the Fenian Brotherhood staged several invasions of the United Canadas, New Brunswick, and the newly formed province of Manitoba.

Punching Above Our Weight picks up the story around the time of Confederation. It touches on the sharp skirmishes with Fenian agitators and then explores the events of the Red River and North-West Resistances. It is during these events that the earliest Canadian military operations were conducted, albeit by a fledgling military against an even more fledgling opponent.

The book then expands on some of the first international military involvements by Canadian soldiers, largely in defence of the British Empire. Canadian voyageurs helped guide a British expedition along the Nile River to relieve the besieged city of Khartoum during the Mahdist War. A decade and a half later, Canadian soldiers were once again on the same continent, this time in South Africa fighting the Boers. Despite the controversial final two years of that war, highlighted by a British-imposed concentration camp system, the Second Boer War contributed to a growing sense of Canadian nationalism — though a largely Anglo one — as a result of celebrated victories at places such as Paardeberg and Leliefontein.

At the conclusion of the Second Boer War in 1902, no one could have foreseen the dramatic transformation the nation would undergo over the next 43 years as a result of two world wars. It was the First World War that tested the fabric of nationhood and the ability for the Canadian military to fight a prolonged and casualty-heavy conflict overseas. While Canadians served in both Britain's Royal Navy and its Royal Flying Corps, it was the soldiers of the Canadian Corps that became the ultimate expression of Canada's war effort. By November 1918, the corps had become an elite fighting formation and had developed a fearsome reputation among its enemies, with its commander, Arthur Currie, considered one of the ablest on the Western Front. Yet this incredible military success, capped off by the tremendously bloody yet successful Hundred Days Campaign, came at a horrific cost in casualties and nearly split the country apart over the issue of conscription. Nonetheless, the First World War was a defining moment in the story of the Canadian nation, helping to propel Canada onto the international stage and toward a redefined sovereignty within the British Empire.

The interwar period proved chaotic for Canada's military. An immediate postwar recession saw violent outbreaks of labour discontent with veterans found on both sides of the battle lines. A brief economic boom was then followed by a traumatic economic collapse. The interwar period thus witnessed dramatic reductions in defence spending, and when war came again the Canadian military was woefully unprepared for the fight to come.

Despite Canada's unpreparedness, the Second World War brought about the apogee of the nation's global military participation. The country's army, air force, and navy expanded to an unbelievable size, peaking at 1.1 million soldiers, sailors, and aircrew, including nearly 51,000 enlisted women. While the Royal Canadian Navy served around the globe, no naval victory was more important than that of the Battle of the Atlantic in which Canada's navy helped secure the vital supply lines to Great Britain. Royal Canadian Air Force personnel (pilots and ground crew) also served with distinction in almost every theatre. Dogfights over the Mediterranean, anti-submarine operations off the coast of Great Britain, flying transportation routes in Burma (today's Myanmar), reconnaissance flights over enemy lines in Northwest Europe — which this author's grandfather participated in — are just some of the areas where Canadian aircrew proved themselves. Most controversially, was the significant role played by the No. 6 Group, RCAF, Canada's largest contribution to the air war, which participated in the merciless bombing campaign of Germany. While two disasters, Hong Kong and Dieppe, marred the Canadian Army's start to the war, by 1945 Canadian infantry had fought its way through Sicily and up the Italian mainland, stormed the beaches of Normandy, and liberated swathes of occupied Northwest Europe.

In the tense environment of the postwar world, the Canadian military maintained the largest peacetime force in the country's history, and it wasn't long before this military faced its first Cold War test. During the Korean War, Canadian pilots fought in the skies of MiG Alley, Canadian naval vessels patrolled up and down the Korean Peninsula, and the Canadian infantry fought off waves of North Korean and Chinese attackers at places such as Kapyong and "The Saddle."

In the aftermath of the Korean War, anxiety over a potential conflict between the United States and the Soviet Union led to Canadian politicians leaning heavily on the United Nations to find ways of preventing localized conflicts from drawing in the superpowers. This ultimately led to Lester B. Pearson's proposal of a U.N. peacekeeping force in the Sinai Desert during the Suez crisis, which, in turn, established the model for interpositionary peacekeeping that the Canadian military and public embraced for much of the rest of the 20th century. Blue-helmeted Canadian peacekeepers served around the world in places such as Haiti, the Congo, Cyprus, the former Yugoslavia, and numerous other war-torn regions.

However, by the 1990s, this "peacekeeping myth" was fractured by a horrific scandal in Somalia and the revelation of a daylong battle between Canadian soldiers and Croatian forces near the town of Medak. What was left of the myth of peacekeeping was completely dismantled when Al-Qaeda executed a series of terrorist attacks on American soil. In the aftermath of 9/11, the Canadian military was once again at war, this time in Afghanistan. While 40,000 Canadians served, and the Canadian military performed its role admirably, the legacy of this conflict is still hotly contested.

Punching Above Our Weight seeks to provide a modern interpretation of Canada's history at war. For those familiar with this subject, the last book to provide such a broad chronological approach was Desmond Morton's excellent *A Military History of Canada*. It was a must-read for any serious student of the subject, but that book is now dated and out of print. It is with great hope that this volume encapsulates the history of Canada at war since 1867 while incorporating much of the new considerable literature that has characterized Canadian military history in the past 20 years. A tall task, indeed, but one that has hopefully been achieved here.

Thus, warfare has been a constant presence in the annals of this country. This is not to say that it is the only major impetus for change — far from it. But the history of war — like the story of politics, economics, gender, labour, culture, technology, society, et cetera — is a vital part of the building blocks that make up the brick wall of the Canadian narrative. To ignore the history of war in this country is to disregard a key part of our past and present.

1

THE EXPANDING NATION

When the Dominion of Canada was formed in July 1867, its constitution, the British North America Act, gave the federal government powers over defence. In May of the next year, this was formulated in the Militia Act, which converted the pre-Confederation militia into an official body known as the Reserve Militia that in theory obligated all fit males between 18 and 60 years of age to serve. By 1869, this force was largely ignored and existed almost exclusively on paper. The Militia Act also created a Volunteer Militia, numbering approximately 40,000, consisting of volunteers who were eligible for 16 paid days of training each year. The country was divided into nine military districts in which these volunteers were recruited and trained as part of district-based militia battalions. There was no professional Canadian standing army at the time, for this the government relied upon the British Army. That became problematic in 1869 when the British government of Prime Minister William Gladstone announced it would be withdrawing most of its troops from Canada, though threats from south of the border delayed this withdrawal.

The Fenian Raids

Between the American Civil War and Canadian Confederation, the Fenian Brotherhood, an Irish Republican organization based in the United States, carried out a series of raids into Canada with the goal of compelling Britain to leave Ireland. In Canada West in June 1866, the Fenians defeated a Canadian force at the Battle of Ridgeway but were eventually forced to withdraw to the United States. In Canada East and New Brunswick, the Fenian forces were chased away with little bloodshed. The Fenian invasions drove home very real concerns about the ability of British North America to defend itself if it remained a collection of separate colonies. Especially in New Brunswick, the Fenian attack at Campobello Island in April 1866 thrust many into the pro-Confederation camp who saw safety in collective security as part of a new nation.

In late May 1870, thousands of Canadian militia were called to the Canadian-American border in Southern Ontario and Quebec as reports came in of Fenian mobilization. It was only in Southern Quebec, however, that Canadian militia were put to the test. The Fenians sought to launch a two-pronged invasion, with

Canadian militia stand over the body of a dead Fenian, slain at the Battle of Eccles Hill, May 1870.

the ultimate objective of capturing the town of St. Jean. One force would cross the frontier at Eccles Hill to the east of the Richelieu River and another would ford where the Trout River entered into Canada to the west of the Richelieu, southwest of present-day Huntingdon, Quebec.

The attack plans were well known by the Canadian authorities by the time the Fenians were on the move. A Canadian spy operated undercover as one of the leading Fenians, and warnings also came from the American authorities, including a U.S. marshal who crossed the border to warn the Canadians of the impending assault. On the morning of May 25, about 200 Fenians entered Canada and were met by a much smaller force of Canadian militia embedded on Eccles Hill. A sporadic firefight ensued, and by the end of the day, the Fenian commander was arrested and the attacking force withdrew in the face of stubborn Canadian resistance.

The western prong consisted of approximately 200 to 300 Fenians who crossed at Trout River in the early morning of May 27. The plan was to enter Canadian territory and then establish a defensive position to await the Canadian militia, which would, of course, be obligated to drive them from the Dominion. A mixture of volunteer Canadian militia and British regulars arrived on the scene and quickly advanced on the Fenian position. The Fenians fired several volleys to little effect and then simply began to melt away. Within 30 minutes, the brief skirmish was over; the Fenian advance had been in Canada for a total of 90 minutes. That evening General George Meade, the commanding officer for the Union Army at the Battle of Gettysburg, arrived in the area with a small force, arrested the remaining Fenian leaders, and made it clear that no more incursions into Canada would be allowed. The Fenian threat to Quebec was over.

In 1871, in an interesting turn of events, a small cavalry of Fenians foolishly attempted to attack across the border in southern Manitoba in support of what they thought was a Métis uprising. The news of this Fenian "invasion" caused immense anxiety within the new province of Manitoba, especially among the English-speaking population, which feared it might trigger an uprising of the Métis. The Fenians did, in fact, have a small number of Métis with them — three members of the extended family of Elzéar Goulet, who lived on the American side of the border near modern-day Pembina, North Dakota. Yet the Métis of Manitoba proved loyal to the new Canadian government. In fact, nearly 200 Métis on horseback gathered at St. Boniface under

Louis Riel, their leader, to ride out to meet the supposed threat. Infamously, for Canadians of the time, Manitoba's lieutenant governor, Arthur Archibald, met Riel there and shook his hand. It was a moment captured by the press and one that caused such a public uproar that Archibald was dismissed from his post.

The Fenian raid on Manitoba was farcical. Most of the Fenians were arrested by the U.S. military before they even got across the border, while the man who organized the raid, William O'Donoghue, was caught by a Métis patrol and delivered promptly to Canadian authorities. There were no further Fenian attacks on Canada.

The Red River Resistance

Canada's first major military operation as a nation stemmed from Ottawa's expansionist dreams and efforts to ensure Canadian control over territory in the West, specifically the Red River Settlement in modern-day Winnipeg. This operation was an expedition across the rough and rugged geography of the Canadian Shield into the Red River Settlement and was followed by a controversial annexation of what became Canada's newest province of Manitoba.

The Red River Settlement was established in the early 19th century and attracted former fur traders and buffalo hunters. It served as an administrative site for governing the economic activities of the Hudson's Bay Company (HBC), which controlled the territory known as Rupert's Land, a vast expanse that covered much of modern-day Canada, including parts of Alberta, Saskatchewan, Manitoba, northern and western Ontario, northern Quebec, and the territories. By mid-century, the Red River Settlement was the largest Western European settlement in British North America before the Rockies. It counted 12,000 souls and had a newspaper; post office; multiple churches; schools; a steamship line connected to Saint Paul, Minnesota; and a network of cart trails and waterways linking it west and east.

In 1870, the population of the Red River area was composed of a heterogeneous mix of francophone and anglophone Métis, a people who had carved out an independent political and cultural identity and had made the Red River basin their home. There were also substantial Cree and Ojibwe, along with newly arrived settlers from Canada and a small number of Americans. The terms of Canadian Confederation, as drawn up in the British North America Act, contained provisions for Ottawa to eventually take control of the HBC-controlled territories of Rupert's Land and the North-West Territories. In July 1868, the British Parliament passed the Rupert's Land Act, which officially transferred the HBC-controlled territories to the British government to eventually be handed over to Ottawa, to be completed in December 1869. The Canadian government agreed to pay the company £300,000 (at the time approximately $1.5 million), though the official transfer of the territories to Canada was delayed due to a concerted resistance effort by many within the Red River Settlement itself.

This resistance stemmed from growing concerns among Red River settlers about what annexation would mean for their continued way of life. Many of those living in the region had serious questions about taxation laws and whether their property rights would be respected under a new Canadian regime. As well, there were serious anxieties over religious and language freedoms among the settlement's French-speaking Catholics, many of whom, though not all, were Métis. Prime Minister John A. Macdonald's first moves only confirmed these fears when government representatives were sent to the Red River Settlement to begin preparing it for annexation by the new Canadian state.

The delegation included William McDougall, who was dispatched to assume the position of lieutenant governor for the new province. McDougall happened to have a reputation for being staunchly anti-Catholic. Furthermore, surveyors preceded McDougall to map the area for a government-sponsored settlement. The problem was that Ottawa had made little to no effort to engage with any of the settlers currently living in the Red River area. Many in the Canadian government saw Red River as an untamed wilderness full of "half-breeds" and "Indians" who would be pushed aside the minute civilization arrived in the form of the Canadian state. Yet the people of Red River grew more and more frustrated with an Ottawa that ignored them. For instance, many only found out about McDougall's appointment through American newspapers.[1] The surveyors arrived almost totally unexpectedly. The inhabitants feared that this was all part of a Canadian scheme to ignore their rights, property, language, customs, and community. With little effort by any in Ottawa to assuage them of these fears, the tension was palpable and the community took action.[2]

One of the leaders to come to the fore during this period was 25-year-old Louis Riel. Born in the Red River Settlement in October 1844 to a Métis father, Louis Riel, Sr., and Julie Lagimodière, Riel lived in a devoutly Catholic household, and as a young man, left for Montreal to become a priest. When his father passed away in 1864, Riel departed the priesthood to find employment and financially support his struggling mother. He found work as a law clerk, then spent time employed in Chicago and Minnesota, finally going back to Red River in the summer of 1868, just as the Rupert's Land Act was passed.

Upon his return, Riel quickly emerged as a leading figure within the community. He was well educated and a strong orator with a good grasp of both constitutional and legal languages. As well, he could speak and write in English and was on good terms with the local religious leadership. As early as August, Riel began a campaign to unite the various factions within the Red River Settlement. While some joined him, others saw Riel as too much of a radical, which hampered efforts to unite all the various Red River groups. Even the "French party," as the francophone Métis were increasingly called, found it difficult to agree on what steps to take in regard to the impending Canadian annexation.

In late September 1869, a Métis council, which included Riel, issued a list of resolutions to the Canadian government. The council expressed its loyalty to the Crown but emphasized to Ottawa that the Métis had been kept in the dark concerning Canadian annexation and demanded their right to be respected by the incoming government. Then, in October, a group of Métis led by a cousin of Riel's stopped the work of a survey team. Over the following days, barricades were erected on roads leading into the settlement and armed patrols were conducted on behalf of a new body calling itself the Métis National Council, with Riel as its secretary.

In November, representatives from the Métis National Council, including Riel, seized the HBC headquarters at Upper Fort Garry, deposing the ineffectual Red River government, the Council of Assiniboia. The seizure of Fort Garry was not only a major political coup but netted Riel and his supporters nearly 400 rifles, ammunition, gunpowder, and most importantly, 13 cannons.

Riel continually sought to achieve a consensus among the various interest groups in the settlement and hoped his new governing authority would reflect that. Riel sought support from the settlement's anglophone population, which

Louis Riel, 1884.

he was able to secure. He also met with various Indigenous leaders who expressed concerns over their rights and privileges as guaranteed by the Crown. Riel even had to deal with a small yet vocal American annexationist group. Nevertheless, he adeptly navigated this complicated political arena, and by the middle of December, a list of rights was agreed upon representing almost all the interested parties except for the American annexationists.[3]

At the same time, Canadians in the settlement who were in favour of Confederation pressured McDougall, currently waiting on the Minnesota side of the 49th parallel, to authorize the raising of a loyalist force to deal with Riel and his followers. This force, numbering 50 men, called itself the No. 1 Winnipeg Company of Volunteers, though this name was as close to professionalism as the unit got. They were a ragtag collection of pro-Canadian annexationists who found themselves outnumbered and outgunned, and despite hefty promises of running Riel out of Red River, surrendered to Red River forces before a shot was ever fired. McDougall and what was left of the "Canadian Party," as it came to be called, withdrew back into Minnesota.

With the successful seizure of Upper Fort Garry and the withdrawal of the Canadian Party, Riel invited delegates from the French and English parishes to join him in formally establishing a Provisional Government that duly elected him as president. This new Provisional Government then drew up terms for Red River's entrance into Confederation and selected three representatives to send as commissioners to Canada.

Meanwhile, the Canadians continued to stir up trouble. Donald Smith, a newly arrived commissioner who had been operating in the settlement clandestinely, had been working hard to break up the fragile union Riel had formed. In February, a young French Métis named Norbert Parisien was killed by a Canadian Party mob that believed Parisien was a spy. Soon after, an armed contingent of Canadians, labelled "rebels" by the Red River press, set out to arrest the Provisional Government and free the captured Canadian prisoners. Despite learning that these prisoners had already been released, this contingent chose to still march past Fort Garry in a show of force. They were met by a well-armed, mounted group of Métis and forced to surrender. In fact, this Canadian force was so poorly armed that some of the men only carried lead-weighted cudgels as weapons.

Regardless, Riel wanted an example made of these men. Their commander, Captain Charles Boulton, was tried, found guilty, and received a death sentence, but Riel commuted it, giving in to pressure from the Canadian representatives in the settlement and others within Riel's own government. However, one of the surveyor-turned-soldiers received no such commutation — his name was Thomas Scott. Considered a troublemaker by nearly everyone who encountered him, Scott had served with the Winnipeg Company of Volunteers, was captured, and escaped, only to once again find himself a prisoner of the Provisional Government. Scott was found guilty of insubordination and armed revolt, and on March 4 was executed. This proved to be a major mistake for Riel.[4]

The Red River commissioners arrived in Ottawa in April to begin negotiations at the same time as the news of Scott's execution reached the Canadian capital, posing a serious challenge for the delegation. Those advocating annexation without negotiation used Scott's execution to fan the flames of anti-Catholic and anti-French sentiment throughout Ontario. Public speeches by leaders of the Protestant Orange Order, sympathetic newspaper articles, political speeches, and public rallies and discussions in taverns and streets favoured a heavy government reaction. More and more voices in English Canada clamoured for the Canadian government to respond.[5]

While the Canadian government listened to the various demands of the Red River representatives, it was already taking steps to bring the crisis to a conclusion. On May 12, Ottawa passed the Manitoba Act, officially incorporating the Red River region into Canada as the Province of Manitoba. Interestingly, much of the demands of the Red River representatives were written into the act. Despite the furor over Scott's execution, the negotiations were seen as a success. Yet on the same day the government passed the Manitoba Act, it also authorized a military expedition to travel to the newest province to enforce the government's peace. Canada's first official military operation was about to begin.

The man chosen to lead the Red River Expedition was Garnet Wolseley. Born in Dublin, Ireland, in 1833 to a prominent Anglo-Irish family, Wolseley joined the British Army at 18 and served in Burma, Crimea, India, and Africa, even spending a brief period in the United States "observing" the American Civil War. In fact, he met Confederate generals Robert E. Lee, James Longstreet, and Stonewall Jackson. In 1870, Wolseley was a full colonel and deputy quartermaster general for Canada, effectively responsible for military supplies.

Wolseley was tasked with leading a contingent of just over 1,000 men and four seven-pounder guns (weighing about 250 pounds each) over 1,240 miles from Toronto to the Red River Settlement. The expeditionary force was a mix of British regulars and volunteer Canadian militia. Two hundred and fifty British regulars from the 60th Regiment of Foot were joined by a smattering of soldiers from the Army Hospital Corps, Army Service Corps, and Royal Artillery. These were supported by units from Ontario and Quebec identified as the Ontario Rifles and Quebec Rifles respectively.

The primary challenge to the whole operation was transportation. There was little road and no rail infrastructure for most of the journey to Red River. Once the expedition left Collingwood in Southern Ontario, it had to rely on waterways, canals, rivers, lakes, and hastily constructed corduroy roads to traverse the wilderness. In the country west of Lake Superior, the expedition would be joined by voyageurs to help navigate the waterways. These auxiliaries, mostly Indigenous, were essential for the survival of the expedition and on numerous occasions saved the men from disaster. On May 21, the leading detachment of the expeditionary force set out from Collingwood by steamer.

The first major obstacle met by the expedition were the Americans. The fastest route from Southern Ontario to the Red River Settlement was through the United States. A far better road-and-rail system existed there, and on the Great Lakes a key American canal connected Lake Superior to Lake Huron. Yet using U.S. transportation networks proved problematic. The United States was still upset with the British over their perceived Confederate sympathies during the American Civil War, and Wolseley himself was reported

Sir Garnet Wolseley, circa late 1880s.

to have been quite friendly with the leading Rebel generals. Thus, when the expedition arrived at the St. Marys River (at the modern-day city of Sault Ste. Marie, Michigan), it was prevented from using the American-operated canal connecting Lake Huron to Lake Superior, despite Canadian claims that these soldiers were on an "errand of peace." To overcome this issue, Wolseley ordered the ships unloaded and the entirety of their supplies carried across land to the Canadian side of Lake Superior. The steamers were then able to pass through the canal, since their captains could now claim they no longer carried any soldiers or military *matériel*, and once through were able to pick up the men and all their supplies waiting bemusedly on the shore.

The going only became more difficult when the expedition arrived at Prince Arthur's Landing on the western shore of Lake Superior. Prince Arthur's Landing (today's Thunder Bay) was a small community still reeling from a massive forest fire that had ripped through the village prior to the expedition's arrival. Wolseley and his men set up camp in a charred and blackened landscape, the peat moss still smoking, and many soldiers wrote home lamenting the depressing scenery surrounding them. The major problem, however, was that there were only small sections of usable road heading westward. By late June, many of Wolseley's men were working as construction crews, hacking roads out of the smouldering wilderness, while others continued to scout for faster ways to move west. Wolseley also ordered that a large depot of supplies and ammunition and a hospital be established at Prince Arthur's Landing in case the expedition was forced to fall back with casualties. A company of militia and two of the cannons were left to guard this position while the expedition continued on its way.

The stretch from Prince Arthur's Landing to the Red River Settlement became one of the most arduous and difficult logistical campaigns in Canadian military history. With dense forest and limited road networks, much of the journey was conducted via a convoluted rivers-and-lakes system that posed immense challenges to Wolseley and his men. The expedition utilized flat-bottomed boats, 30 feet in length, similar in construction to pinnaces used in the Royal Navy. Each boat carried eight or nine soldiers, provisions, and supplies for 60 days of travel, along with two or three civilian auxiliaries hired as pilots and guides.

When rapids, waterfalls, or impassable stretches were encountered, Wolseley's men were forced to portage. The boats were brought up to shore and the supplies unloaded. The men then carried the supplies until a new stretch of navigable water could be reached. The boats were transported overland by placing the keels on logs and rolling the boats forward. Time and time again, this gruelling task was accomplished, frequently overcoming steep inclines as high as 100 feet. By the end of June, it was not uncommon to see soldiers carrying upward of £400 worth of supplies on their backs via a method borrowed from their Indigenous guides — a strap wrapped around the forehead allowing for the weight to be distributed evenly along the back and neck. Spontaneous competitions erupted between the men to see who could carry the heaviest load, and while the going was difficult, the work demanding, and the mosquitoes plenty, the morale of the troops remained surprisingly high.[6]

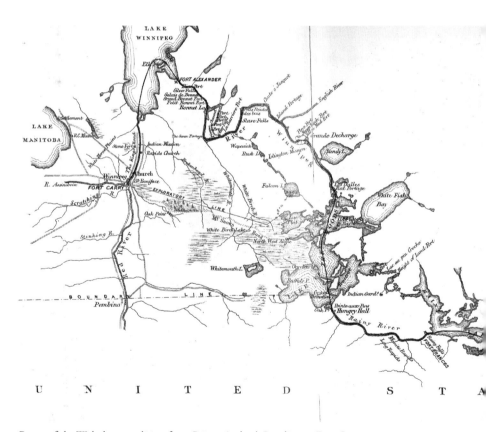

Route of the Wolseley expedition from Prince Arthur's Landing to Fort Garry.

As the expedition moved westward from Prince Arthur's Landing, it stretched to over 186 miles in length. The vanguard established temporary supply dumps, scouted forward routes, and sometimes engaged in constructing passable roadways while the rest of the column followed in time. The daily routine saw the men awake just before sunrise and in their boats as daylight illuminated the undulating patterns of the Canadian Shield. They breakfasted for one hour at 8:00 a.m., took another one-hour break at 1:00 p.m., and the day came to an end sometime around 6:00 or 7:00 p.m. Every day, for weeks on end, this pattern was repeated as the expedition carved its way methodically through the dense and unforgiving wilderness.

The men became experts at rapidly taking down their tents, packing up their supplies, and loading the equipment into the boats to get as much

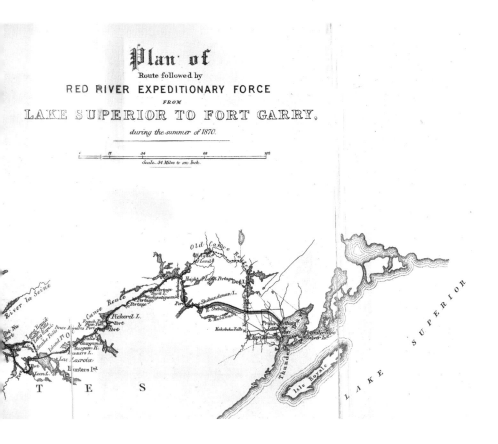

daylight as possible, then doing the opposite as quickly as possible in the evening to maximize rest time. By August 4, the leading men of the expedition arrived at Fort Frances, just west of Rainy Lake. Along this route, they began to regularly encounter Anishinaabe families engaged in fishing and passed by a series of small villages. From Fort Frances, the column headed west along the Rainy River where it finally arrived at the southern end of Lake of the Woods. Here the expedition turned northward, rowing into the wild and dangerous Winnipeg River, which took the men on a harrowing journey to Fort Alexander at the mouth of Lake Winnipeg, home to the Sagkeeng First Nation.

By mid-August, Wolseley received word from loyalist settlers that all haste had to be made as Riel continued to build up his defences — reports that proved false. Wolseley thus decided to push ahead accompanied by the 60th Regiment of Foot and two cannons, leaving the rest of the expedition to catch up. On the morning of August 24, Wolseley and his vanguard disembarked from the Red River to travel the final few miles via land. At this point, it was still unknown whether they were going to meet any resistance. Seven hundred yards from the fort not a soul stirred, no flag flew, the gates were closed, and yet the guns of Upper Fort Garry could be seen mounted on the walls. The men expected enemy fire to erupt any minute as they approached the outer bastions. Yet, as they came closer, it became clear that Riel and his supporters had fled, most of them to the U.S. Wolseley thus took possession of the fort in what he saw as a bloodless victory, disappointed not to have had the chance to engage Riel and his followers in open battle.

By the end of August, the entire expedition was in the Red River Settlement. While some welcomed the Canadian contingent, others bristled at what was perceived as an unnecessary occupation. When the British regulars left in September, law and order broke down as some of the Canadian militia who remained began to terrorize the local population, particularly the Métis. Wolseley, for his part, was unable to effectively control his men. Fights broke out frequently, and many from the pro-Canadian contingent carried out acts of revenge against Riel's supporters.[7] Four men were killed, including Elzéar Goulet, one of Riel's top lieutenants, who was chased into a river by a mob where he drowned. Riel's cousin, André Nault, was beaten and left for dead. A Catholic priest was shot at, and the editor of the local newspaper was attacked. There were even unconfirmed reports of sexual assault against women in the settlement. Many within the community referred to this period as the "Reign of Terror." Despite the controversial nature of this occupation, Canada's first military operation had officially come to an end and Manitoba was now a province of Canada.

In the aftermath of the Red River Resistance, Riel and most of his followers were seen as rebels, traitors, and murderers by most of English Canada, while French Canada was far more sympathetic. Riel, in particular, was seen by many as a defender of both French-language and Catholic rights. Regardless, Riel was forced to flee to the United States, where he was eventually granted a general amnesty by the Canadian government with the condition of a five-year exile. Despite the troublesome occupation, the soldiers who participated in the Wolseley expedition were celebrated as heroes throughout English Canada, and many of them settled in the new province.

Looming over Ottawa during the Red River crisis was anxiety over an expansionist United States. Canada's ability to deliver a military force into the West and impose order was certainly about ensuring Manitoba's entry into the country, but it was also about sending a message to the Americans.[8] The successful completion of the Wolseley expedition made it clear to any Americans still clamouring for full continental control — U.S. Manifest Destiny — that the West was Canadian territory and Canada was willing to use force to ensure it remained that way. This, of course, ignored the fact that a Canadian military made up primarily of poorly trained and badly equipped militia would have struggled to defend itself against an invading American army.

Any serious possibility of war with the Americans, however, was averted with the signing of the Treaty of Washington in May 1871 between Great Britain and the United States. This treaty soothed American grievances over Great Britain's actions during the U.S. Civil War, and most importantly for Ottawa, normalized relations between Canada and the United States.

With the American threat diminished by the Treaty of Washington, almost all British soldiers were withdrawn from Canada so that by 1872 what remained were small garrisons at Esquimalt and Halifax. The Canadian military was slightly reorganized with new designations. The Permanent Active Militia, or the Permanent Force, was the closest equivalent Canada had to a standing army, though it was still a volunteer-based militia, just with more extensive training. The much larger Non-Permanent Active Militia, or the Non-Permanent Militia, was made up of part-time soldiers who generally trained one weekend a month. Added to this was the North-West Mounted Police (NWMP) created in 1873. This was a paramilitary police force designed to enforce government policy in the West while ensuring that tensions between settlers and First Nations did not escalate into an "Indian war."

Defence spending by Ottawa was limited in these early years. There was a general lack of public support for the military despite the celebrated success of the Wolseley expedition, as well as an economic depression that rocked the country in the 1870s. Defence budgets continually fell, hitting a low of $650,000 in 1876, well below the million-dollar mark deemed necessary for appropriate upkeep. One notable addition to Canada's military infrastructure, however, was the founding of the Royal Military College in Kingston, Ontario, in 1876. Staffed mostly by British officers, many of the college's most promising graduates went on to careers in the British Army as opposed to the much smaller and underfunded Canadian active militia. Canada's defence was simply a low priority for the Canadian government during these lean financial years. This was made particularly clear to the British when in 1878 Britain seemed on the brink of war with Russia. Canada was asked to spend $250,000 to upgrade its coastal defences, yet the Liberal government of Alexander Mackenzie authorized a paltry $10,000.

The militia was still spoken of with pride by Canadian political and military leaders. But while 40,000 active militia members on paper and another 620,000 in reserve looked impressive, the reality was that Canada's army was badly managed, under-equipped, and poorly trained.[9] Most Non-Permanent Militia regiments relied on the philanthropic nature of wealthy benefactors to ensure they had the necessary equipment and clothing. Urban regiments often had newer uniforms and better equipment than their poorer rural counterparts. For both rural and urban regiments, however, officers were often appointed based on their political connections regardless of skill or suitability for the position. Training primarily consisted of a 12-day summer camp, often the highlight of that year's social calendar. During this 12-day period, the men lived in tents, participated in daily marches, underwent weapons training, and then engaged in a mock battle to close out the camp, afterward descending en masse to the nearest tavern, much to the chagrin of local townsfolk. Besides this, most regiments attempted to meet for a few days every month to continue training, but these were haphazard, with some holding regular, well-attended monthly sessions and others meeting only occasionally.

By the early 1880s, the economic depression had faded, and John A. Macdonald's returning Conservative government increased defence spending to the magic $1 million mark. New Non-Permanent Militia regiments were authorized from the growing Prairie population, while new training centres were established and older ones improved. In this spirit of affluence, the 1883 Militia Act authorized the creation of a small Permanent Force of cavalry, artillery, and infantry. A professional standing army in Canada was now taking shape, and confidence in it was high when conflict erupted in the North-West Territories in 1885.

The North-West Resistance

The annexation of Rupert's Land and the North-West Territories was an important step in Ottawa's plans to open the West to settlement. Yet similar tensions to those that existed in the Red River basin reared their heads in the North-West Territories district known as Saskatchewan, along the southern branch of the Saskatchewan River.

While the Manitoba Act legislated respect for Métis property rights and even laid aside land for Métis descendants, the flood of immigrants into the province after 1870 pushed many disaffected Métis off their traditional land and sent them farther west into what is today the province of Saskatchewan. By the late 1870s, various Métis leaders, including Louis Riel's future right-hand man, Gabriel Dumont, were writing letters to the federal government requesting that it implement policy clarifying recognition of Métis land grants within the newly settled territory along the South Saskatchewan River, primarily in the parish of St. Laurent centred around the village of Batoche, which had become the unofficial centre of the Métis community. By the early 1880s, the demands for land recognition grew louder and became blended with a greater call for French representation in local government and support for French-language schooling. It seemed that 1869 was repeating itself all over again. A government intent on preparing the region for more white

settlement appeared to be generally disregarding the rights of current oc-
cupants on the land. Frustration with the federal government's inadequate
response to repeated requests to address the land issue led a delegation of
Métis to seek out Riel.

The Riel that the delegation found in Montana in 1884 was quite a different man than the one who had led the Red River Resistance. After fleeing
Manitoba in 1870, Riel was voted into the House of Commons as a Member
of Parliament but was prevented by the federal government from taking his
seat. He continually petitioned Ottawa for an amnesty, and in early 1875,
finally received it on the condition that he live outside Canada for five years.
That same year, Riel had a religious epiphany, which his friends attributed to
a mental breakdown, and was shuttled into an insane asylum in Quebec for
nearly two years. When he was released in 1878, he returned to the United
States where he settled down, married, had children, and prepared to live the
rest of his life as a devout Catholic and modest schoolteacher in Montana. In
1884, however, fate came calling. Riel was convinced to return to Canada to
lead the Métis once again to challenge the federal government's expansionist
policies. As Riel was to discover, Canada's response would be far stronger
than that of 1870.

No. 6 Company Victoria Rifles of Canada, 1889.

While Riel had the support of much of the French-speaking Métis in the Saskatchewan region, he struggled to gather wide-scale support from the English-speaking community. Furthermore, he only found a small number of individual supporters among the Cree and Blackfoot, not nearly as many as he had anticipated or hoped for. This was surprising to him. By the early 1870s, the buffalo, a crucial source of food, had been hunted to near-extinction, which led to widespread starvation among many of the Prairie First Nations. With their people starving, many leaders agreed to permanently settle on small chunks of their traditional territory in exchange for government support, primarily in the form of food and equipment for sedentary farming.

In 1876, this reserve system was codified in the Indian Act, which designated First Nations as wards of the state and effectively governed how they were to be looked after on said reserves through government representatives known as "Indian agents." The problem was that the government continually failed to meet its obligations. Whether it was corrupt Indian agents, a lack of government funds, or politicians who simply did not care, most Indigenous people found their lives became more difficult on reserves as promises of food, supplies, equipment, and training were rarely if ever provided. Indigenous peoples were abandoned by the Canadian government and left to starve on small plots of their once-large traditional territories.[10] By the early 1880s, frustration with the government reached a boiling point. Despite this, most Chiefs would not declare support for the Métis, while a number openly professed their continued loyalty to the Crown. Many were, in fact, suspicious of Riel and concerned that his actions would undermine ongoing Indigenous efforts to secure the aid promised by the Canadian government.

Riel's intention was not open rebellion. In fact, there was significant hope that he could negotiate with the Canadian government as he had in 1869. In December 1884, a petition was sent to Ottawa. Some of the key concerns expressed in this petition were increased rations for Indigenous people, land to be guaranteed for the Métis, recognition of the rights of established settlers (both titled and untitled), and a reduction in the price of government land for settlers seeking to expand their current holdings. Finally, this petition requested that representatives be allowed to go to Ottawa to negotiate terms for the region's inhabitants, with a potential view to gaining provincial status. While the petition was received by Macdonald's government and confirmed by the undersecretary of state, no formal response was ever received.[11] As a result of the failure by the government to respond, in early March 1885, Riel formed a provisional government. Even then, Riel hoped the provisional government would be enough to induce Ottawa to negotiate.[12] He was wrong.

The first action of the conflict in the North-West Territories broke out at Duck Lake on March 26.[13] Word had gotten to Riel that a mixed force of Canadian militia and the NWMP had ridden out from Fort Carlton, about 28 miles west of Batoche, with the intention of preventing a cache of weapons from falling into the hands of Riel's supporters. Gabriel Dumont, Riel's military commander, dispatched a force of 30 Métis led by his brother, Isidore, with orders to intercept this column. Isidore Dumont was under strict orders not to open fire. When the Canadian force of almost 100 men approached Isidore Dumont's skirmish lines at Duck Lake, a parley between the two leaders turned into a scuffle. One of the interpreters for the NWMP then pulled out his revolver and opened fire, killing Isidore and mortally wounding an unarmed Cree Elder attempting to defuse the situation. The two sides then erupted into a Wild West shootout, with the excellent marksman skills of the Métis winning the day. The Canadian force retreated; first blood had been spilled.

Word of Duck Lake spread, leading to a small number of younger First Nations warriors joining Riel's forces. Yet the majority of First Nations remained neutral, and many Indigenous leaders continued their peaceful diplomatic efforts to secure food. Unfortunately, one of these attempts went awry. Days after Duck Lake, a starving group of Cree men, women, and children from three different nations descended on the settlement of Battleford. They came to reaffirm their loyalty to the Crown while hoping to receive desperately needed food supplies from government stores. Panicked by what they thought was a massive war party, the nearly 500 settlers withdrew into the walls of the local NWMP barracks. Despite a messenger being sent ahead declaring the peaceful intentions of the arriving Cree, the community saw this group as hostile and no one in the fort would go out to meet the Cree leaders. With the town empty and the Cree people starving and desperate, the Chiefs lost control over their people, who began to loot the abandoned town before fleeing back to their reserves.[14]

Things turned far more violent at Frog Lake on April 2 when a Cree war party led by Wandering Spirit killed a particularly cruel and corrupt Indian agent along with eight other settlers, including two priests, while taking three hostages, including two women who had just witnessed their

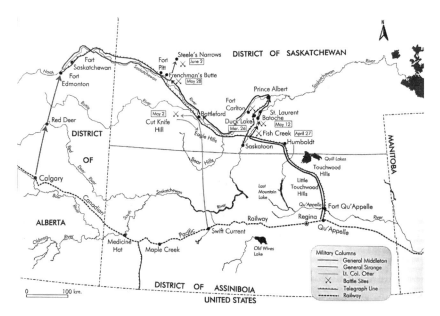

Major actions of the North-West Resistance.

husbands being shot and killed.[15] The war party then moved on to Fort Pitt where the small garrison of mounted police abandoned its post (the commander scandalized over this controversial retreat was Francis Dickens, son of famed author Charles Dickens). The supplies and weapons at Fort Pitt were seized by the war party and the unprotected civilians taken hostage. These events, particularly the Frog Lake Massacre as it became known in the English press, unjustly cast all Prairie First Nations as sympathetic to Riel if not outright allied to his cause. The fact that most of the nations remained on their reserves was of little concern to the Canadian government or the English-speaking press, which now spoke of a "Métis-Indian uprising."

Back in Ottawa, news of open violence led the government to immediately mobilize a large military response that included members of the Permanent Force as well as a large contingent of Volunteer Militia. Thousands of enthusiastic volunteers in Montreal, Quebec City, Toronto, Halifax, and throughout the Prairies rushed to join local militia regiments. Within days, two Ontario regiments, the Queen's Own Rifles and the 10th Royal Grenadiers, and two Quebec regiments, the 9th Voltigeurs of Quebec and the 65th Carabiniers of

Montreal, along with Canada's two Permanent Force artillery batteries, were travelling on the newly constructed Canadian Pacific Railway line westward into the heart of the rebellion. Despite claims made by the railway, the line was not fully completed yet and a long march lay ahead for the men. The detachment from Canada would join formations already mobilizing in the West, including the NWMP, a smattering of militia from Winnipeg and the Prairies, and cowboys-turned-light-cavalry from the District of Alberta. Most of the militia regiments sent were selected based on the political loyalty of their officers to the ruling Conservative government, not for any recognition of skill or experience. While some of the men had participated in regular monthly training sessions, others had barely ever fired their weapons. Equipping the men also posed issues in the first few days, since uniforms, weapons, and kit in all states of repair were handed out to the men.

The man chosen to lead the entire Canadian contingent was 59-year-old Frederick Middleton, a British major-general who, like Garnet Wolseley, was born in Ireland to a prominent Anglo-Irish family. He joined the British Army at 17 after attending the Royal Military College at Sandhurst and went on to serve in New Zealand during the Māori wars and in India during the Indian Mutiny. His service led to him being appointed the commandant of the military college at Sandhurst and then in 1884 he was given the position of general officer commanding the militia of Canada and thus was the top military man in the country when conflict broke out in 1885. At its peak, Middleton's force numbered 6,000 men, though the fighting would be over before the majority of them got close to the front.

While Middleton's initial plan was to concentrate all his forces and descend on Batoche, there was great fear among the white settler population in the region that a First Nations uprising was in the making. Pressured to defend a scared and scattered settler population, Middleton chose to divide his force into three columns, one to capture Batoche and the others to provide protection for the settlers. One column, under the command of Major-General Thomas Bland Strange, a retired British artillery officer, marched northward from Calgary to Edmonton and then eastward along the North Saskatchewan River into the District of Saskatchewan to engage the Cree who had attacked Frog Lake and Fort Pitt. The middle column under Canadian-born William Otter, a lieutenant-colonel and veteran of the Fenian invasions, drove northward from Swift Current toward Fort Battleford. General

Middleton commanded the largest column, which travelled north from Fort Qu'Appelle on a 200-mile trek to Batoche.

At Fish Creek on April 24, Middleton's force, numbering approximately 900 men, stumbled into a Métis ambush led by Gabriel Dumont. The Métis had set up in a coulee along the South Saskatchewan River with a smaller force on horseback hidden in nearby woods. When Middleton's force triggered the ambush, the battle turned into chaos. Despite Middleton outnumbering Dumont and even being able to bring up artillery, the Métis were protected in the coulee, and every time Middleton's force attacked, his soldiers were silhouetted against the prairie sky, becoming easy targets for the sharpshooting Métis.

Dumont's force had established a strong defensive position despite it being the low ground, and the Canadians could not dislodge them. Nonetheless, small groups of them began to quietly retreat as ammunition and water ran low and the Canadian attacks continued. Dumont himself ran the length of the battlefield multiple times, trying to maintain the cohesion of his lines. The tide of the battle turned, however, when Dumont and a small group of his men were able to get behind Middleton's position where they proceeded to fire from the cover of a small copse of trees. The Canadian soldiers now thought themselves surrounded and started to fall back. Middleton, believing

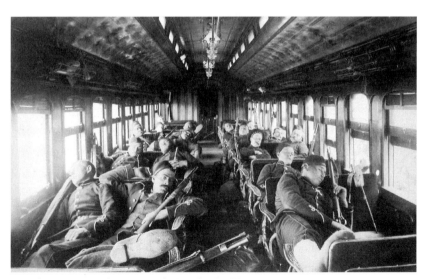

Canadian troops on their way to the North-West Territories, 1885.

the Métis position too strong for continued frontal attacks, eventually ordered the withdrawal.

As Middleton regrouped and licked his wounds, Lieutenant-Colonel Otter stumbled into a military defeat at Cut Knife Hill in a battle that never needed to happen. In the aftermath of the looting of Battleford, the Cree and Assiniboine who had taken part sought refuge on Chief Poundmaker's reserve near Cut Knife Hill, a natural defensive position named after a historic Cree victory. As news of violence spread throughout the region, more Indigenous people came to join the Cut Knife camp until it numbered more than 1,000 men, women, and children. Many were concerned that the Canadian forces would conduct a punitive campaign in response to the events at Battleford and Frog Lake and thus sought security in numbers. Riel seized this opportunity and sent agents into the Cut Knife camp to spur them into joining him but with little success. Poundmaker, though only nominally in charge of this growing band, was still able to exert some influence over his younger warriors and prevent the growing camp from joining Riel.

Meanwhile, as Riel's agents struggled to gain converts from the Cut Knife camp, Otter arrived at Fort Battleford with a force of 500 men. He had explicit orders from Middleton to defend the fort against possible attack. However, Otter was not content to sit by and wait. He sought to deliver himself a victory and requested permission to go on the offensive. Middleton denied this request, but Otter went anyway. He set out with a flying column of 325 men to engage Chief Poundmaker's force, hoping to swoop down and surprise the Cut Knife encampment. But on the evening of May 1, Otter's force was spotted and light skirmishing erupted.

Otter was in over his head. The next day, he brought up two cannons and a Gatling gun and opened fire on the village. While women and children ran from the battle, the warriors returned fire from hidden positions along the river. For six hours, battle raged as Cree and Assiniboine warriors, led primarily by War Chief Fine Day, slowly encircled Otter's men. Despite Otter having a significant advantage in both numbers and firepower, the natural cover utilized by the Cree-Assiniboine warriors rendered these advantages useless. Eventually, Otter realized the precariousness of his position and was forced to call for a full retreat. At this point, many of the warriors prepared to give chase on horseback when Poundmaker, who up till then had played little to no role in the battle,

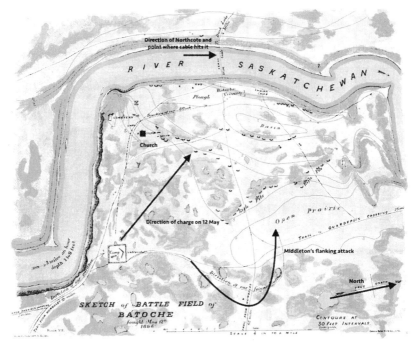

Battle of Batoche, May 9–12, 1885.

intervened. By preventing the warriors from moving out, he no doubt saved Canadian lives that day.[16]

Despite his losses, Middleton had always stressed that the focus of the campaign should be on the Métis headquarters at Batoche where Riel, Dumont, and 250 followers were preparing for a climactic battle. Middleton understood that if he could inflict a decisive defeat there, he might capture the leaders and bring a swift end to the conflict. After the experience at Fish Creek, Middleton was aware that he would once again find himself up against a well-fortified enemy. Under Dumont's supervision, the rebels had built a series of interconnected rifle pits dug in concentric circles along a ridgeline surrounding the village. These were well camouflaged and manned by excellent marksmen, though with limited ammunition. Middleton devised a plan whereby he would avoid throwing his men at these dug-in positions as he had at Fish Creek. Instead, he would send a steamship loaded with 50 soldiers and artillery up the Saskatchewan River. The plan was for the ship to land in the rear of the Métis defences, just north of the village, while the main body would attack from the south. Caught in this pincer movement, Middleton hoped the Métis would be forced to capitulate. Things did not go as planned, though.

On the morning of May 9, Middleton's steamer, the *Northcote*, began its journey up the Saskatchewan River. It was spotted before Middleton's southern attack could commence. The ship was thus exposed, and while Métis small-arms fire did little damage, it was finally incapacitated when Dumont ordered a ferry cable stretched across the river, cutting through its smokestack and masts. It now had no way to steer and was at the mercy of the river's current. Unknown to Middleton, by the time he launched his ground attack, the *Northcote* had become lodged on a sandbar where it remained for the rest of the battle.

Meanwhile, Middleton's first wave attacked the dug-in rebels. The camouflaged rifle pits posed problems for the Canadian soldiers, who for the most part were simply guessing where to shoot. Rebel bullets smacked all around the Canadians as Middleton used all of his arsenal, which included artillery and a Gatling gun crewed by members of the Connecticut National Guard. Despite the Canadians' advantage in firepower, Riel's defences held firm. Yet Riel's men were unable to launch any serious attack against the Canadian lines, nor could the Canadian soldiers seem to make any headway against enemy positions. Elie Dumont, Gabriel's nephew, led a group of Métis on a flanking attempt using a brush fire as cover. This manoeuvre was beaten back while the fire spread, nearly threatening Middleton's camp. The battlefield became covered in smoke, fire, and bodies. By 3:00 p.m., Middleton ordered his men to retreat to a constructed zareba for the night.

For the next two days, the Canadians probed for weaknesses in the Métis line. Small groups attempted to outflank the enemy, while Middleton's cannons and Gatling gun blanketed the battlefield with incessant fire. At the end of the day on May 11, Middleton was informed by two disaffected priests who had crossed over from the Métis lines that the defenders were close to breaking and short on ammunition. Riflemen could be spotted leaving their rifle pits, hunting among the brush in search of bullets dropped by Canadian soldiers. Others were forced to simply fire rocks or nails. What Middleton did not know was how fatigued the rebels were. A number were dead or wounded, and only 50 or so could mount any effective defence. Middleton, meanwhile, could still call on roughly 800 soldiers.

Matters came to a head on May 12 when Middleton decided to launch a final assault. He would personally lead a flanking attack against the rebels from the east, followed shortly after by an attack from the main body from the south-southwest. Confusion, however, plagued the operation. The officer in charge of the main body never heard the signal to commence the attack, and Middleton's smaller group threw itself against the rifle pits to no avail. Middleton retreated to his headquarters, screaming at his subordinates before retiring to lunch. Unknown to the British general, his flanking attack had succeeded in one way: it had drawn rebel defenders to the eastern side of the ridge. The main line of defence facing south-southwest was now significantly weakened. While Middleton was eating his lunch, several Canadian officers chose to take the initiative and without orders launched a charge against the depleted enemy lines. As Middleton was mid-bite, he heard the bugle call and roar of his men, quickly supported by the artillery and Gatling gun. This final charge broke the enemy who were short on ammunition, low on water, and exhausted. They scampered from their rifle pits back into the village of Batoche, and after a short flurry of house-to-house fighting, they surrendered. The Battle of Batoche was over by early afternoon. Three days later, despite Dumont and others successfully escaping to the United States, Riel surrendered to the authorities.

The fighting was not quite done yet. General Strange's column coming in from the District of Alberta engaged Wandering Spirit's war party at Frenchman's Butte on May 28. Much like the situation at Cut Knife Hill, the Cree at Frenchman's Butte refused to join Riel at Batoche. Yet, like Otter, Strange was dead set on attacking, and only when a fight seemed unavoidable did the Cree dig a series of defensive rifle pits into a hillside to provide cover and protect the women and children travelling with them. When Strange attacked, his men were beaten back, and despite his nine-pounder cannon inflicting some damage, Wandering Spirit had chosen an excellent defensive position. Strange, wanting to avoid a "Custer," was forced to retreat. A few days later there was another attack against Wandering Spirit's war party as it fled northward. His group by this time was much diminished through desertion, hunger, and cold but once again found itself in a defensive struggle. This final attack was led by NWMP officer Sam Steele as the Cree retreated across the narrows of Loon Lake.

✦ ✦ ✦

The aftermath of the North-West Resistance played out differently among different groups. In English Canada, the victory of Canada's army was celebrated. The militia myth, that being the erroneous belief that Canadian militia were somehow more effective than professional soldiers, remained as strong as ever.[17] This was despite the fact that the force was poorly prepared for the campaign and struggled to defeat a numerically, technologically, and logistically inferior force. If there was any criticism, it was lobbed against Middleton, the British officer who was thought to have acted too slowly and kept too tight a rein on his eager Canadian soldiers.[18]

For French Canada, Louis Riel became a symbol for the French-Catholic struggle against an assimilationist English-Protestant nation. Riel obtained near-martyr status in Quebec when he was found guilty of treason, and despite the jury recommending mercy, was given a death sentence.[19] Riel was hanged for treason on November 16, 1885. One juror famously quipped, "We tried Riel for treason, and he was hanged for the murder of Scott."

The hardest blow fell on the Métis and First Nations, 81 of whom were eventually charged with crimes ranging from arson to murder to treason-felony.

Louis Riel in custody, 1885.

Eight Indigenous men, including Wandering Spirit, were found guilty for their actions at Frog Lake and hanged in the largest mass hanging in Canadian history. Two others found guilty were the prominent Cree leaders Poundmaker and Big Bear, who had no real involvement in the uprising at all. Both leaders were imprisoned, and though both were eventually granted early release, they died shortly after. Even though only a few hundred Indigenous warriors fought against the Canadian government, the conflict was used as an excuse to further control and oppress the people of the Prairies.[20]

While Métis rights continued to be ignored, Canadian policy toward First Nations became even harsher, highlighted by the implementation of the "pass" system, a process by which First Nations had to present travel documents signed by the local Indian agent to travel to and from their own reserves. In effect, the marginalization of Indigenous peoples not only continued unabated but was, in fact, accelerated in the aftermath of the fighting, regardless of whether one had participated or not. These greater restrictions on First Nations further facilitated Prime Minister Macdonald's strategy of increasing white settlement in the West.

For the Canadian military, there were some glaring issues that for the most part were conveniently ignored. Most soldiers sent to fight in the

Big Bear (seated, second from left) and Poundmaker (seated, right) and unidentified men in North-West Mounted Police barracks, 1885.

North-West Territories were simply not prepared for an actual sustained campaign. There were no supply lines, no transport organization, very few medical personnel (though the force did include a dozen female nurses), and no engineers. Despite some voices emphasizing the ineffectiveness of the Canadian military and calling for the expansion of the Permanent Force, most politicians balked at this. They cited budget issues and claimed that expanding the force was a direct challenge to the citizen soldier ideal that made up the heart of the Canadian military and thus the Canadian nation.[21]

So, in the immediate aftermath of the North-West Resistance, no real improvements were made to the Canadian military structure. It continued to be an organization that looked strong on paper but was largely ineffective. Its Permanent Force was too small while its Non-Permanent Militia was corrupt, inefficient, and rampant with political appointments for officers and beset with equipment and training issues.

2

FIGHTING FOR THE EMPIRE

The challenges of empire facing Great Britain in the final decades of the 19th century created significant debate in London concerning the role its colonies would play. The Liberals in Britain saw the colonies as burdens upon the Crown and treasury, while Conservatives viewed the empire as a source of strength, both in manpower and *matériel*. There was no question that Britain's empire was posing significant challenges to the British military. Revolts, rebellions, insurrections, and crises were erupting frequently, and the British Army in particular was overstretched dealing with these. At the same time, the final decades of the 19th century saw the emergence of a unified Germany seeking to assert itself as a continental power while also challenging British might at sea.

The challenges facing the British and their empire influenced discussions within Canada about the Canadian military and how it should or should not be used to help in various imperial conflicts. Prime Minister Macdonald showed little enthusiasm for sending the Canadian military overseas to assist the British. Certainly, he did not challenge the right for the British to recruit within Canada for the British Army, nor did he object to Canada's Royal Military College graduates or Permanent Force officers transferring into the British military to see action, but Macdonald's priority was domestic issues. His final years in power were driven by the desire to encourage immigration into Canada, both to provide much-needed labour in Canada's urban centres and to settle the rural West. It was unlikely that new Canadians were going to accept the low pay and harsh conditions of a life in the military when better financial opportunities were available in industrializing and expanding Canada.

As well, public views toward imperial military participation were complicated, revolving around the split between English and French Canada. For most English-speaking Canadians, especially those from the British Isles or descendants of those from the British Isles, heeding the call of the empire was an integral aspect of being a Canadian subject of the British Crown. It was one's duty. For many young English-speaking Canadians, the opportunity to prove themselves on the battlefield in service of the empire was both the ultimate expression of Anglo-Saxon masculinity and a way to prove the fortitude of a young Canadian nation.

In French Canada, however, the feeling was far more ambivalent, if not outright hostile. While French Canadians certainly served in the Canadian military, the idea that young French-Canadian men might be forced to fight and die for the British Empire overseas was anathema to the beliefs of many. The British conquest of New France in 1763 still echoed within the French-Canadian consciousness, especially in Quebec, and fighting for an empire that had not only conquered French Canada but was seen as both anti-Catholic and anti-French was a hard sell.

Volunteerism thus formed the basis of Canadian participation in British imperial adventures. When such an adventure presented itself in August 1884 and a call went out for Canadian voyageurs to assist in a British campaign in Egypt, these volunteers were found.

The Nile Expedition

At the very same time Riel was organizing along the banks of the Saskatchewan River, an Islamic religious leader known as the Mahdi led an uprising against Anglo-Egyptian forces in Sudan. Egypt was technically an autonomous province within the Ottoman Empire. However, British military intervention in 1882 on behalf of Tewfik Pasha, the Khedive and nominal ruler of Egypt,

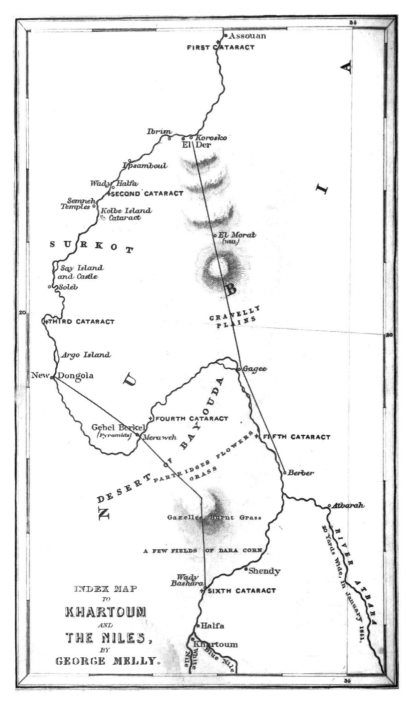

Sketch by George Melly of the Nile River and its cataracts, 1851.

brought this province into the British sphere of influence, often called the "veiled protectorate." British military action in 1882 also secured British control over the all-important Suez Canal, a waterway that immediately constituted one of the most crucial pieces of infrastructure in the British Empire.

By March 1884, Mahdi forces had lain siege to the key city of Khartoum on the Nile River. The British were concerned that the fall of Khartoum could potentially trigger an uprising among Islamic sympathizers within Egypt, thus threatening British control of the region and British control of the Suez Canal. Pressure from both the British public and the military led London to authorize a relief expedition under the command of General Garnet Wolseley, the Red River veteran, who wanted to avoid a march overland to relieve Khartoum and chose instead to take the shorter route via the Nile. To do this, however, he needed experienced boatmen, and who better than the same voyageurs who had helped him in 1870?

Three hundred and eighty-six men were recruited for Wolseley's Nile Expedition; half spoke English, half spoke French, and one-third of the contingent was Indigenous. Only a small number of the volunteers were veterans of the Red River Expedition, though the contingent's commanding officer, Lieutenant-Colonel Frederick Denison, was one of them. The expedition arrived in Egypt in October 1884, and by the end of the month, it, along with just over 5,000 British soldiers, began its ascent of the Nile. It was clear from the start that these "Nile voyageurs," as the press hailed them, were crucial in allowing the expedition to move rapidly along the untamed river. The expedition made good progress but not without casualties. Louis Capitaine was the first. Capitaine was a father of three and a Kanien'keha:ka from just outside Montreal. He drowned after capsizing while guiding his boat through a section of rapids. By December, seven more Canadian voyageurs had died. Unfortunately, despite the speed of the expedition, it did not arrive in time; by early February, news reached Wolseley that Khartoum had fallen. At this point, Wolseley shifted his campaign inland to seek out and destroy the Mahdi forces.

The voyageurs were no longer needed and began their long journey home. On their way, they stopped in London where they were celebrated. Even Queen Victoria sent them a personal message thanking them for their service in Egypt. Wolseley was proud of the men. He wrote: "The Dominion of Canada supplied us with a most useful body of boatmen. Their skill in the

Sketch of a whaleboat navigating a cataract on the Nile River.

management of boats in difficult and dangerous waters was of the utmost use to us in our long ascent of the Nile. Men and officers showed a high military and patriotic spirit, making light of the difficulty and working with that energy and determination which have always characterized Her Majesty's Canadian Forces."[1]

There was growing uncertainty in London about Britain's ability to maintain its dominant global position. Despite still having the most powerful navy in the world, numerous imperial crises erupting during the 19th century found Britain stretched dangerously thin protecting its global empire. By the 1880s, the United States and a newly unified Germany were challenging Britain's position as the world's industrial leader, and Germany was openly contesting Britain's position as the dominant European power. Britain's army, in fact, remained almost laughably small compared to those of the other major European powers, and most of its standing military was scattered throughout the empire on garrison duty. There was, for many, an increasing anxiety over Britain's security, both within Europe and throughout the world. Pressure was therefore placed on Britain's dominions to improve their military situations to support the mother country in case of war.

The Mahdist conflict and Canada's participation in the Nile Expedition highlighted the tension between British imperial interests and Canadian defence spending. Despite the government's clear loyalty to the empire, reforms to its military were resisted at almost every step. Both the Permanent Force (PF) and the Non-Permanent Militia (NPM) were hotbeds of political patronage. If any sort of reforms were to occur, this had to be dismantled. This system, however, was an important cog within the Conservative and Liberal political machines and attempts to do away with patronage often failed. One of the major issues confounding reform attempts was that throughout the 1890s they were often initiated by British officers who held the role of General Officer Commanding (GOC) the Militia.[2] A nationalistic element thus arose when reforms were tried, with Canadian politicians resisting efforts by a British GOC to reform the Canadian militia system.[3]

Despite this resistance, some reforms were successfully implemented. Major-General I.J.C. Herbert, GOC from 1890 to 1895, successfully reorganized the PF, amalgamating the four infantry schools into the Royal Canadian Regiment of Infantry (later the Royal Canadian Regiment), the various cavalry and mounted infantry schools into the Royal Canadian Dragoons, and the PF artillery regiment into the Royal Canadian Artillery. His attempt, however, at creating a PF artillery unit in Esquimalt on Vancouver Island met with failure when he could not find any Canadians willing to enlist. (Canada was forced to pay Royal Marines to man the battery.)

The PF was put to the test in 1898 when gold was discovered in the Yukon and tens of thousands of prospectors, mostly Americans, flooded into the region within weeks. The few Mounties already there were overwhelmed, and there were growing fears that the United States might use the combination of a large American population coupled with growing lawlessness to make a claim on the territory.[4] In response, the Canadian government created the Yukon Field Force. This numbered just over 200 men — infantry, cavalry, and artillery, including machine guns — composed entirely of soldiers from the PF. After a long journey by train, canoe, and then over land, the Yukon Field Force arrived at Fort Selkirk in the Yukon where it was successful in calming the situation. The Yukon Field Force finally withdrew in 1900 because Canada was once again going to war.

The Yukon Field Force on parade in Vancouver, 1898.

The Second Boer War

The Second Boer War had its roots in decades of hostility between the British, settled primarily in Cape Colony, and descendants of Dutch settlers known as Boers, who lived primarily in the Orange Free State and the Transvaal. The conflict, however, was triggered by the discovery of riches. In the mid-1880s, gold and diamond deposits were found in these two Boer territories, and as in the Yukon, the discovery of minerals triggered a flood of immigration. This time, however, it was scores of British *uitlanders* arriving to seek their fortune. The Boer people and the British already had a tense history, going to war with each other in the First Boer War in 1880–81, and tension only increased as reports filtered back to Britain of British subjects being treated poorly by Boer authorities. Newspapers throughout the empire published dramatized accounts of oppressed British subjects, and public condemnation of the Boers grew. Jingoism ruled the day, and for many in Great Britain and throughout the British Empire, this affront to Great Britain could not be tolerated. For others, the idea of adding the mineral-rich Boer states to a larger British South Africa would be a great boon to the imperial treasury.

Canadian prime minister Wilfrid Laurier had no desire to fight in South Africa. Laurier and the Liberal Party had come to power in 1896 with significant political support from French Canadians, especially in Quebec. He was in a precarious political situation and fully aware that many within Quebec sympathized with the Boers, who were seen as a fellow minority group oppressed and bullied by the assimilationist British Empire. Others, like prominent French-Canadian nationalist Henri Bourassa, were concerned that participation in this war would set a precedent for automatic Canadian entry into future wars. For Laurier, any support for Canadian participation in a war against the Boers could very well damage his standing among the all-important Quebec political base.[5]

The Colonial Office in London and the governor general of Canada, Lord Minto, were well aware of Laurier's reluctance to commit Canada to war. London was hoping that Canada, like the other dominions, would eagerly offer men and *matériel*, and so the Colonial Office reached out to Lord Minto in July 1899 to see if Canada would commit troops in case of war. Lord Minto knew he was going to get nowhere with Prime Minister Laurier or with Frederick Borden, his minister of militia and defence, so he skipped

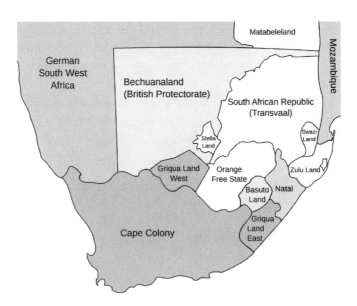

Map of South Africa in 1885.

right past them and went straight to the GOC, General Edward Hutton, asking him if he could prepare a military response in the case of war.

Hutton, a career British soldier from Devon who had served in the First Boer War, immediately promised a force of 1,200 soldiers. Hutton then leaked this vow to a variety of newspapers. When, in September, Hutton finally informed Minister Borden of his commitment to the Colonial Office, various English-language newspapers were already celebrating Canada's would-be pledge. Laurier, furious, was now trapped. Momentum within English Canada for a Canadian commitment was too strong for him to ignore.[6] When the Boers declared war on the British on October 11, Laurier's hand was forced, though not entirely. Ever the great compromiser, Laurier declared that this would be a volunteer force, hoping that would appease some of his base in French Canada. Furthermore, while Canada would pay to equip and

Prime Minister Wilfrid Laurier, 1906.

transport its force, once in South Africa the first contingent would be paid for entirely by the British.

Canada's initial contribution to the Second Boer War included four nursing sisters and 1,000 men comprising the 2nd (Special Service) Battalion of the Royal Canadian Regiment of Infantry, or 2 RCRI. The regiment was made up of eight regional companies, one from western Canada, three from Ontario, and two from Quebec and the Maritimes, with French-speaking recruits specifically allotted to F Company. Laurier was not going to allow Canada's first overseas contingent to be commanded by anyone but a Canadian. The man chosen to lead 2 RCRI was 56-year-old Lieutenant-Colonel William Otter of Cut Knife Hill infamy. While not a particularly impressive officer, he was Canadian, and the best the country had to offer.

Lieutenant-Colonel William Otter, 1904.

The regiment set sail in late October 1899, proudly displaying its new badges of a crown superimposed on a maple leaf with *Canada* written below. Morale was high. The good humour was not to last, however, for the men were disgracefully packed into a cattle boat turned troop transport wholly unfit to house a contingent that size. Seasickness combined with an outbreak of dysentery made the voyage a brutal start to the experience, and the men were more than happy to disembark in Cape Town on November 30.

The Second Boer War can be divided into three phases.[7] The Canadians arrived during the first phase, which lasted from October 1899 to January 1900. This first phase was characterized by a series of British failures in the face of an aggressive Boer enemy. In fact, the first phase went so badly for the British that in December 1899 the call went out for any and all help from Britain's dominions, including a second contingent from Canada. For most of the first phase, the Canadians drilled and trained to the point that the men began to openly detest Otter. Regardless, Otter was intent on making sure his men were as well prepared as possible for the rigours of the South African battlefield.

The second phase, starting in February 1900, was characterized by a series of British counteroffensives inflicting several defeats on the Boers. One of the most significant of these victories was the Battle of Paardeberg, which became a shining military moment in the Canadian public imagination.

On February 12, the regiment joined a British force marching out to relieve the siege of Kimberley, a diamond-mining town under attack by General Piet Cronjé, the Boer commander. Cronjé attempted to slip away from the numerically superior British but was caught by British cavalry at the Modder River near a place called Paardeberg Drift. Instead of continuing to flee, Cronjé made the questionable decision to halt and go on the defensive. Adhering to time-honoured Boer defensive doctrine, he formed his force up into a laager, effectively a circular defensive position using his wagons as cover. Repeated British attempts to attack Cronjé's position failed, but the British were able to bring their superior artillery to bear on Cronjé and his army, including many of their wives and children, who were subject to days of withering artillery fire.

The Canadians arrived on February 18 and were immediately ordered to cross the fast-flowing river, which they did while under fire, and later that afternoon joined a British charge against the Boer lines. The charge was beaten back, with 21 dead. Ten days of miserable siege followed. The weather

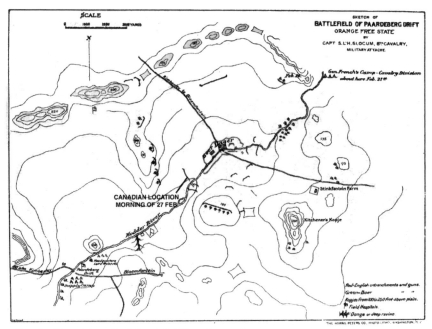

Sketch of Paardeberg Drift battlefield by John Fawkes.

was bad and supplies were scarce, since Boer commandos had effectively disrupted the British supply lines. Potable water was limited, and the Modder was so full of dead bodies and horses that it was undrinkable, a terrible fate to befall thirsty men as they stood beside a raging river.

By February 26, the British were facing a surrounded Boer enemy that had been thoroughly demoralized and worn down from days of incessant British artillery fire. The 2 RCRI was ordered to take part in a pre-sunrise attack the next day. In the pitch-black early morning hours of February 27, the 2 RCRI gingerly moved into no man's land. Some of the men even held hands so as not to lose one another as they advanced over the ground. The advance went slowly as the Canadians quietly edged toward the Boer lines. The Canadians got within 30 yards of the Boer trenches when, suddenly, someone tripped an alarm and the Boers opened fire. Chaos ensued. Entire companies were now pinned down.

Clearly in a desperate situation, with the sun now coming up, the call went down the line to retreat. G and H Companies, on the right flank of the Canadian attack, did not hear the call and remained in place. Due to

Canadian soldiers crossing the Modder River to attack Boer positions at Paardeberg, 1900.

blind luck, the two companies had, in fact, stumbled into a fairly strong position and had even been able to dig themselves some protection while their comrades remained exposed to accurate Boer fire. The men of G and H Companies held their position and continued to pour fire into the Boer lines. With daylight came the realization that these Canadians, just under 120 strong, commanded the dominating position on the field.

This was the final straw for the demoralized Boers. A white flag was raised, and a Boer officer stepped forward and announced to a Canadian officer his intent to surrender. White flags then appeared all along the Boer lines. The Battle of Paardeberg was over. Almost 10 percent of the entire Boer military was captured at Paardeberg. The British had finally gotten a much-needed victory, and the 2 RCRI, despite the confusion and chaos of the attack, was hailed as the victor.

Paardeberg was one triumph in a successive series of British victories culminating in the capture of the two Boer capitals — Bloemfontein in March and finally Pretoria in early June. At this point, with the British enjoying numerical and *matériel* superiority and the two capitals in British hands, it was felt the war was all but over. Yet the Boers stubbornly refused to surrender. After the fall of Pretoria, the Boers shifted to hit-and-run tactics and the war went into its final and most controversial phase — guerrilla combat. From June 1900 until the end of the conflict, Boer operations were characterized by attacks from small units of mounted Boer commandos, hitting hard and fast and then disappearing quickly into the wide-open veldt.

The British felt that the most effective way to counter the Boer commandos was with similar mounted units, and the second Canadian contingent was just that. Having arrived in early 1900, it comprised three batteries of the Royal Canadian Field Artillery and two mounted regiments: the Royal Canadian Dragoons, made up primarily of recruits from the Permanent Force regiment of the same name, and the 1st Canadian Mounted Rifles, consisting primarily of recruits from the North-West Mounted Police. As well, a mounted regiment, privately raised by Lord Strathcona, Canada's High Commissioner in London, arrived in April 1900. Lord Strathcona's Horse regiment included recruits from the ranks of the NWMP and was, in fact, led by Lieutenant-Colonel Sam Steele, a former superintendent of the force and veteran of the North-West Resistance.

As Canada's military presence in South Africa grew, combat continued. In April at Israel's Poort, Lieutenant-Colonel Otter was shot in the neck while rallying his retreating men, but he survived. The Royal Canadian Field Artillery participated in the relief of Mafeking in May, which had been under siege by the Boers since October 1899. In June, elements of the first and second Canadian contingent helped in the capture of Pretoria. In July, at Witpoort, Harry Lothrop Borden, the son of Frederick Borden, was killed when the Royal Canadian Dragoons successfully counterattacked a Boer position. That same month at Wolwespruit, Sergeant Arthur Richardson of Lord Strathcona's Horse earned the Victoria Cross when he rode an already wounded horse back through enemy fire to rescue an unhorsed Canadian comrade.

In November 1900, more Victoria Crosses were awarded to Canadian soldiers, this time at Leliefontein, Canada's second-most famous battle of the South African war. In the early hours of November 6, a British column rode out to capture a Boer commando unit reported to be camped 18 miles south of the town of Belfast along the Komati River. Skirmishing between the two sides became more frequent as the British and Boer forces came close to each other. The British commander, Major-General Horace Smith-Dorrien, who had camped his column at a farm called Leliefontein, decided to withdraw to the safety of Belfast the next morning. A detachment of the Royal Canadian Dragoons and a section from D Battery of the Royal Canadian Field Artillery were placed as the rearguard when the column set out on the morning of November 7.

When the Boer commander realized the British were withdrawing, he decided to attack, seeing an opportunity to capture the Canadian artillery pieces. The enemy launched a series of cavalry charges to attempt to overwhelm the Canadian rearguard. During the first assault, Toronto-born Lieutenant H.Z.C. Cockburn placed himself and his men between the Boers and the Canadian cannons, stopping the assault while losing all his men in the fighting (Cockburn himself was wounded but made it to safety). Another Boer charge came soon after, commandos riding fast and firing from the hip. This time they ran into Quebec-born Lieutenant Richard Turner and a dozen men who beat back the attack, helped greatly by the actions of Sergeant Edward Holland, from Ottawa, who kept his Colt machine gun firing until the enemy nearly overran him. In what was the most desperate fighting for Canadians of the entire war, they had successfully held back the Boers, protected the rear of the British column, and ensured the Canadian guns remained in Canadian hands. Cockburn, Turner, and Holland all received Victoria Crosses for their actions at Leliefontein. Not until the Battle of Vimy Ridge in April 1917 would more Canadians receive the British Empire's highest decoration for a single action.

Two months before the Battle of Leliefontein, the British began implementing a strategy designed to destroy the economic and social bases of the Boer commandos. Tens of thousands of Boer civilians were forced into what the British deemed "concentration camps." British — and Canadian — soldiers rounded up mostly women and children, often destroying property and burning crops. The civilians were imprisoned in sections of the veldt that were surrounded by barbed-wire fences, living in hastily constructed blockhouses where they suffered greatly from harsh discipline, poor administration, and terrible public health measures. The camps were segregated, as well. An even greater number of them were established for the Black population, many of whom were forced into manual labour.

By 1902, long fencelines, thick belts of barbed wire, and blockhouses had been erected throughout the Transvaal and Orange Free State. The Boer republics had effectively become large, enclosed camps that at their peak were manned by 50,000 British Empire soldiers. In the Transvaal, 8,880 square miles were enclosed, and in the Orange Free State just over 10,400 square miles were cordoned off via this elaborate concentration camp system. While no honest comparison can be made to the genocidal camps of the Second

Lieutenant H.Z.C. Cockburn, VC.

Lieutenant Richard Turner, VC.

World War — the British did not intend to eradicate the Boers — the death toll was shockingly and shamefully high for these civilians. Disease was the main killer. Of the 116,000 civilians placed in camps, at least 28,000 died, a disproportionate number of them Black.[8]

By 1901 set-piece battles were rare, and for most Canadians the war had become one of patrolling, rounding up civilians, and long marches into the veldt to hunt small groups of Boer commandos still holding out. In March 1901, just over 1,200 Canadian volunteers arrived to serve in the South African constabulary, a large police force that would try to impose order on the conquered territories once the war ended. More mounted rifles continued to come from Canada, as well. A second regiment of the Canadian Mounted Rifles arrived in mid-March 1902 and was thrust right into battle, finding itself engaged in one of the bloodiest days of the entire war for Canada — the Battle of Hart's River.

By late March, the 2nd Canadian Mounted Rifles, 900 strong, was part of a British force stalking one of the last of the larger Boer contingents still operating in the field. The Boer force, numbering approximately 2,500 soldiers, had disappeared into the desolate terrain of the western Transvaal. The British column chasing them totalled just under 2,000, though the British commander, Colonel G.A. Cookson, believed they, in fact, outnumbered the Boers. When the two sides finally clashed on March 31, Cookson realized he was outmanned and chose to set up a defensive position around a farm called Boschbult, the other name often given to the Battle of Hart's River. The 2nd Canadian Mounted Rifles had, in fact, been assigned to protect the baggage train, so that by the time the regiment arrived at the farm, the Boers were already launching attacks against the British position.

Artillery rained down on the British and Canadian soldiers while Boer snipers continued a deadly fusillade. At one point during the battle, 21 Canadians from E Squadron under Lieutenant Bruce Carruthers, from Kingston, Ontario, were separated from the main force and became entangled in a vicious fight. Carruthers ordered the men to dismount and they fought off waves of Boer attacks until out of ammunition, at which point they engaged the enemy in hand-to-hand combat. When the Boers broke off fighting later in the day, 18 of the 22 men had been wounded or killed. Carruthers himself appeared to be briefly captured. The British suffered 159 casualties on the day, 53 of whom were Canadians. Besides Paardeberg,

Indigenous Africans in a British concentration camp in South Africa, 1901.

Hart's River was the bloodiest day of the war for Canada but also the last Canadian action of the conflict. In May of that same year, the Boers officially surrendered, and the Treaty of Vereeniging brought the Transvaal and the Orange Free State into the British Empire. These two territories eventually merged into a greater South Africa in 1910.

Eight thousand three hundred and seventy-two Canadians served in the Second Boer War. Two hundred and twenty-four were killed (135 of those from disease) and 252 wounded. Although little comfort to those families grieving, the toll for Canada was light. Canada's army, which included men from all over the country, had performed admirably: four Canadian soldiers were awarded the highest decoration in the empire, Canadian units played key parts in important battles, and the optimism that characterized the Canadian spirit at the turn of the century was further reinforced by what was broadly seen as a successful military participation. February 27 was now officially known as Paardeberg Day and acted as Canada's unofficial day of military commemoration, eclipsed by November 11 at the end of the First World War. Despite the participation of much of the Permanent Force, the majority of those who served were from the militia, and thus the Canadian militia myth remained as powerful as ever in the aftermath of the war. In fact, many Canadians, such as future minister of militia Sam Hughes, himself a veteran of South Africa, championed the narrative that the militia of the British Empire had "come to the rescue" of the British professionals.

The idea that the Second Boer War was some kind of unifying event in Canada failed to resonate for French Canadians in Quebec. While Quebec had begrudgingly accepted Laurier's commitment to volunteerism and limited participation in the war, helped by the Catholic Church declaring its support for the British call to arms, many in Quebec still deplored what was seen as British imperial aggression. Furthermore, many pointed out the Canadian Parliament's seeming impotence in deciding when the country went to war.

Henri Bourassa led the charge. As Member of Parliament for the riding of Labelle, he had been elected in 1896, resigned in 1899 to protest Laurier's decision to send soldiers to South Africa, and was re-elected in 1900. He was not shy in using his platform to decry Canada's involvement in South Africa.[9] Bourassa was also quick to condemn the British policy of scorched earth on the Boer population, including the establishment of concentration camps. While Bourassa represented the political opposition to the war within Quebec, the one event that best showcased French-English tensions was the Montreal Flag Riot in March 1900.

On March 1, an inebriated loyalist crowd of almost 2,000 people made up of McGill University students and English-speaking Montreal residents celebrated Canada's role in the recent victory at Paardeberg. The mob eventually attacked two French-language newspaper offices. They forced office staff to raise the Union Jack and then turned their attention to the campus of Laval, Montreal's French-language university, where they successfully bullied the caretaker into hoisting the Union Jack, as well. The next day, Laval students tore down the flag and organized a countermarch. Fear of escalation led to the archbishop of Montreal personally stepping in to send the students home. Later that night, an armed mob, led by McGill students, returned to the Laval campus. They were met by Laval students and professors, as well as police, and chaos ensued. Fights broke out, the police trained water hoses on the crowd to disperse them, shots were fired, people were hurt, but eventually the police restored order. In the aftermath, Laval students planned a counterattack on the McGill campus, but the authorities from both universities, the city, the police, and the church intervened and further violence was avoided.[10]

Aftermath of the Second Boer War

The Second Boer War certainly sparked tension between French- and English-speaking communities, but it also generated serious reforms to the Canadian military establishment. In 1902, the man spearheading this was GOC Major-General the Earl of Dundonald (Laurier successfully had Hutton recalled). With full support from Frederick Borden, who was still reeling from the loss of his son in South Africa, Dundonald enacted reforms that saw Canada's army further take on the trappings of a modern professional force. Specifically, these reforms created the necessary infrastructure for Canada's army to sustain itself in the field, theoretically without help from the British. This included engineers, signals for communication, ordnance for resupply, an army service corps to organize logistics, and a medical staff. Dundonald oversaw the creation of a permanent training facility at Petawawa, Ontario, which continues as a training base today. He also increased the amount of training required for officers in the Permanent Force, including the practice of sending Canadian officers to the British Army's Staff College at Camberley.

Dundonald, however, ran into trouble when he targeted the militia. The GOC pulled no punches when he highlighted serious flaws in the militia structure: its lack of training, its dearth of funding, and most significantly, its use primarily as a vehicle for patronage and thus the plethora of unqualified personnel holding officer rank as a result. Once again, a British GOC attempting to reform the militia clashed with nationalistic beliefs due to the sacrosanct nature of the militia system, and Dundonald was fired in 1904.[11]

Yet Dundonald's reforms, his insistence on improving the Canadian military, and his perceived "attack" on the militia all influenced Frederick Borden to make further changes with his 1904 Militia Act. One piece of the act stipulated that Canada no longer required a British officer to be General Officer Commanding. In fact, the position of GOC was scrapped and in its place was a new Chief of the General Staff. British-born Sir Percy Lake held this position until 1908 when none other than Canada's most experienced officer, Major-General William Otter, assumed the role, becoming Canada's first Canadian-born Chief of the General Staff.

Borden's act established a Militia Council, consisting of both civilian and military personnel, which reported directly to the minister and was given wide-ranging powers to act on his behalf. Reforms included the incorporation of nurses into the military as well as giving them equivalent officer rank. He also increased the size of the Permanent Force to 2,000 members. Under Borden, Canada took further steps to reduce its domestic security reliance on Great Britain when it took over command of the two key coastal bases of Esquimalt and Halifax in July 1905. It was, however, a constant struggle for the Canadian government to recruit soldiers to garrison the isolated Esquimalt base at the meagre pay of 40 to 50 cents per day. Nonetheless, this was a dramatic four years of reform, and improvements were obvious. Perhaps no one said it better than accomplished military historian Jack Granatstein when he wrote: "These were major, long-overdue changes and, when added to Dundonald's reforms, they left Canada better prepared for war than it had ever been."[12]

Certainly, as the 20th century progressed, Canadians became aware of a growing militarism both within the British Empire and throughout Europe.

Two Canadian nursing sisters and a Miss L. Trotter (centre) in South Africa, 1900.

Germany's ascension as a major European power coupled with a series of diplomatic crises led many in Canada to clamour for greater military preparation. Perhaps no movement better reflected this nascent militarism than the cadet program. In 1908, the first province to wholly embrace cadets was Nova Scotia, Frederick Borden's native province, where every male teacher was expected to have some sort of military training while all teachers were expected to qualify for drill and physical training. Instructors, arms, books, and examinations were all provided by the federal government with bonuses and monetary prizes awarded to both teachers and students who displayed cadet excellence. By 1911, six provinces, including both the Catholic and Protestant education committees of Quebec, had enrolled in this federal program. By 1913, 40,000 boys had signed up for the cadet initiative, up from 9,000 in 1908.

Yet 40,000 boys in a country of seven and a half million people does not a militaristic nation make. Many people were opposed to the cadet movement; protests rang out from farm organizations, trade unions, pacifist religious sects, and conscientious objectors newly arrived from all over Europe. Even Prime Minister Wilfrid Laurier decried any sort of movement toward "the vortex of militarism," as he saw it.[13] Nonetheless, it was also clear that Europe was edging closer to war and that subjects of the British Empire could very well be called upon. The issue of imperial defence once again began to split Canadian public opinion.

Creating a Canadian Navy

No other debate characterized the controversy of imperial defence in the years leading up to the First World War as much as the debate over the navy. The unveiling of the powerful dreadnought-class vessel by the British in 1905 had suddenly made numerous ships obsolete within the Royal Navy and thus gave rivals an opportunity to catch up. In March 1909, it was announced in the British House of Commons that the Royal Navy risked losing supremacy on the high seas in the face of an aggressively expanding German navy. Now London began asking for naval help from its colonies.

Canada had no navy in 1909. The closest thing to it were armed patrol vessels operating along the coasts for the Fisheries Protection Service. These were

HMCS *Niobe*, circa 1910.

HMCS *Rainbow* in Burrard Inlet, 1910.

meant to keep poachers out of Canadian waters while at the same time project some sense of Canadian sovereignty. One ship, CGS *Canada*, even sailed to Bermuda and cruised the Caribbean for three months, visiting ports, delivering salutes, and training with a local British naval squadron.

Traditionally, the belief was that if Canada's coastlines were ever seriously threatened the Royal Navy would come to defend them. Even after Canada took over responsibility for Halifax, that belief persisted, since it only took about five days for ships to sail from Great Britain to Canada's East Coast. Pacific defence was more unsure once the Royal Navy's Pacific squadron was called back to the British Isles. Yet Canada had very few serious threats to its waters or its borders, which led to many Canadians disregarding any serious need for a navy. Regardless, by the end of 1909, Laurier was pressured by London to enhance Canada's naval capacity. While the British government wanted a substantial commitment in naval construction, Laurier was able to settle on a compromise of four cruisers and six destroyers for an estimated cost of $11 million.[14]

When news of Laurier's proposed navy reached the public, Canadian naval commitments became wrapped up in broader French-English tensions and Liberal-Conservative rivalries. For French Canadians in Quebec, the navy was seen as a tool to draw Canada deeper into British imperial commitments. As with the arguments made during the Second Boer War, Quebec nationalists decried any government steps that automatically drew Canada into another British war. The navy, many in Quebec believed, meant committing Canada to such a conflict.

For Conservatives, despite what at first seemed to be bipartisan support for a Canadian navy, Laurier's navy was seen as too small and ineffectual to make any serious difference for Canada or the British. Many in the Conservative Party argued that what Britain really needed were financial contributions to continue building modern dreadnoughts, not some "tinpot navy" that would make little difference among oceanic belligerents. Laurier found himself in a very difficult political position, one that proved his undoing.

The Naval Service Act was passed in early May 1910 amid raucous debate. Canada's navy was officially created, becoming the Royal Canadian Navy (RCN) in August 1911. Two destroyers — HMCS *Niobe* on the East Coast and HMCS *Rainbow* on the West — were given to Ottawa by London and began service almost immediately. Many of the personnel from the Fisheries

Protection Service provided the nucleus for the crews, yet shortages persisted and Royal Navy sailors and officers were seconded to make up for the lack of trained officers and sailors. Rear-Admiral Charles Kingsmill, from Guelph, Ontario, a 40-year veteran of the Royal Navy, was appointed as the Canadian navy's first director and helped oversee the establishment of a naval college at Halifax.

From day one, however, the navy became a political target on the back of Wilfrid Laurier. In a rare show of co-operation, Quebec *nationalistes* such as Henri Bourassa banded together with Conservatives to attack Laurier and his government, one side claiming it betrayed the French-Canadian people, the other that it betrayed the British Empire. When Laurier's party lost a Quebec by-election in November 1910, he realized how much the naval issue had weakened his political hold on what was his most crucial base of support. Despite some last-minute political wrangling, Laurier could not shake the two-pronged attack of Conservatives and *nationalistes*, and in the election of 1911, he and the Liberals were defeated.[15]

Robert Borden, the new Conservative prime minister, set about rescinding the naval bill and instead proposed a contribution to the British of $35 million to support the construction of three new dreadnought battleships. When this was blocked by the Liberal Senate, Laurier's navy died. Recruiting stopped, the vessels of the Fisheries Protection Service continued their coastline patrols, and the *Niobe* and the *Rainbow* languished on their respective coasts. When war came in 1914, Canada's East Coast was defended by the Royal Navy while Canada's West Coast was jointly protected by the Royal Navy and the Imperial Japanese Navy, much to the chagrin of the strongly anti-Asian population of British Columbia.

3

THE FIRST WORLD WAR: 1914-1916

The reasons for the outbreak of the First World War are complex, but it was, in essence, the result of decades of tension between various European rivals. Germany, which had only formed as a country in 1871, had by the early 20th century positioned itself as the dominant continental military power. As such, the leader of Germany, Kaiser Wilhelm II, sought to increase Germany's global power through the acquisition of overseas territories. Germany even briefly flirted with the idea of building a navy that could potentially challenge Britain. While the naval-building program never achieved such a level, Germany's ascendancy became a problem for both Great Britain and France. Great Britain was not going to allow Germany to challenge its imperial global hegemony, while France saw Germany as an existential continental land threat. This common enemy led to the two ancient foes entering into an alliance with Imperial Russia, thus forming the Triple Entente. Effectively, if war broke out, Germany would find itself threatened now on both its western and eastern flanks. To counter this, Germany secured a pact with the Austro-Hungarian Empire, Italy, and, later, the Ottoman Empire — what historians have labelled the Central Powers.

When Archduke Franz Ferdinand, heir to the Austro-Hungarian throne, was assassinated by a Serbian radical on June 28, 1914, Austria demanded restitution from Serbia. Russia backed Serbia, Germany supported Austria, and the series of alliance systems clicked into place, dragging Europe and then the wider world into the first global industrial total war. While conflict erupted in Africa, Asia, and the Middle East, the main theatre of war was in Europe where fronts opened along its eastern, southern, and western borders. When Germany steamrolled through Belgium on its way to invading France, Britain entered the conflict, ostensibly defending Belgian neutrality. With its declaration of war against Germany on August 4, Canada, as a member of the British Empire, was once again at war.

Within Canada the response to war hinged on where you lived, what you did, and where you were from. Generally speaking, it was in the urban centres of Canada where enthusiasm for war seemed strongest. As well, surprisingly, considering French Canada's antipathy toward imperial participation, news of the outbreak of war appeared to receive support in both English and French Canada,[1] though that waned within French Canada over the coming months. Within English Canada support was, not amazingly, highest among those who were born in Great Britain and those first-generation Canadians

Minister of Militia and Defence Sam Hughes, 1914.

descended from British immigrants, while support was more diminished among those Canadians descended from non-British immigrants.[2]

In those excitable days of early August, these nuances of support were buried behind tens of thousands of young men and boys flocking to recruiting stations desperate to get to Europe before the conflict was over. The man most associated with this early phase of Canadian military recruitment was the controversial, eccentric, bombastic, megalomaniac Sam Hughes, minister of militia and defence. Born near modern-day Bowmanville, Ontario, Hughes was the Conservative MP for the Victoria riding in Ontario, today part of the Haliburton–Kawartha Lakes–Brock federal constituency.

Hughes was a Tory, an Orangeman, both a British imperialist and an ardent Canadian nationalist, a lifelong militia member, a crack shot, and a firm believer in the effectiveness of citizen soldiers. He had served during the Fenian raids but was denied service in the North-West Resistance. In 1899, his enlistment was once again denied, but he went to South Africa, anyway, finding service with the British Army. Despite proving himself quite a capable soldier on the battlefield, he was an absolute pest off it and was eventually dismissed from service. The overbearing officer had written several letters condemning the British military for cowardice. These were published in Canada and South Africa. This, combined with a penchant for disobeying orders, led to his brief tenure in South Africa coming to an end. None of this, however, stopped him from campaigning unsuccessfully to be awarded the Victoria Cross.

Back in Canada, Hughes's reputation was far more intact. He was a diehard Conservative and a fanatic cog in the Conservative Party political machine. When Robert Borden won the 1911 federal election, Hughes was a natural choice for the ministerial post as head of the militia. After war broke out in 1914, Hughes saw it as his divine mission to ensure that Canada contributed as much as it could to the war in Europe. That involvement, however, was going to be tightly controlled by Hughes.

The first step for Hughes was to scrap the mobilization plan already in place, one drawn up in 1911 and modified as recently as early 1914. Instead of forming Canada's first contingent from already existing militia units and using the already functioning base at Petawawa, militia commanders were ordered to send recruits to Valcartier, just north of Quebec City. The problem was that there was no camp at Valcartier. Even as the first recruits were arriving, the camp was being carved out of the wilderness,

East end of grounds at Camp Valcartier, September 1914.

from barracks to latrines to rifle ranges. Nonetheless, Valcartier was to be Hughes's own mini-kingdom.[3] He personally appointed officers, promoting and demoting at will, and oversaw all aspects of the training process while touring the grounds in his colonel's uniform, accompanied by an honour guard of cavalry.

Hughes scrapped the traditional regimental names in favour of a new numbered battalion system, a decision that did not go well with the long-service members. He quickly damaged the recruitment of French Canadians by demanding that only English be spoken. Hughes also rejected the application of one of the most capable officers in the entire Permanent Force, François-Louis Lessard, a French-speaking Catholic from Quebec City who had served with the Royal Canadian Dragoons during the Second Boer War. Yet the chaos and inefficiencies within Hughes's recruitment system were hidden beneath the enthusiasm and eagerness of the tens of thousands of young men who enlisted. It seemed as if a ready supply of Canadian volunteers would be endless.

By late 1914, the First Canadian Contingent set sail for Europe. The make-up of this group spoke heavily to the demographic nuances of Canada's support for the war. There were 36,267 men in the first contingent — 23,211 of these, or 64 percent, were born in Great Britain; 1,245, or 3.5 percent, were French-speaking Canadians. While most recruits were British-born, two-thirds of the officers were Canadian-born, drawn primarily from the militia. After arriving in England in October 1914, the force was eventually transformed into the 1st Canadian Division, made up of three brigades, each with four battalions, each battalion with around 1,000 men. Also included were three brigades of field artillery, each consisting of four batteries of four guns each. Along with these six brigades were the required ancillary services such as signallers, engineers, service corps, and medical personnel.

One segment of the population that controversially found its way into the ranks were adolescent boys. Despite the initial recruitment age set at 18 (later raised to 19), it is estimated that more than 20,000 adolescents served in the Canadian Expeditionary Force, as it came to be called. While most of these lads were 16 and 17 years of age, one 10-year-old successfully enlisted, while a 12-year-old even made it into the trenches. Many of these underage soldiers were able to enlist because they carried with them letters of permission from their parents. Others simply forged documents or outright lied about their age. The ability for these boys to enlist depended entirely on the local situation. Different recruiting sergeants at different recruiting stations turned a blind eye to these youngsters if they still had a quota to meet. Some of these underage recruits found themselves on a train or boat back home once their parents found out and demanded their return. Far more of them spent the war in Europe. It is likely that upward of 2,300 underage soldiers were killed during the conflict.[4]

Hughes was far too busy to worry about underage recruits. He was adamant that a Canadian command the first contingent. Instead, the commander of Canada's 1st Division was British-born Lieutenant-General Edwin Alderson. His brigade commanders, however, were Canadian. The 1st Brigade was handed to Lieutenant-Colonel Malcolm S. Mercer, a Toronto lawyer and officer in the Queen's Own Rifles. The 2nd Brigade was given to Lieutenant-Colonel Arthur Currie, a real-estate and insurance broker in Victoria, British Columbia. Despite being a Liberal, Currie, who was an artillery officer in the militia, was friends with Hughes's son, Garnet, which was enough to get him appointed. The 3rd Brigade went to the most accomplished of the three brigade commanders, Brigadier-General Richard Turner, who had won the Victoria Cross at Leliefontein and was running his family's grocery business in Toronto when war broke out.

The insistence of Hughes for a Canadian commander was symptomatic of his overall reputation taking a beating in England. His attempt at creating a Canadian air force failed miserably and was met with derision by the British. Hughes's insistence on Canadians wearing Canadian-made gear also became a fiasco. The cold and wet weeks training on Salisbury Plain, the training ground in England, eventually led to the inadequate Canadian boots and kit being replaced with British-made substitutes. The MacAdam Shield-Shovel, designed by Hughes, was meant to be a shovel that stopped bullets; it could

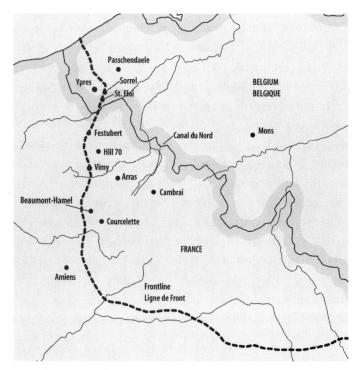

Map of major Canadian battles along the Western Front, 1914–18.

barely lift dirt or stop a bullet. The shovels were quickly melted into scrap metal. Even the Canadian-made trucks and wagons that arrived with the first contingent were found to be unsuitable for life at the front and thus replaced. When the Canadians finally got to France, the only piece of equipment they still had from Canada was the Ross rifle, a weapon Sam Hughes was personally fond of. Despite being a great sporting rifle, it proved to be wholly unsuitable to the dirty and muddy conditions of the Western Front. It jammed frequently, and despite Hughes's insistence on it being kept, was officially replaced in 1916, though many Canadians had already discarded their Rosses for any British Lee-Enfield they could find.

The type of war these young men entered was like nothing they could have ever imagined.[5] The lethality of industrial technology had outpaced almost all tactical thinking of the day. Artillery was so powerful and accurate that it could kill from miles away, and machine guns turned battlefields into bullet-swept killing zones. Simply put, it was no longer safe above ground

Minister of Militia and Defence Sam Hughes holding the MacAdam Shield-Shovel, date unknown.

and soldiers began digging in. By the end of 1914, a complex series of inter-connected trench lines stretched from the North Sea all the way to the border of Switzerland. Each side's trench was protected by thick belts of barbed wire. Separating the two sides was no man's land, a pockmarked hellish landscape where the detritus of war was deposited. As the months went on, the trench systems got deeper, the barbed wire thicker, and the body count higher. The very nature of modern war had become defensive. Soldiers in their trenches held a distinct and brutal advantage over an attacking enemy exposed above ground to the modern killing technology of the day.

Second Battle of Ypres

After a brief acculturation period in a quiet sector of the front, the still under-trained 1st Division was ordered into the Ypres Salient in mid-April 1915. The salient was a six-division frontage protecting the city of Ypres and pushing eastward into German-held territory. On their left was the 45th Algerian Division, made up primarily of soldiers from French-controlled territories in North Africa, and on their right was the British 28th Division. When the Canadians arrived, they found the trenches in terrible condition and spent most of the next week rebuilding and fortifying their stretch of the line. Then, on April 22, all hell broke loose.

The Germans had experimented with the use of gas previously in the war, but never on the scale that was to be used on the opening day of the Second Battle of Ypres (the First Battle of Ypres took place in the fall of 1914). Following a German bombardment, 5,730 cylinders containing chlorine gas were opened, and 160 tons of the poisonous fumes drifted slowly across no man's land backed by a gentle westward wind. An eerie sight emerged as a greenish-yellow smog, roughly 15 to 20 feet in height, crept slowly over the battered topography of no man's land. The target was not the Canadians, though; the gas and the follow-up barrage were directed at the North Africans on their left. Wholly unprepared for gas warfare, the division panicked and broke. Men barely accustomed to the wet and cold weather of Northwest Europe were now choking, vomiting, and dying as their faces turned from blue to a ghastly green. The effect of the gas caused the membranes in the bronchial tubes to swell, eventually turning to a liquid mass. A man effectively choked to death on his own insides. Major Andrew McNaughton recalled the horrific sight: "They literally were coughing their lungs out; glue was coming out of their mouths. It was very disturbing ..."[6] Those who were lucky enough to escape the gas ran. Within minutes it seemed as if the entire Algerian division was gone and a gap in the line now led straight to Ypres. The only chance of stopping the Germans lay with the 1st Canadian Division.

Turner's 3rd Brigade was the first to step into the breach. He launched a chaotic series of counterattacks that temporarily paused the German advance. Once reinforced by elements of Currie's 2nd Brigade, they fought through the course of that evening, and by the morning, battalions from the 1st Brigade were also thrown into the fight and the Canadians were able to finally establish a shaky yet continuous line of defence.

In the early morning of April 24, fresh German troops wearing rudimentary gas masks followed another deadly cloud directed against the Canadians. A bacteriologist working with the Canadian Army Medical Corps, Lieutenant-Colonel George Nasmith from Toronto recognized the gas for what it was and sent word down the line: urine-soaked cloth, specifically the ammonia in urine, could be used to mitigate the worst effects. While this was an extremely crude method, it did enough to allow for Canadian machine-gun and rifle fire to continue. But the Germans kept coming. The 15th Battalion from Toronto was all but destroyed, their commander found drunk and disorientated well to the rear. Turner's 3rd Brigade, with its centre now smashed, began a fighting withdrawal. He tried to get reinforcements forward, but confusion led to him ordering men to the wrong part of the line. This opened the door to the village of Saint-Julien, immediately to the Canadian rear, and Turner was forced to retreat, handing it to the enemy.

The Germans were now pressing General Mercer's 1st Brigade farther south of Saint-Julien. With support from effective Canadian artillery and flanking fire, the brigade held. Arthur Currie's 2nd Brigade still controlled most of its original line, but it was starting to collapse under the weight of the German assault. Lieutenant Edward Bellew from the 7th Battalion and Sergeant Hugh Pearless were at the apex of this. The last two men remaining in their machine gun section, Bellew and Pearless continued firing their Colt machine-gun even when surrounded by the enemy. Pearless was killed, but Bellew kept up the fight; he was eventually taken prisoner but not until he smashed his machine gun to prevent it falling into enemy hands. Bellew was awarded the Victoria Cross, Pearless the Distinguished Conduct Medal.

By the afternoon, Currie was extremely concerned that his lines were about to totally collapse. It was here that he made the questionable choice of leaving his headquarters to personally find reinforcements. Despite rallying several hundred men and getting them back into the line, Currie's decision to leave his command post was controversial.[7] A decision like that could have ended his career as a battlefield commander, yet by the end of the day his brigade held. However, it had suffered so many casualties that the next day, April 25, it was forced to withdraw.

The Germans had advanced three miles by the end of that day, yet because of the Canadians, the Entente lines had not collapsed. More fighting was to come, but Canadian participation in the Second Battle of Ypres had effectively ended. It was quite incredible that the almost totally untested 1st Division had prevented a route and halted the German push to Ypres. Despite facing a terrible new weapon with little to no protection, using a rifle that continuously jammed, facing an experienced and numerically superior enemy, as well as being led by officers with little experience in modern warfare, the Canadians had saved Ypres. If anything, the Second Battle of Ypres highlighted the significant advantage held by the defender in this new modern war. The cost was not cheap, though: the 1st Division suffered 6,000 casualties.[8]

Between Ypres and the Somme

The Canadians soon learned the terrible price of going on the attack. At Festubert in May 1915, backed by what many at the time considered more than sufficient artillery support, Turner's 3rd Brigade followed by Currie's 2nd Brigade suffered 2,500 casualties in seven days of fighting that earned them a total of 600 yards. On June 15 near Givenchy, just south of Festubert, the 1st Division once again went on the attack, achieving even worse results. This time it was Mercer's 1st Brigade, and even though Mercer's men had ample time for reconnaissance and preparation, the attack was a failure. The Canadian and British artillery was simply not powerful enough to neutralize enemy artillery and machine-gun nests or cut through enemy barbed wire. More artillery was needed, in particular more heavy artillery that could actually destroy dug-in enemy positions. The Canadians were now experiencing the trench deadlock that perplexed commanders for much of the war, resulting in continued costly frontal attacks for little gain with very little chance of a real breakthrough.

By the end of that summer, the 1st Division had been shredded in combat. Its infantry strength of 11,000 men had suffered 9,400 casualties, a staggering loss of 85 percent. But reinforcements were on their way. The 2nd Division arrived in September and the 3rd Division in December. General Alderson was given command of the newly created Canadian Corps. General Turner got the 2nd Division, and Currie the 1st. Most of the staff officer positions were filled with British officers, despite Sam Hughes's protestations; there simply weren't enough experienced Canadians to fill those roles effectively.

That winter was brutal. The Canadians spent it near the village of St. Eloi on the southern edge of the Ypres Salient. Freezing temperatures mixed with constant rain and the wet, muddy conditions of the trenches led to low spirits among the men. Their clothes were constantly soaked and caked in mud, lice infested every part of their bodies, and they could rarely stay warm for any extended period of time. Trench fever and other sicknesses spread like wildfire through the ranks. Trench foot, the rotting of one's foot from constant overexposure to damp, unsanitary conditions, became such a problem that routine checks of the men's feet were required. Men slept, ate, and went to the bathroom in the same stretch of trench they occupied. An officer might be lucky enough to find accommodation in a dugout, relatively dry and warm as long as one did not object to sleeping with rats. For the other ranks, one simply passed out wherever they could: a carved-out niche in the wall or simply at the bottom of the trench along the duckboards.

The daily routine included refilling sandbags, patrols, sentry duty, and the odd excursion into no man's land coupled with general labour on any number of trench or road improvement projects. Most soldiers considered the daily routine quite boring. Sometimes this boredom was broken up by a harrowing trench raid, a practice first developed by the Princess Patricia's Canadian Light Infantry. These raids provided much-needed experience and certainly kept the Germans on their toes but often led to an artillery barrage in response. Sometimes live and let live was a safer policy. Comparatively, casualties were relatively light during the winter period. Yet raids, patrols, random shelling, and sniper fire combined with sickness meant a slow and steady drain of men. From January to March 1916, the Canadian Corps suffered 2,500 casualties, including 546 killed.

Most of the men looked forward to the respite of the rear areas. Policy deemed that soldiers would serve for one week in the front lines, followed by a second week in the support lines, a third week in reserve, and finally a fourth week out of the trenches entirely in the rear areas. The amenities naturally got better the farther away from the front lines one got. The rear areas meant hot food, hot baths, clean clothes, entertainment, and an opportunity to escape the constant threat of death. Alcohol was often a priority, as was the companionship of females. Sex was, in fact, a major problem, since the Canadians suffered from one of the highest rates of venereal disease in the entire British Expeditionary Force — a shocking 209.4 per thousand as compared to the British rate of 36.7 per thousand.[9]

Venereal disease was the least of the men's worries when, in March 1916, the Canadian Corps returned to the Ypres sector near the village of St. Eloi. The St. Eloi battlefield by this point had gone deep underground. Vast networks of subterranean tunnels stretched well into no man's land. A prior British assault had seen six mines detonated beneath the German lines. When the 2nd Canadian Infantry Division entered the trenches on the

Canadian soldiers take a bath near the front line.

night of April 3, they found the battlefield entirely changed from what they had studied and observed prior to the mine detonations. Dead bodies, destroyed trenches, disconnected defensive positions, little to no actual working communications equipment, and six massive craters provided a confused landscape that Turner's men now had to occupy and hold. Forty-eight hours later, the Germans attacked. The 6th Brigade's 27th Battalion was utterly destroyed, and then for 10 days both sides went back and forth fighting and dying for control of the craters. By the morning of April 17, they belonged to the Germans. The Canadians lost the "battle of the craters," as it came to be known, at a cost of 1,373 men.

In the aftermath, General Alderson wanted the heads of several Canadian officers he felt performed poorly during the battle. However, Sir Douglas Haig, the British commander-in-chief, was concerned about offending the prickly Canadians and instead let the axe fall on General Alderson himself.[10] His replacement was Sir Julian Byng, one of the most important leaders of the Canadian Corps.

An aristocratic cavalry officer, Byng had served in India, Sudan, South Africa, Egypt, and, most recently, in the disastrous Gallipoli campaign. He was initially quite miffed at being given the command, famously writing,

Canadian soldiers at rest in the trenches.

"Why am I sent the Canadians? I don't even know a Canadian.... I am ordered to these people and will do my best, but I don't think that there is any congratulations in it."[11] Regardless of this early snobbish attitude, Byng came to respect his men and in turn earned their respect.

Byng took over a Canadian Corps positioned just to the northeast of St. Eloi, along the easternmost portion of the Ypres Salient, holding the only part of the Ypres ridge not currently in German hands. The centre of the corps's line was the dominating feature of Mount Sorrel, and in early June, the Germans tried to take it.

The morning of June 2 was a relatively warm one when Major-General Mercer, General Officer Commanding the 3rd Division, and the 8th Brigade's Brigadier-General Victor Williams, set out to the front to personally observe the enemy positions. As Mercer and Williams were peering through their binoculars, the German attack struck. A massive artillery barrage, the largest that most Canadians had faced up to that point in the war, landed right on top of the officers. Mercer was killed and Williams seriously wounded (later taken prisoner). At the same time, several mine detonations exploded

Julian Byng (left) walking with a French officer, May 1917.

in and around Mount Sorrel followed by waves of German attackers. The 4th Canadian Mounted Rifles, the battalion directly in the way of the German assault, suffered nearly 90 percent casualties in less than half an hour. Any Canadians left were mopped up quickly, and the Germans, some wielding brand-new flame-throwers, were able to secure the ridge.

The next day, the Canadians counterattacked and, as at St. Eloi, a see-saw battle ensued. The Germans would capture a position and then meet a Canadian counterattack while any Canadian-captured position quickly faced a German one. On June 13, the only division still relatively fresh was Currie's 1st, and thus it was ordered to attack. Behind an incredibly effective and well-planned artillery-and-smoke barrage, Currie's men were able to drive the Germans back to their starting point. For the next 24 hours, the corps artillery, commanded by Quebec-born Henry Burstall, dealt the counterattacking Germans a series of vicious and accurate blows, and by the end of June 14, the Battle of Mount Sorrel was over. The Canadians had regained their lost ground but had suffered 8,500 casualties in the process. Of particular note, the work of Currie's division to restore the line highlighted the effectiveness when infantry and artillery prepared and co-operated closely. These were lessons that Byng would not let the corps forget.

By the summer of 1916, the war had cemented along global fault lines. In the east, the Russians desperately held on against the Germans. In southern Europe, in the rugged mountains of the Alps and Dolomites, the Austrians had reached a stalemate with the Italians, who had switched to the side of the Entente powers in April 1915. In the Middle East, the teetering Ottoman military faced multiple attacks from British, Indian, and dominion forces, while in Africa, fighting raged between bodies of African soldiers commanded by white European officers. At sea, the Royal Navy began tightening the noose of a continental blockade of Germany. In the air, the war had evolved from planes used simply for reconnaissance to machines engaging in terrifying air combat, while Zeppelins and bombers rained down death and destruction on civilians and combatants alike. The reality of modern war had become one of attrition. But simply killing more of your enemy was not going to be enough. Belligerents had to wear down not only their enemy's army but their civilian population and industry until that very state collapsed. Some of the more forward-thinking commanders had recognized this and given up hope of any single war-ending battlefield victory. Others, including Field Marshal Douglas Haig, commander of all the British forces on the Western Front, had not.

The Somme Offensive

Haig had a plan for decisive victory. His French allies were desperately engaged at Verdun in one of the largest battles on the Western Front. In February 1916, the Germans had launched a massive offensive focused around that ancient and historic city and the numerous fortresses protecting it. To stave off defeat, the French called upon their allies for help and British assistance indeed came. In July, the British, along with a smaller number of French troops, launched an offensive along the Somme River. Haig was the architect of the Somme Offensive and believed that with the Germans engaged in the southeast at Verdun, a breakthrough was now possible — a single decisive victory could truly crush the German military. Using unprecedented amounts of artillery, Haig planned for the British Fourth Army to seize the strategically crucial Pozières Ridge and then, if the German defences remained strong, consolidate and prepare to support further attacks by both the Fourth and Second

Armies. If the German defences were deemed to be weakening, a series of cavalry attacks would be launched to exploit whatever opportunities arose. Haig was optimistic that this offensive would deliver a significant blow to German martial strength along the Western Front.[12]

While it did inflict serious damage on the Germans, the Somme also witnessed the worst single day in the history of the British Army. The first day, July 1, just over 57,000 casualties were sustained. Attacking that day at Beaumont-Hamel was the Royal Newfoundland Regiment. Within 30 minutes of the attack, it was nearly wiped out. Of the 800 soldiers in the regiment, only 68 were available for roll call the next day. Haig's Somme Offensive never got its breakthrough. Instead, the British became bogged down in a lengthy, brutal, and unrelenting attritional offensive.

By simple luck, the Canadian Corps had escaped the early phase of the Somme. The corps did get bigger, though. On August 4, the 4th Canadian Infantry Division was added to it, commanded by Quebec-born Major-General David Watson. Watson had started the war as commander of the 2nd Battalion, Canadian Expeditionary Force, then was promoted to lead the 5th Brigade before being given the 4th Division.

Watson's rise to command spoke to a very real sense of professionalism that now permeated the corps's leadership. The pre-war Canadian idea that amateur soldiers with spirit were somehow more effective than professional soldiers with experience was long gone by 1916. The Canadian Corps had undergone extensive combat trials, and the leadership from non-commissioned officers to senior officers had experienced a brutal form of meritocracy. Those who could command in the chaos of the modern industrial battlefield made themselves known, and those who could not were gone. Thus, the 1916 Canadian Corps not only had a professional and experienced leadership group but one that had risen, like Watson, through the corps itself.

This was one of the elements that by then had made the corps so effective as a fighting force. Further to this, its divisions were kept within the corps structure, unlike other British corps where divisions were constantly swapped out and moved around. This not only meant that the leadership group stayed within the broader corps administrative structure but that a corps-wide fighting doctrine was embraced and practised throughout. Simply put, in terms of fighting doctrine and leadership, the Canadian Corps was one of the most homogenous organizations within the British Expeditionary

Force. While other corps commanders had to deal with new divisions and new officers coming in and out of their formations, Byng (and later Arthur Currie) dealt with mostly the same people. Successful officers moved up the ranks and stayed within the corps. By 1916, many not only had months of combat experience but also months of experience working together. It was no great challenge for Byng to work with Watson because Watson was already very familiar with how the corps went about its violent business.

In early September, this large and experienced corps went into the line near Pozières Ridge. Its objective was the French village of Courcelette, which lay on its northeast slope. The 2nd Division launched the attack on the village in the early-morning hours of September 15, supported by six brand-new Mark I land battleships (tanks). By the end of the day, the village was in Canadian hands, and the next two days were spent defending against determined German counterattacks that were frequently beaten back by vicious hand-to-hand combat. With the 2nd Division securing the village, it now fell to the 3rd Division to clear out two German trench systems key to the entire area. Fabek Graben, the first of them, fell quite rapidly, but Zollern Graben, the second one, became the site of furious back-and-forth combat as the Canadians captured it, lost it, and recaptured it. During this back-and-forth action, Private J.C. Kerr, from Fox River, Nova Scotia, won the Victoria Cross when he ran along the top of the enemy trench dropping grenades, despite having most of his fingers blown off earlier that day. His bravery forced the Germans to surrender a 250-yard stretch of trench. By September 22, the Battle of Flers-Courcelette, as it came to be called, had come to an end. The Canadians had delivered one of the most successful days of the entire Somme Offensive, a victory measuring 3,000 yards.

The success of the Canadian attack highlighted how the corps was undergoing a transformation from an inexperienced militia-based organization to a professional fighting force. It effectively utilized a creeping-barrage tactic, learned from the French, whereby the artillery acted as a screen, moving forward with the advancing infantry and forcing the German defenders to remain in their trenches while the infantry advanced across no man's land toward its objectives. As well, Canadian units were given limited objectives, and when captured, they were bypassed by fresh units moving toward the next objective. This "leapfrogging" technique became standard practice.[13]

Less of a contribution to their success was the tank. Early tanks were bulky, slow-moving, inflexible machines, and while at first they were successful in instilling terror in the enemy, the shock value eventually faded and the tank became just another addition to the modern industrial battlefield.

The Canadian experience at the Somme was not done yet. A series of attacks were launched from the end of September onward, attempting to capture an extremely well-fortified German position known as Regina Trench. The Canadians paid dearly for every yard of trench line secured, edging their way forward. Finally, on November 18, the remainder of Regina Trench was captured by David Watson's 4th Division, experiencing its first taste of combat on the Western Front. The Canadian participation during the Somme Offensive cost them just over 24,000 casualties in seven weeks of fighting. The British and French lost more than 620,000 and the Germans, 670,000.

✦ ✦ ✦

With the continually growing casualty lists, more pressure was placed on the recruitment drive back home, and with it, a greater spotlight was shone on Sam Hughes. His time as militia czar was coming to an end. By 1916, many were questioning Hughes's fitness for the role of minister of militia. He had wholly bungled equipping the initial contingent of Canadians going overseas and had stuck rigidly to his support for the Ross rifle despite the fact it was unsuited to war on the Western Front. Hughes was also the architect of the scandalous Shell Committee, which fattened the pockets of his friends while continually sending poor-quality munitions to the front (see later in this chapter for more about the Shell scandal). Furthermore, he had alienated many leading French Canadians, angered both British and Canadian officers, and even begun to run afoul of some people within the Conservative Party itself.

The recruitment and training system Hughes had devised resulted in men arriving in England under-equipped and deficiently trained for the job at hand. One soldier writing home called Hughes "a stupid bastard," while Joseph Flavelle, head of the Imperial Munitions Board, labelled him "insane." Another Canadian officer nicknamed him the "Mad Mullah of Canada." Despite both Hughes and Borden continually increasing Canada's military commitment — promises of 500,000 by January 1916 — many within Borden's circle as well as opposition Liberals in Parliament were demanding change. By August 1916, pressure on Borden was so great that he took control of recruitment away from Hughes and handed it to a civilian-run National Service Board, which implemented a far more centralized and effective model for Canada's manpower needs.

Instead of taking this as a sign that his position was precarious, Hughes continued to overstep. In September 1916, word got back to Borden that Hughes had created his own militia council while in London, effectively trying to take charge of the Canadian war effort overseas. This had been done without Borden's approval and proved to be the last straw. The prime minister demanded Hughes's resignation and tearfully Hughes obliged. By mid-November, just as the Canadian fight for Regina Trench was ending, Hughes was gone. Many cheered.[14]

The intensity of fighting that characterized the Canadian role during the Somme Offensive saw an increase in the cases of operational stress injuries, what was then labelled "shell shock," which was really just a catch-all phrase to describe a soldier's nervous breakdown on the front. These breakdowns were often the culmination of prolonged exposure to danger combined with physical and mental exhaustion. The symptoms of shell shock were variable, from chattering teeth to stuttering to uncontrollable anger or lapsing into comatose behaviour. It could manifest in unrelenting laughter, constant crying, or the inability to walk, sleep, eat, or even talk. Some men recovered quickly, often only needing some rest and an escape from the battlefield before returning to the line. Others were damaged for life.

For most of 1914 and 1915, concerns over "nervous illness" — an earlier diagnostic term for what later was deemed shell shock — were not yet significant enough to warrant any serious attention by senior command. Certainly, cases increased as the Canadian Corps became involved in more operations. At the Battle of Mount Sorrel in June 1916, for instance, 11 percent of casualties were classified as shell shock or some other form of nervous breakdown. However, it was the unprecedented carnage of the Somme Offensive that led to a shell-shock crisis within the British Expeditionary Force, where it seemed as if unsustainable numbers of men were being lost due to psychological trauma. This in turn revealed that the medical system within the

Minister of Militia and Defence Sam Hughes (far left) visits Arras, France, August 1916.

British Expeditionary Force and thus the Canadian Expeditionary Force, the former heavily influencing the latter, was wholly unsuited to cope with the dramatically increasing number of cases.

When a soldier was deemed by a medical officer to be suffering from shell shock, he was often sent to a rest station in the immediate rear area known as a divisional rest station. Here the soldier could receive warm food, bedrest, and an escape from immediate danger while all the time being observed. If his symptoms continued and were deemed legitimate, he was then moved to a casualty clearing station well to the rear where, once again, if symptoms continued, he would often end up back in Britain for treatment. For those at the divisional rest station who were deemed to have recovered, or whose symptoms were thought to be illegitimate (labelled "malingerers"), they would be ushered back to the front.

The sharp increase in shell-shock cases during the Somme Offensive became a serious concern for Douglas Haig and other senior commanders within the British Expeditionary Force. Many felt the British military medical professionals, particularly the ones who were civilians prior to the war, were too lenient with shell-shock cases, and a series of steps were taken to delegitimize shell shock as a wound, effectively trying to shame soldiers into not reporting symptoms while pressuring military doctors to actively reduce the increasing casualty counts.

From 1916 onward, a whole series of policy directives, treatment and triage centres, evacuation procedures, and classification systems were adopted, discarded, and manipulated to try to reduce the growing casualty numbers from shell shock and other combat stress injuries, an estimated 17 percent of all non-fatal Canadian casualties during the corps's peak fighting on the Somme. None of this was ever really effective in dealing with the root problem: how to prevent, mitigate, and cure shell shock. Returning men to active duty as quickly as possible was always the paramount objective, a policy that led to disastrous consequences for tens of thousands of surviving veterans.[15]

The Home Front: 1914 to 1916

The home front was also changing in ways that would prove challenging for many returning veterans. The War Measures Act, passed in August 1914, was a crucial tool in ensuring that the Canadian home front was mobilized to support the war in unprecedented ways. The act gave the sitting government sweeping powers over the Canadian state and the Canadian people. Policies or procedures that would not have been legal or acceptable in peacetime could now be implemented in the name of the war effort. It also allowed the government to censor the press and to control communications, transportation, trade, and industry. Under the act, the government could arrest, detain, and even deport individuals suspected of antiwar activities without a trial. It even allowed the government to seize private property if deemed necessary for the war effort.

The control of information was a primary objective under the War Measures Act. Canada's chief censor during the First World War was Lieutenant-Colonel Ernest J. Chambers, whose actual title was Gentleman Usher of the Black Rod. Chambers was born in England but grew up in Montreal, becoming a journalist for the *Montreal Daily Star* before taking his post with the government. Active in his role, he reprimanded *Maclean's* magazine for publishing a report that briefly mentioned a Canadian defeat and ordered the *Sault Express* to pull its June 1916 article entitled "No More

Soldiers at the Front." Chambers was particularly mistrustful of any literature not in English or French and frequently banned publications that were in
neither language. Over the course of the war, Chambers's power expanded to
all facets of communications, including the media, telephone and telegraph
communications, movies, photographs, and even pieces of music (he, in fact,
banned 31 pieces of music). By the end of the war, Chambers, backed by the
powers of the War Measures Act, became one of the most powerful men in
the country.

The War Measures Act also allowed the government to limit and even sus-
pend civil liberties once guaranteed to residents of Canada. People originally
from nations now at war with the British Empire were deemed "enemy aliens."
Eighty thousand of these enemy aliens were forced to report regularly to local authorities and carry identity papers on them at all times. Of particular
concern to the Canadian government were those enemy aliens without employment. For these indigent enemy aliens, internment became the solution.

While the German-Canadian community was generally well off, many of
the ethnic communities originally from the Austro-Hungarian Empire were
not so fortunate. One of the largest groups of these were Ukrainian Canadians
(most Ukrainians would have identified as Ruthenian, but Ukrainian became
the common identifier in Canada). In the late 19th century, tens of thousands
of Ukrainians had come to Canada lured by promises of good, cheap land.
Most of them came from territory split between the Austro-Hungarian and
Russian Empires, generally in the area known as Galicia. Thus, when war
broke out, entire immigrant communities of Ukrainians who had come from
the Austro-Hungarian Empire were now classified as enemy aliens.

Eight thousand five hundred and seventy-nine enemy aliens, mostly men
but some women and children, were rounded up, including Ukrainians,
Poles, Croats, Germans, Turks, Bulgarians, and a smattering of other nation-
alities, many of whom were unemployed. These people were sent to isolated
internment camps throughout the country. Those internees with property
had theirs confiscated and few were compensated after the war.[16]

To limit the financial strain on the federal government, the internment
program became a partnership between federal and provincial government
departments. The entire program was run by none other than William Otter,
who had come out of retirement for the job. Under Otter, internees lived in
prison-like conditions and were made to work on various mining and logging

projects, helping to repair and improve military infrastructure, clearing land for settlement in Northern Ontario and Quebec, and repairing rail lines in Atlantic Canada, as well as assisting in the development of Banff National Park, including the final nine holes of the modern-day Fairmont Banff Springs Golf Course. Paid less than half the daily wage of normal government labourers, this was an accessible and readily available source of cheap labour. In fact, numerous petitions were made to the government by municipal and provincial authorities to get access to these internees for their own projects.

Life in these camps was difficult, despite Otter's attempt to clean up some of the worst abuses. Internees were regularly mistreated by their overseers, including beatings, solitary confinement, and food restrictions. Six internees were shot and killed while attempting to escape, dozens perished from sickness and accidents, while a few died by suicide. At one point, reports on abuses in these camps by both Swiss and American diplomats made their way to Berlin where an incensed German government threatened reprisals were this program to continue. By 1917, however, this issue became moot as most internees were paroled to meet the growing demand for labour in Canada's expanding war industries. The internment program was officially ended in 1920. Sadly, this would not be the last time in the 20th century the War Measures Act allowed the Canadian government to intern residents of Canada.

Besides dealing with enemy aliens, one of the major challenges faced by the Canadian government was how to finance the war. The federal budget and the nation's debt were rapidly increasing as the war progressed. Traditional sources of revenue such as customs duties, postal rates, and tariffs were not enough to sustain the war effort. Borrowing from the Americans certainly helped, but for nationalistic and economic reasons it could not continue unabated. More cash was needed. War bonds, the precursor to modern-day Canada Savings Bonds, became a quick source backed by a focused propaganda effort extolling Canadians to show their support by purchasing the bonds. The Canadian government also passed a few radical tax initiatives. A luxury tax was enacted on tobacco and alcohol in 1915. A Business Profits War Tax was instituted in 1916. Most controversially, Canada's first income tax was approved in 1917. All of this, thought temporary at the time, helped generate much-needed revenue for the war effort and became major revenue sources for future Canadian governments.

Morrissey Internment Camp near Fernie, British Columbia, 1915.

The demands of total war rapidly accelerated Canada's economic growth. By 1915, the country had been pulled out of a two-year pre-war recession, and while Prime Minister Robert Borden had made early promises that the government would not interfere in business, by 1917, Canada's laissez-faire approach to the economy was over. A fuel controller threatened punishment for people caught hoarding fuel. A food controller established price guidelines and promoted food consumption awareness. But the two main industries driving Canada's wartime economy were wheat and munitions, and the government took unprecedented steps to regulate both industries.

The global demand for wheat skyrocketed with the outbreak of war, and the Canadian Prairies became the breadbasket for the British war effort. As wheat prices continually rose, more and more people migrated to the countryside to take advantage of the lucrative trade. New farms appeared and old ones expanded their operations. To police the rapidly growing wheat industry, and the ensuing inflationary consequences, Borden removed wheat from the open market and placed it under the jurisdiction of the Board of Grain Supervisors. The board would be responsible for controlling the price and sale of wheat for the 1917 and 1918 harvests. By the end of the war, wheat prices had tripled, the Prairie population had increased by over a million, and the number of farms had increased by 28 percent.

Like wheat, demand for munitions skyrocketed. In 1914, the Department of Militia and Defence under Sam Hughes convinced Britain that Canada could supply much of its munitions needs. Hughes created the Shell Committee to oversee the contracts to manufacture and deliver munitions from Canadian factories to Great Britain while maintaining a competitive market model. His committee was scandalously incompetent, since it became a source of patronage and profiteering. Orders either never showed up or arrived in Britain incomplete. The munitions that did arrive were often of poor quality and this was only tragically discovered on the battlefields of the Western Front.

By 1915, a full-out Shell crisis had emerged, and the British government took steps to centralize the Canadian munitions industry under its control. With Robert Borden's blessing, the Shell Committee was scrapped and replaced in December by the Imperial Munitions Board. This board was a British agency answerable to the Ministry of Munitions in London but run by Joseph Flavelle from Peterborough, Ontario.[17] The Imperial Munitions Board worked. It solved the Shell crisis and effectively organized and managed Canada's largest wartime industry. At its peak, 200,000 men and women worked in 675 factories across Canada, with the board operating at a budget three times the size of the federal government's.

As the Canadian government sought to transform Canada's home front to a total war footing, the common Canadian soldier in Europe was also transforming. To survive the horrors of trench warfare, the men of the Canadian Corps developed a unique and powerful trench culture that allowed them to make the best of the violent world around them. Numerous techniques were employed by the soldiers to acclimate themselves to life on the front line, from naming trenches after familiar geographical locations back in Canada to a distinct use of swearing (in particular the varied use of the word "fuck") and slang ("napooed," meaning gone from the trenches as a result of being wounded or killed).

Sometimes it would be a macabre embrace of the dead, one company developing a daily ritual of shaking hands with a corpse's arm that remained dangling from a trench wall. Music, storytelling, battalion newspapers, acting troupes (like 3rd Division's famous group The Dumbells), along with souven-iring and trench art, all played a part in informing the soldiers' culture that would have been quite alien to any non-combatant back in Canada. Some Canadian soldiers took advantage of educational opportunities through the "University of Vimy Ridge." Although beginning informally by only offering a smattering of courses, the program was soon formalized back in England as the "Khaki University." Courses ranged from basic reading and writing to technical courses and even academic graduate work.

These various methods of coping with the strain of war became crucial to the mental well-being of the men. Even their officers came to realize how important this soldiers' culture was in keeping up morale. Acceptance by the leadership class meant that various aspects of this culture provided an outlet for regular Canadian soldiers to challenge and even criticize their leaders in a manner that fell within acceptable boundaries of regular mili-tary discipline. Through satirical cartoons, poetry, literature, and anonym-ous griping, trench newspapers became a particularly favourite way for the "rankers" to negotiate the authority of the officer class. Griping, complain-ing, and making fun of officers occurred in almost all the newspapers and was generally accepted by officers as a means for the men to let off steam.

As the war progressed, trench culture came to define life on the Western Front and became important in helping mitigate the psychological stresses of combat. This cultural support was sorely needed as the Canadian Corps en-tered 1917, a year that saw it face some of its toughest challenges of the war.[18]

4

THE FIRST WORLD WAR: 1917-1918

At the beginning of 1917, the Canadian Corps was stationed in the line near the city of Arras in a region dominated by the German-held position of Vimy Ridge. The corps had spent the winter training, rebuilding, and improving its fighting doctrine. Much of this improvement was encapsulated in Arthur Currie's "Verdun Report." Currie, along with several senior British officers, visited the Verdun battlefield to glean important tactical lessons from the French. Currie's subsequent report went straight to Julian Byng as well as other senior commanders within the corps.

The French emphasis on strong reconnaissance and on rehearsing major attacks was highlighted, two elements that reinforced Currie's own personal belief in the need for ample preparation before any battle. However, what really stood out in his report was his praise for the French empowerment of the infantry platoon. Using fire and movement and the coordinated employment of machine gunners, bombers (grenade-throwing infantrymen), and riflemen, the French infantry platoon could deal with most enemy strong points without waiting for artillery, which allowed for greater speed of movement across the battlefield and better flexibility in attack. While the British Expeditionary Force was certainly experimenting with more

Lieutenant-General Arthur Currie (left) with Field Marshal Douglas Haig, February 1918.

flexible platoon and section tactics, one of the major issues still facing the Canadians — and British — was that they operated within an attack style dominated by a continual reliance on artillery.[1] This reliance limited manoeuvrability and speed of advance on the battlefield. Currie strongly recommended adopting French platoon-style tactics, and Byng readily agreed.

Besides inflexibility, another major problem facing the Canadian Corps was the devastating impact of enemy artillery. The "creeping-barrage" technique was fairly effective in neutralizing enemy soldiers, but enemy artillery continued to wreak havoc on attacking Canadians. The man responsible for trying to solve this problem was Lieutenant-Colonel Andrew McNaughton from Moosomin, Saskatchewan. McNaughton was an electrical engineer in civilian life, and by 1917 was in command of the Canadian counter-battery corps.

To this command, he brought a scientific approach to gunnery. Known to have kept a pet lion cub in his headquarters, supposedly because he enjoyed watching how it scared British officers, McNaughton embraced a wide array of scientific methods to detect enemy artillery. He utilized state-of-the-art aerial photo reconnaissance from both planes and hot-air balloons and advocated flash-spotting, using a mathematical process that could identify an enemy gun based on the location or "spot" of the flash. An even newer technique championed by him was sound ranging, which relied on cutting-edge

Brigadier-General Andrew McNaughton, October 1918.

microphones placed throughout no man's land to pick up the sound of an enemy gun firing. A mathematical formula could then triangulate the location of the enemy gun based on the interval between a gun firing and the "bang" it made. Under McNaughton, these techniques were used effectively, and his counter-battery corps became one of the finest in the entire British Expeditionary Force.

Vimy Ridge

The skills, techniques, and practices adopted during the early months of 1917 made the Canadian Corps's fighting doctrine cutting edge and would be put on display at the Battle of Vimy Ridge.[2] Vimy Ridge was the dominating geographical feature in the Arras sector and had been held by the Germans since late 1914. The British and French had both launched unsuccessful attempts to capture it. By 1917, it was considered one of the strongest positions along the entire German front. Since 1914, it had been continually reinforced and its trenches further improved. It was now a complex defensive array of interconnected strong points with deep bunkers, heavily fortified trenches, machine-gun emplacements protected by concrete, and thick belts of barbed wire with the enemy artillery hidden by the reverse slope of the ridge. The Canadian assault on the ridge was going to be an opening thrust for the larger Battle of Arras, securing the left flank for the attacking British Third Army.

The attack plan was carefully constructed by Julian Byng and his staff. The infantry would advance along a strict timetable in co-operation with the artillery whose barrage would once again "creep" across the battlefield in support of the attacking infantry. The Canadians would also be supported by more heavy artillery than they had ever used before in an attack: one heavy gun for every 20 yards of frontage. This also included the use of the new 106 fuse, which detonated on contact with enemy wire, cutting through the sharp metal. Extensive battlefield rehearsals were conducted in the weeks leading up to the attack. Senior officers all the way down to junior non-commissioned officers knew their objectives inside and out, as well as the objectives of those around them. Long underground subways dug into the chalky soil allowed

Canadian soldiers overlooking the village of Vimy, France, from the crest of Vimy Ridge, April 1917.

the corps to build up its supplies and reinforcements without detection by the enemy. The Germans knew something was coming; they just didn't know what or when.

On the snowy morning of April 9, 1917, after a brief let-up of what was a week-long artillery barrage of the German trenches, Canadian soldiers from all four divisions attacked. Within nine hours, the 1st, 2nd, and 3rd Divisions had captured all their objectives, while McNaughton's counter-battery corps neutralized 80 percent of the enemy guns. The 4th Division ran into complications, however, at Hill 145 and "The Pimple." Both were dominating high points along the ridge. Refocused attacks saw Hill 145 fall on April 10 and The Pimple finally captured amid a blizzard on April 12. It was in the seizing of this last objective that Lance Corporal Henry Norwest, a Métis cowboy from Fort Saskatchewan, Alberta, earned a citation for bravery by covering the attack with deadly and accurate sniper fire (he went on to earn the Military Medal but was killed in August 1918). With the capture of The Pimple, all of Vimy Ridge was now in Canadian hands.

The victory of Vimy Ridge was celebrated in France and throughout the British Empire. A Paris newspaper hailed it as an "Easter gift" to the French by the Canadians, while British newspapers celebrated the Canadian Corps and its magnificent triumph. Even King George V personally congratulated the men on their achievement. Now it was French officers arriving at Vimy Ridge to study the Canadian battle.

Capturing the ridge meant taking 4,500 yards of German-held ground. Yet, because the Canadians now held the high ground and could see out across the Douai Plain, the Germans were forced to fall back several miles. The battle vindicated the advanced fighting doctrine of the Canadian Corps, and the Germans were stunned by the rapidity of its success. The battle also led to Julian Byng being promoted to command the British Third Army. However, the victory came at a heavy cost. The corps suffered 10,602 casualties, most of those on the first day. This gave April 9 the dubious distinction of becoming the bloodiest single day in Canadian military history. The fighting was so severe that three Victoria Crosses were awarded on that initial day alone, with a fourth bestowed on the second. The battle itself was an incredible tactical win, but it had very little impact on the broader course of the war. Strategically, the Battle of Arras devolved into another of Haig's attritional offensives. More fighting was to come. Vimy Ridge was a renowned victory, certainly, but not the only stellar achievement for the Canadian Corps. It was, in fact, an early part of a long string of uninterrupted successes that continued until the end of the war.

Vimy Ridge, however, may have had one very unintended yet important consequence for Canada and the larger British Empire. While the corps was fighting for the ridge, an Imperial War Conference took place in London. Here, representatives of the dominions as well as Great Britain met to discuss issues related to the war. The victory at Vimy came at a perfect time, since it shone a spotlight on Canada's contribution to the war effort, and in turn to the broader impact of Britain's dominions. In late April, with the victory at Vimy Ridge still fresh, Prime Minister Robert Borden was able to pass Resolution IX, of which he was a principal author.[3] This measure called for a future conference to restructure the relationship between Great Britain and its dominions and to recognize them as equal nations and part of an imperial commonwealth. Canada was now on its way to full autonomy.

Conscription

Vimy Ridge also contributed to one of the greatest domestic crises in the history of Canada: conscription.[4] In the aftermath of Vimy Ridge, Prime Minister Borden, who himself had just returned to Canada in May, was faced with the stark reality that recruitment numbers were decreasing while casualty rates were increasing. He and his War Cabinet quickly came to the realization that the current volunteer system was not sufficient to support continued Canadian Corps operations, especially since Borden and most others assumed the war would carry on into 1919. Although in 1915, he had promised no conscription and had repeated his promise again in 1916, Borden was now faced with a hard decision. If he wanted the Canadian Corps to continue to operate at a high level and earn Canada a battlefield reputation that could translate to greater postwar recognition, he had to ensure it maintained its combat effectiveness. To do so, the corps needed men, thus Borden announced that his government would impose conscription, passing the Military Service Act in August.

The public response was immediate. In rural Canada, the reaction was largely negative, fearing a depletion of farm labour because of conscription.

The outcry among Indigenous leaders was swift. Many argued that based on historical treaties Indigenous warriors could not be forced to fight against their will. Others argued that because "status Indians" did not hold the rights of citizenship, they could not be legally conscripted. These arguments worked, and in January 1918, the government exempted Indigenous men from conscription.

In Quebec, the reaction was downright hostile. Conscription was seen as an instrument of English Canada to force young French Canadians to fight and die in a British imperial conflict. As Henri Bourassa stated, Borden's conscriptionist agenda was the "antithesis of everything we [French Canadians] love, everything we believe, everything we want. It is the synthesis of all we hate …"[5] In much of urban English Canada, the belief was that conscription would finally force Quebec to "do its part" in terms of enlistment. Yet among the first class of men called up (Class 1 being unmarried men or widowers aged 20 to 24 years of age), nearly 94 percent of all Canadians applied for an exemption. It was clear it wasn't just French Canadians who were hesitant to serve in the meat grinder of the Western Front. The eagerness and enthusiasm for enlistment seen in 1914 and 1915 were gone, carried away with the bodies of the dead and wounded from Canada's early battles.

Conscription was also not going to go unchallenged by Wilfrid Laurier and his Liberals. It thus became the focus of the federal election that December. To try to avoid an election, Borden attempted to form a coalition with Laurier, leader of the Official Opposition, but Laurier was against conscription and believed the issue would destroy Borden's party. Laurier was wrong. Borden was able to outmanoeuvre Laurier with two key pieces of legislation. The Military Voters Act enfranchised all members of the Canadian Expeditionary Force, including people of colour, non-British subjects, and serving nurses, while allowing Borden to place pro-government votes in the riding of his choosing if the voter did not select his or her own constituency.

His second political volley was the Wartime Elections Act, which enfranchised mothers, wives, and sisters of serving soldiers — the first time women were allowed to vote in a Canadian federal election. Suddenly, Borden enfranchised hundreds of thousands of new voters, most of whom would support his new Union Party. Ninety-two percent of Canadian Expeditionary Force members voted Union. Although his party was abandoned by a small number of Conservative MPs from Quebec, Borden was able to lure several pro-conscription Liberals across the floor to join his new Union government, making it almost entirely English-speaking. The conscription issue shattered the Liberals, and when the returns for the election were in, Borden's new party had swept the country except for Quebec. In that province, the Liberals won 62 of the 65 seats (Prince Edward Island's four seats were split evenly between Laurier and Borden). Yet with 57 percent of the popular national vote, Borden had his mandate and could now pursue conscription.

Anti-conscription rallies and protests had already erupted since Borden first announced his government's plan in May 1917. These became more and more violent. Riots erupted in Montreal and Quebec City. Crowds assaulted recruiters, soldiers, and government officials, while government offices were attacked. In August, the home of Lord Atholstan, owner of the pro-conscription newspaper *Montreal Star*, was bombed.

The year 1918 began with federal agents actively enforcing conscription within the province and arresting those who refused to report. On the evening of March 28, a young man in Quebec City was removed from a bowling alley and taken into custody by police when he was unable to provide his exemption papers. Angered at the arrest, a crowd began to form outside the police station, and despite the man being released, the crowd attacked. The next evening an even larger mob gathered and ransacked the headquarters of two pro-conscription newspapers before pushing past a police barrier and destroying the local Military Service Registrar office. The dispatch of 300 troops from the Citadelle de Québec finally restored order late that evening, but more violence was to come.

Borden became increasingly concerned these riots could spark a province-wide insurrection, with insurrectionists arming themselves from a major weapons and munitions factory located in the city. The prime minister thus took the radical step of declaring that Quebec City was now under federal control. Seven hundred and eighty soldiers were dispatched to protect federal buildings, with a further 1,000 coming in from Ontario. Violence continued as the arriving military clashed with large, angry crowds. Reports arriving in Ottawa warned that the politicians, police, fire department, and even local French-Canadian soldiers were sympathetic to the rioters. Three thousand more soldiers were requested from western Canada. On March 31, mobs of rioters once again fought with soldiers, some groups being dispersed

Anti-conscription rally in Montreal, May 1917.

at the point of bayonets while a contingent of Canadian soldiers protecting an arms shipment opened fire on an attacking crowd, wounding three civilians. Local firearms dealers were ordered to move their goods to the Citadelle de Québec for protection from looting. There were now 1,800 soldiers in the city, including General François-Louis Lessard, who had come from Halifax to take command of the Canadian force. French-Canadian soldiers were ordered to remain in barracks while the city streets were patrolled almost exclusively by English-speaking soldiers.

On April 1, thousands of Quebec residents once again took to the streets and attacked soldiers using bricks, rocks, and snowballs. Suddenly, shots rang out from rooftops, and several Canadian soldiers were hit. The troops responded, opening fire on the crowd. Four rioters were killed, upward of 70 were seriously injured, while 32 soldiers were wounded in the fighting that followed. The violence of the Easter Riots shocked the nation. Civic leaders, including Henri Bourassa and senior clergy of the Catholic Church in Quebec, immediately called for calm, and in the ensuing days this appeal prevailed. Nonetheless, on April 4, martial law was declared and the city was completely cut off from outside travel. A tense but stable peace ensued. By

April 15, most of the soldiers were off the streets and back in their barracks, and 10 days later Lessard returned to Halifax.

The crisis had passed. Robert Borden got the nearly 100,000 conscripts he wanted, and 24,000 of those conscripted made it to France and became crucial reinforcements for the Canadian Corps as it fought its way through the Hundred Days campaign. Had the war gone into 1919, as many believed, far more would have found themselves arriving on the Western Front. Borden barely avoided open revolt.[6]

Demographic Changes in the Canadian Expeditionary Force

The continuing casualties also led to a demographic shift within the Canadian Expeditionary Force (CEF). Declining enlistment numbers had been a growing concern since mid-1916. Despite the reorganization of the recruitment system and the sacking of Hughes, the enlistment numbers continued to drop while casualties mounted. More and more pressure was put on the military to accept non-white volunteers. The acceptance of non-white volunteers was fairly radical, since the war was viewed by many as a "white man's war," specifically rooted in a form of Anglo-Canadian nationalism that celebrated both "Britishness" and "whiteness." Even though there was no official policy of discrimination, local recruiting officers turned away most visible minorities because of absurd ideas about racial characteristics and deeply embedded prejudices. For the Canadian government, permitting Indigenous people or Canadians of Asian descent to serve might in turn lead to demands for full citizenship, something that was simply out of step with the common assumption that Canada was a "white man's nation." Yet the casualties sustained at Vimy Ridge highlighted the shocking disparity between casualty numbers and enlistment numbers. By the end of April, the corps had sustained 23,939 casualties, while only 4,761 men enlisted. Steps needed to be taken to increase enlistment, and despite continued prejudice, more and more visible minorities were allowed to enlist in the CEF.

In Nova Scotia, which at the time had Canada's largest Black community, numerous young men of African descent had been rejected by recruiters because of the colour of their skin. After nearly two years of lobbying by the Nova Scotian Black community, however, the government relented, and in

July 1916, the all-Black No. 2 Construction Battalion was formed — Canada's first and only segregated unit, though it was commanded by white officers.[7] Eight hundred Black Canadians served in the CEF. Later that same year, 160 Japanese Canadians, who had been rejected by recruiting stations in British Columbia, crossed into Alberta where they successfully enlisted in the CEF.

While the CEF began to accept more and more non-white recruits, tens of thousands of young Chinese men were being transported across Canada via rail to Halifax where they were to end up on the Western Front as part of the Chinese Labour Corps. As early as 1916, both the British and the French were becoming desperate for men to fulfill labour roles behind the front lines. Based on an earlier proposal by the Chinese government, all three countries engaged in diplomatic talks to begin recruiting young men, particularly from the coastal province of Shandong in northeast China. Recruiting agreements were signed that year, even though China did not formally enter the war as an Entente ally until August 1917, and the first of these labourers began to arrive in France by early 1917. Canada agreed to help facilitate the transportation of those men intended for the British Expeditionary Force, and upward of 84,000 of these Chinese labourers were thus transported from Canada's West Coast to Halifax via specially designated, heavily guarded Canadian Pacific

Chinese Labour Corps personnel celebrate Lunar New Year, February 1918.

Indigenous soldiers and elders, 1916–17.

Railway trains. This transportation operation was conducted under strict secrecy, and the Canadian government even quietly, and temporarily, waived the $500 Chinese head tax that had been in force since 1903.[8]

At the same time, more and more Indigenous men were accepted into the CEF. In 1914, the government's official position was that no Indigenous men should be allowed to enlist. Deeply held racial stereotypes about their "savage" nature and propensity for "scalping" led to some arguing they had no place in a "civilized" European war. At the same time, others argued that while the British military would welcome Indigenous soldiers, the Germans would not afford them the privileges of "civilized" warfare under the Geneva Conventions. Yet some recruiting stations simply turned a blind eye, and Indigenous men entered into the service as early as the fall of 1914. By late 1915, Indigenous men were officially allowed to enlist.

Support for the war varied greatly among Indigenous communities. Some nations raised money to donate to the government war effort via the Patriotic Fund. Others, such as the Mi'kmaq, Maliseet, and Six Nations, saw significant numbers of their young men enlist, while other nations simply refused to support the war effort at all. Many did volunteer, though, and by the war's end, between 3,500 and 5,000 had served (one Kanien'keha:ka woman from the Six Nations reserve, Charlotte Edith Anderson Monture, was a nurse in the U.S. Medical Corps). Roughly one-third of all eligible Indigenous men took part in the CEF, a ratio nearly equal to that of non-Indigenous volunteers.[9]

✦ ✦ ✦

The year 1917 was a tumultuous one outside Canada, as well. In May, French soldiers frustrated with the apparent futility of their constant offensives began to mutiny. Then, in November, a Bolshevik-led insurrection led to the toppling of the Russian provisional government, and by December, Russia was negotiating its way out of the war. Yet it was not all bad news. German unrestricted submarine warfare, coupled with attempts to gain Mexican support in a war against the United States, allowed President Woodrow Wilson to finally convince the U.S. Congress to declare war on Germany in April, though it would be many months before the Americans arrived in any significant numbers.

Third Battle of Ypres (Passchendaele)

The Canadian Corps received a new commander in June, none other than 41-year-old Arthur Currie. A Canadian now led the largest military force in Canadian history. Currie was also the youngest officer in the British Army to achieve the rank of lieutenant-general. His first test came shortly after his appointment when he was given the task of capturing the city of Lens. About three miles north of Vimy Ridge, Lens was a coal-mining town that had been utterly destroyed in the fighting. Giant heaps of rubble and detritus were piled around skeletons of former buildings in all that remained of the city. Douglas Haig was hoping that with the capture of Lens, the Canadian Corps could prevent German troops from moving farther north where Haig had launched yet another offensive, the Third Battle of Ypres.

After surveying the battlefield, Currie realized the city of Lens was not the most strategically important position in the area. Hill 70 situated just to the north of the city was, its base spreading into the suburbs of Lens to its

King George V (left), Lieutenant-General Arthur Currie (centre), and Lieutenant-General Henry Horne (right) surveying Vimy Ridge, August 1917.

south. If Currie could capture Hill 70, he could direct murderous artillery fire onto the Germans in Lens and hopefully force their withdrawal. With this logic, Currie was able to convince First British Army commander Henry Horne to allow him to shift his objective from the rubble-strewn city to the heights of Hill 70.

Currie's plan was to use "bite-and-hold" tactics. His corps would capture the hill (the "bite" portion), then hold it against expected German counter-attacks. To do this, Currie made sure his men were equipped and prepared to bring up heavy machine guns shortly after the capture of their final objectives. Each Vickers heavy machine gun brought up would constitute an interlaced defensive web of supporting fire designed to meet the Germans when they counterattacked. As well, Currie made sure his artillery sighted the most logical transportation routes the Germans would take. When the treeless slope of Hill 70 was captured, the Germans were going to have to pay in blood to try to take it back.

At 4:25 a.m. on August 15, the men of the 1st and 2nd Divisions launched their attack. Despite the Germans being well prepared, the same skill and co-operation that characterized Vimy Ridge was once again showcased by the

Canadian soldiers investigating a German sniper position at Hill 70, August 1917.

corps. Small-level platoon tactics using fire and movement rapidly overcame German defensive positions, and McNaughton's counter-battery corps once again proved its worth. By the end of that first day, the hill was in Canadian hands at a cost of 1,000 dead and 2,400 wounded, and the men had prepared their positions to receive the expected German counterattacks.

The Germans would not disappoint. For the next 72 hours, 21 different German counterattacks were beaten back. Withering machine-gun fire and deadly Canadian artillery ravaged five different German divisions. It was during this chaotic period that Japanese-born Private Masumi Mitsui of the 10th Battalion earned the Military Medal when on August 16 he recaptured a Lewis light machine gun and maintained fire, holding back German troops from capturing a key position (he was later promoted to sergeant). Mitsui was not the only Japanese Canadian to earn a medal that day. Hiroshima-born Private Tokutaro Iwamoto, from the same section as Mitsui's, earned the Military Medal when he single-handedly cleared out a position known as the Chalk Pit, capturing 20 Germans in the fighting.

Despite the seizure of Hill 70, the Germans would not abandon Lens, and Currie showed a rare lapse in judgment when he ordered the 4th Division to

Masumi Mitsui (standing) and Masajiro Shishido, 1916.

attack the city.[10] Very little time had been spent on reconnaissance or preparation for the attack. The Canadians had limited information on enemy strength or positions. On top of all that, the attackers would be engaging the Germans in terrain that heavily favoured the defenders. Lens had been absolutely demolished in the fighting, and piles of bricks and debris had been turned into trench lines that carved through its streets and the remains of its buildings. The Germans had constructed tunnels and passageways that allowed them to move in behind the Canadians even as they advanced. The result of the ensuing attack on Lens was a failure. From August 20 to 25, battalion after battalion was thrown into Lens only to be repulsed with extremely high casualties. Even when the Canadians supposedly captured an objective, it seemed as if more Germans emerged from cellars, dugouts, and

Canadian soldiers explore a German bunker at Lens, September 1917.

apparently unoccupied piles of rubble. By August 25, the attack on Lens was called off.

The 10-day struggle for Hill 70 and Lens cost the Canadians 9,198 casualties, 44 percent of those sustained in the attempt on Lens itself. Currie's capture of Hill 70 was a masterstroke of "bite-and-hold" doctrine and gave the British another dominating high-ground feature looking out over the Douai Plain. His attempt on Lens itself was a rare mistake, an attack without proper time for preparation or reconnaissance, and the 4th Division paid the price. He would not make that error again.

In early October, the corps was moved back into the Ypres sector to participate in the ongoing Third Battle of Ypres, another Haig offensive that began with lofty goals and degenerated into a months-long attritional calamity. By the time the Canadians entered the fray, Haig was using the offensive to draw German forces away from the French who were dealing with widespread mutinies. The area occupied by the Canadians embodied the worst of the First World War battlefield. Years of fighting over the same ground had left the earth utterly destroyed. The natural drainage of Flanders' fields was totally blocked, and bodies and equipment littered the ground or were brought up with every new barrage, as if the very earth was trying to rid itself of the detritus of war. The battlefield was so wet that it was impossible to create any sort of continuous trench line. Most of the men were forced to simply hunker down in a loosely connected line of water-logged shell holes. The mud was so thick that it could trap a soldier where he stood. It stuck to guns, clothes, and equipment, making movement near-impossible. Artillery pieces, horses, even men were known to be sucked into the earth, completely disappearing. The Canadians were soaked to the bone, covered in thick mud, and trying desperately to avoid being swallowed by the earth.

The Canadian Corps was given the task of capturing the nearly destroyed village of Passchendaele that sat atop Passchendaele Ridge. After careful reconnaissance of the objective and a good look at the terrain, Currie was utterly appalled. At first he refused to carry out the attack while under the questionable leadership of Sir Hubert Gough, commander of the British Fifth Army. Relenting, Haig placed the Canadian Corps under the command of Sir Herbert Plumer's Second Army. Currie still protested. One of the unique advantages for Currie was that he represented a national military formation. He was answerable to both Ottawa and the British High Command and had

A flooded German pillbox at Passchendaele, Belgium, November 1917.

the rare ability to challenge his superiors if he felt the Canadian Corps was being employed improperly. He did so here. Currie pointed out the futility of sending the Canadians forward and estimated an attack would cost him 16,000 casualties.[11] Despite his protests, Haig's order remained, and Currie's corps went to work.

The attack commenced on October 26, and over the course of 16 days, all four divisions were deployed to push toward the small Belgian village. Slowly but surely, the Canadians did it. Each day saw the corps measure their success in hundreds and sometimes thousands of yards. It was a slow, methodical, violent march over some of the worst battlefield conditions humans had ever encountered. On October 30, Sergeant George Mullin, from Portland, Oregon, who had been with the Princess Patricia's Canadian Light Infantry since 1914, single-handedly captured a German pillbox and forced 10 enemy soldiers to surrender. He would be awarded the Victoria Cross (the first of nine awarded to the corps at Passchendaele). On the night of November 6, Canadian sniper-scout Corporal Francis Pegahmagabow, an Anishnabe soldier from the Shawanaga First Nation in Ontario, earned a bar to his Military Medal (effectively meaning he was awarded it for the second time) when he successfully guided lost reinforcements to key spots in the Canadian line while exposed to continuous and heavy enemy fire.

By November 10, the Belgian village of Passchendaele and the ridge that bore the same name was in Canadian hands. The corps had once again captured its objective, this time at the extraordinary cost of nearly 16,000 casualties. Currie made sure to brief Prime Minister Borden in detail about the battle, his concerns about the attack, and the results. Months later, Borden was said to have told Prime Minister David Lloyd George of Britain that if Passchendaele was ever to be repeated "not a single Canadian soldier will leave the shore of Canada so long as people entrust the Government of my country to my hands."[12]

By this point in the war, so many bloody offensives like the Third Battle of Ypres had left the British facing a serious manpower crisis. To alleviate this, they reduced the size of each brigade by one battalion. British divisions would thus have three infantry brigades of three battalions instead of the original four. Diluting the strength of a British brigade allowed the British Expeditionary Force to better meet reinforcement demands. Pressure was placed on Currie to do the same with his corps. One of the other benefits for Currie commanding this semi-autonomous Canadian Corps was that he was able to resist this British pressure to reorganize. Haig even dangled the carrot of converting the corps into an army formation, potentially making Currie the first-ever commander of a Canadian army in the field. Currie refused and lobbied aggressively to make sure his position was supported by officials back in Ottawa.

Despite the historic and national significance of a Canadian army being in the field on the Western Front, Currie argued that the increase in size to an army, and thus the natural increase in logistical and support services, as well as inexperienced staff officers to help run it, would dilute the combat strength of the corps. In his mind, weakening combat strength would only lead to greater casualties. For instance, a British brigade, now using three battalions, had to employ two battalions up front with one battalion in reserve. This made it far more difficult for any follow-up attack to succeed, since it was conducted by only one battalion, whereas Canadian brigades, still with four battalions, could rely on two battalions in reserve. The Canadian follow-up attacks were just as strong as their initial assault, and both battalions could support each other in such an attack.

As well, by early 1918, the Canadian Corps was further reinforced by the breaking up of the 5th Division still in England (commanded by Sam Hughes's son, Garnet). The redistribution of Hughes's division meant that each battalion at the front now gained 100 extra soldiers. This was not the only area whereby Canadian units were stronger than their British counterparts. Canadian divisions had nine engineer field companies, compared to the British three. Canadian divisions were able to rely on far more machine-gun power, one automatic weapon for every 13 men as opposed to one for every 61 men in a British division. The Canadian Corps was, by 1918, more powerful than any British corps along the Western Front, its only equivalent being the Australian Corps. It could call on more trucks, more artillery, more men, more reserves, and more firepower. It was, in effect, a small national army without the actual designation and accompanying administrative, logistical, and bureaucratic weight.[13]

The Canadian Corps was also lucky. In March 1918, panic struck when the Germans launched General Ludendorff's Michael offensive. Nearly 50 divisions that had transferred from the now-defunct Eastern Front attacked, spearheaded by elite storm trooper units whose job it was to rapidly advance deep into enemy territory, causing havoc and chaos. This offensive saw the Germans make some of the largest territorial gains of the entire war in the west, including the recapture of lost ground such as the village of Passchendaele, so bloodily gained only five months prior. In response to the crisis, the British and French unified their command under French general

Map of German spring offensive, March 21 to July 18, 1918.

Field Marshal Ferdinand Foch. Despite Entente fear of total collapse, the German offensive stalled by the end of April and the crisis passed without the Anglo-French lines breaking.

At the peak of the offensive, however, immense pressure was placed on Currie to release his divisions from their positions in the relatively quiet Vimy sector to reinforce the crumbling British Fifth Army. Once again, the paradox of Currie as a subordinate within the British Expeditionary Force while also being a commander of a national formation made itself apparent when Currie resisted and took his case to his Canadian political superiors. He argued that his corps should be placed in the line as a homogenous formation instead of being broken up into piecemeal reinforcements for the British. Some Canadians were already in the fight. This included the Canadian Cavalry Brigade, which was attached to the British Cavalry Corps, as well as a smattering of medical units. One of those units included Katherine Macdonald, from Brantford, Ontario. She was one of 2,845 Canadian nursing sisters who served in the war. On May 19, a German bomber run over Étaples, France, hit the 1st Canadian General Hospital, killing Macdonald. She was one of 58 Canadian nurses to die in the war.[14]

Currie was adamant that the corps stay together, and Douglas Haig was furious at his obstinacy. Eventually, after back-and-forth messages between Ottawa and London, Currie released parts of the 2nd Division as well as the Canadian Motor Machine Gun Brigade, but by then the crisis had passed. This outcome was fortuitous, since the Canadian Corps largely escaped the brunt of the German offensive, thus leaving no one in any doubt that by the summer of 1918 the Canadian Corps was one of the most powerful corps formations on the entire Western Front.

The Hundred Days Campaign

As the last of the German attacks subsided in July 1918, Field Marshal Ferdinand Foch was already preparing for the counterstrike, a multinational coordinated offensive at several key points along the Western Front: a Belgian push in the north, a British drive supported by the French in the centre, and an American thrust from the south. The Canadian Corps, along with the

Australian Corps, would spearhead the British operation in the centre, which would begin just east of the city of Amiens.

In preparation for the attack, Currie made sure his corps had moved into the line in complete secrecy, knowing that his position in the line near Amiens would signal to the Germans that an attack was imminent. To deceive them, he sent several units north to Flanders to drop falsified orders and allow for meaningless messages to be intercepted, thus giving the Germans the impression the Canadians were farther north. At the same time, the Canadians began extensive training at the Australian tank school, since the attack itself would be supported by the largest numbers of tanks yet used in the war — this time the much-improved Mark V.

The Anglo-French forces launched the Battle of Amiens on the mist-shrouded morning of August 8, the "Black Day" for the German Army. The attack was one of the most successful single-day assaults of the entire war and reflected all the major developments in modern warfare. Canadian artillery disabled German defensive pockets, tanks provided effective cover to German machine-gun fire, and airplanes were used for bombing runs and tactical support, while the infantry utilized advanced fire-and-movement tactics to rapidly overcome enemy positions. The Canadians advanced a total of eight miles, the Australians nearly seven. In a war where success had generally been measured in yards, Amiens was a turning point. Yet it was still incredibly difficult fighting that saw the Canadian Corps receive 10 Victoria Crosses.

One of the more astonishing acts of bravery was by Lieutenant Jean Brillant, a French Canadian from Assemetquagan, Quebec, (modern-day Routhierville). In the early morning of the first day, Lieutenant Brillant captured a machine-gun nest, killing two Germans and suffering a wound in the process. Instead of returning to a dressing station, he continued leading his men into battle. Later that same day, he led his unit in a second attack on a German machine-gun position, knocking it out of action and capturing 150 Germans. Brillant was wounded a second time but was not done yet. He pressed on and headed his unit in another attack on a German artillery position where he was wounded a third time, finally passing out from blood loss. Brillant died on August 10.

Two days later, the Battle of Amiens ended. The Germans had been roundly defeated. But the butcher's bill was high. The Canadians suffered a total of 11,822 casualties. Fortunately, much-needed reinforcements were already

Lieutenant Jean Brillant, VC, June 1918.

arriving in the form of the first draft of conscripts.[15] These men were put to the test right away, since the Canadian Corps was shifted farther north to face the heart of the main German defensive position, known as the Hindenburg Line.

The ultimate objective at this point was the city of Cambrai, an important transportation hub that acted as the rear link to the Hindenburg Line. Capturing the city would effectively mean the collapse of the line itself, but a significant series of interconnected German defensive networks stood in the way. The first was the Drocourt-Quéant Line. This was an important fortified section that saw some of the deepest belts of barbed wire along the entire Western Front, running between the French towns of Drocourt and Quéant. Yet even to get to there, the Canadians had to grind their way past a series of German trenches. Starting on August 26, that was what they did. At a cost of 6,000 men, the Canadians finally forced their way into a position just to launch the attack on the Drocourt-Quéant Line.

This attack commenced on September 2, with the 1st and 4th Divisions leading the way. Artillery, using the effective 106 fuse, smashed the German

Canadian engineers bridging the Canal du Nord in France, September 1918.

wire, while infantry and tanks rolled over the German positions. By September 3, the Canadians had aggressively pushed through the thick belts of barbed wire, forcing the Germans to begin falling back. Sir Julian Byng, still in command of the Third Army, told Arthur Currie that the breaking of the Drocourt-Quéant Line was, in fact, the turning point in the entire campaign. In the two days of fighting through the line, the corps suffered another 5,000 casualties.

The Germans now fell back to a defensive position — Canal du Nord — that was key to protecting the western approaches to Cambrai. Once on the west bank of the canal, the Canadian Corps was afforded a short pause while it prepared to attack. Currie drew up his attack plan while more conscripts arrived to take their place in the front line.

The battle for Canal du Nord proved to be one of Currie's most daring victories and one that highlighted the effectiveness of his engineers.[16] The portion of the canal facing the Canadians was a long, deep, waterless stretch roughly 100 feet wide. Crossing it was going to be a significant challenge, since the Germans had extensive artillery and machine-gun fire covering its length. While infantry could cross the dry canal bed, artillery and vehicles

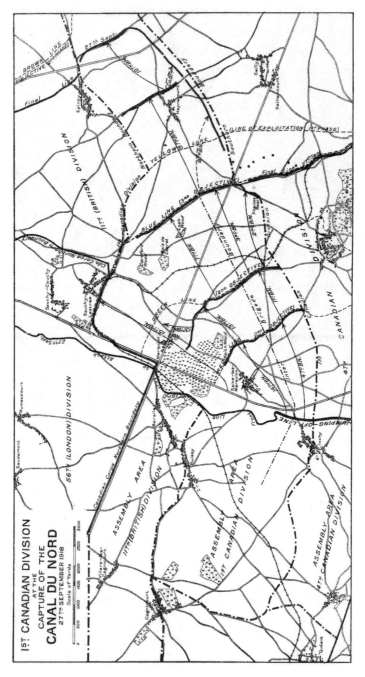

The 1st Canadian Division at the capture of the Canal du Nord, September 27, 1918.

could not. This meant that the engineers were going to have to erect several bridges the morning of the assault to allow all elements to cross, all this, of course, while under fire. Overlooking the canal farther east was another key German defensive position — Bourlon Wood — a hill of thickly wooded terrain where much of the German artillery was hidden.

To win the coming battle, Currie devised a daring and risky tactical plan. He sought to cram the corps into a very narrow space (two divisions in front, two behind), punch through the canal defences with this narrow thrust (led by the 4th and 1st Divisions), and then fan out quickly so that all four divisions (the 3rd Division and a British division temporarily attached to the corps) advanced side by side. Once across the canal, the four divisions would then advance toward Cambrai, squeezing it between a northern and southern pincer movement. Many were worried about this tactical plan. Byng famously told Currie that if anybody could do it, it was the Canadians, but if the plan failed, it would cost Currie his job.

Nonetheless, on the morning of September 27, the Canadian Corps attacked. The engineers were superb and became the key to victory. Seven bridges were constructed within the first few hours of the assault. Ten more were built across the canal within 24 hours. A massive artillery barrage supported the Canadians, helping to protect the exposed engineer. By September 28, the Germans had abandoned their positions around the canal and the dominating heights of Bourlon Wood and had fallen back in a chaotic manner to defend Cambrai. The Canadian Corps pushed itself nearly to the breaking point, and by October 1, the advance was finally halted. Arthur Currie wrote later that the Battle of Canal du Nord was the toughest victory earned by the corps in the entire war. In many ways it was the pinnacle of Canadian First World War achievements. It was a total combined-arms operation that saw a daring tactical plan executed by experienced soldiers crossing a daunting obstacle while utilizing all elements within that corps structure. But the cost again was heavy. The corps sustained so many casualties (31,000 in six weeks) that it was difficult to maintain its current tempo of operations.

Regardless, after a week's rest, the corps launched its attack on strategically vital Cambrai. If this crucial transportation hub fell to the Canadians, the Hindenburg Line would officially be broken. The Canadian Corps thus attacked on October 8, and two days later it reached the outskirts of the city.

German barbed wire at the Hindenburg Line, October 1918.

The Germans were forced to withdraw. The Hindenburg Line was no more; the Germans were officially on the run.

The Canadian Corps, which had started 100,000 strong, had lost 42,600 soldiers in the fighting since early August 1918. Reinforcements were rushed into the front line as fast as they arrived, but there was no question that the infantry battalions were beginning to suffer from exhaustion. Yet the corps continued forward, nipping at the heels of the rapidly retreating Germans. By November 2, after some difficult urban fighting, the Canadians liberated Valenciennes, the last major French city occupied by the Germans.

At this point, many Canadian soldiers began to feel as if the end of the war was in sight. A level of mobility not seen since early 1914 had returned to the battlefield. German soldiers surrendered in larger and larger numbers, and it seemed as if the German will to resist had been irreversibly destroyed. On November 9, Kaiser Wilhelm II abdicated his throne. By November 10, the Canadians were in Belgium, facing the city of Mons where the British had first exchanged fire with the Germans back in 1914. Unknown to Currie or his men at the time, the Germans were secretly seeking a ceasefire, and even though most Canadians felt the end was near, the orders were to continue fighting. Thus, in the early hours of November 11, 1918, the Canadians attacked Mons. But the advance into the city was extremely cautious, and most soldiers were told to keep their heads down. At 10:58 a.m., Private George Price was shot and killed by a German sniper while conducting a patrol in a village just outside Mons. He was the last Canadian soldier to die in battle. At 11:11 a.m., word came down that a ceasefire had been declared. The war to end all wars was now over.

The Hundred Days Campaign broke the back of the German Army, and the Canadian Corps was right at the centre of it. Yet the price was almost too high to imagine. The corps sustained 45,835 casualties during the campaign, nearly 20 percent of all casualties sustained by the Canadian Expeditionary Force during the entire war and 45 percent of its total strength on August 8, 1918. For most soldiers, news of the end of the war was simply met with relief, not with celebrations or parties or flowers but a grim and resigned acceptance of the horrible cost that had been paid.

Demobilization

In the aftermath of the armistice, as the men slowly started to acclimatize to peacetime activities, the dominating question for most was "When are we going home?" Currie had committed two of his divisions to help in the occupation of the German Rhineland, but in regard to the rest, he wanted them to return with their units and bask in the glory of a victory parade in their hometowns with the men and officers they had served together with. For many, however, they merely wanted to get home and were not too concerned with whom they went home. Many veterans argued strongly for a "first-in, first-out" policy, meaning those who had gone to Europe first got to go home first.[17] This posed challenges to Currie's vision of his heroically returning battalions.

It quickly became clear that getting home was going to be a serious issue for the CEF. There were significant logistical challenges in trying to get 300,000 men onto ships and across the ocean. With so many soldiers in Europe waiting to return home, troop transport became a hot commodity and obtaining enough ships to get the men home proved nearly impossible in the short term. Even back in Canada, logistical issues stymied return efforts. Canada's railways were overworked and buckling under the wartime strain.[18]

The Canadian government announced that only 20,000 to 25,000 soldiers per month could be accommodated. It appeared as if it was going to take well into 1919 to get all the members of the CEF home, and tension began to mount. In the Rhineland, in Belgium, and back in England, no number of sports tournaments, university classes, or countryside excursions could alleviate the growing frustration over how long it was taking to get the men back to Canada. In January and then again in March, this boiled over into full-out riots at the Canadian camp at Kinmel Park in southern Wales. The first one saw knives and clubs used in a racially fuelled rumble in response to the attempted arrest of a white soldier by a Black sergeant major of the all-Black No. 2 Construction Battalion. The second riot was an alcohol-fuelled brawl in response to rumours that conscripts were going to be given priority return over volunteers; five soldiers died and 25 were wounded in the ensuing violence. The March riot and the public, disgruntled nature of the Canadians received so much media attention that transport for the troops miraculously appeared shortly after. By mid-1919, the CEF was finally home.[19]

Not all Canadians were enjoying peace yet. In October, 4,000 Canadians were shipped from Victoria, British Columbia, to Vladivostok in Siberia to support the White forces in the Russian Civil War that had erupted after the Bolshevik seizure of power. While these men saw very little action, 500 Canadians serving in an artillery brigade in northwest Russia took part in heavy fighting in the area around Archangel. By this point, however, public support for any continued Canadian military action was declining rapidly, and the Canadians in Archangel, as well as the Canadian Siberian Expeditionary Force, returned to Canada in June 1919, much to the relief of the Canadian government and public.[20]

Canada's military contribution to the First World War was certainly something above and beyond what anyone expected for such a small country. With just under eight million people and a pre-war military that included an under-equipped regular force of 3,000 soldiers and a poorly trained militia of 60,000, Canada was able to put into uniform nearly 620,000 soldiers and form what eventually became the finest corps formation on the Western Front.

Up until 1917, all of those in the CEF were volunteers. Yet a significant portion of these volunteers were born in Britain, with volunteer rates declining

Soldiers of the Canadian Expeditionary Force arrive in Montreal for demobilization, 1919.

among the Canadian-born and dropping further within rural Canada and French Canada. Only with conscription did the ratio of Canadian-born to British-born finally reach parity. The conscripts were sorely needed too. Without them the Canadian Corps could have never kept up its tempo of operations during the Hundred Days Campaign.[21] The success of the Canadian Corps was a major military achievement for such a small country, yet it came at a terrible cost. Close to 62,000 Canadians lost their lives, with more than 172,000 physically wounded and tens of thousands psychologically damaged, with almost no support system waiting for them back home. It would be no exaggeration to claim that every single community in Canada was in some way affected by the casualties sustained in this most terrible of wars.

✦ ✦ ✦

The war had some lasting effects for Canada's growth as a nation. The work of the Canadian Corps certainly gained Canada a greater international reputation. From its seat in the newly created League of Nations, it harangued the nations of Europe about their violent predilections, citing peaceful North America as an example of global co-operation. As well, the military contribution of Canada became valuable rhetoric in the interwar period as both Prime Minister William Lyon Mackenzie King and Prime Minister R.B. Bennett solidified Canada's growing independence from Britain. By 1939, Britain would not be declaring war on behalf of Canada; Canada would do it itself. At the same time, the war pushed Canada into the powerful U.S. economic orbit and kick-started the process by which Canada slowly detached itself from Great Britain.

The veterans themselves seemed to have mixed feelings about the war. Many voiced their opinion that it was a war fought for nothing and the sacrifices were in vain, especially in 1939 when war erupted once more, while others strongly believed it was a good war. Regardless of this, the large number of veterans who returned from Europe became a very powerful voting bloc that successfully lobbied the Canadian government to pass some of Canada's first social welfare measures in the 1920s and 1930s to take better care of those who had risked everything during the conflict.

The war was fought over many ideas: the defence of Christianity and civilization, coming to the aid of Belgium, capturing or recapturing historically important territory, stopping an aggressive Germany, and in some cases, simply a feud between rival dynastic houses. The Entente won but at the cost of millions of people. For what? A more stable geopolitical environment? The League of Nations that was created in the war's aftermath to do just that was impotent from almost day one. Was it to create a more peaceful world order? If so, it totally failed. Numerous smaller wars erupted in the aftermath of the First World War. And, of course, the heavy reparation payments and peace terms imposed upon Germany would be central to the propaganda of Adolf Hitler. Was it to create a more stable and strong global economy? The Great Depression that started in 1929 and only really ended in 1939 wrecked any hope of that.

Simply put, the war to end all wars was the first of two catastrophic total global industrial conflicts to rock the world in the 20th century. The First World War became an important part of a growing notion of Canadian identity and certainly helped fashion a sense of "Canadianness." However, such a perception was heavily dependent on whether one was French- or

English-speaking. Nevertheless, the death of so many was a cautionary tale about the tragedy of blindly going to war.

When war was once again declared in 1939, there were no jubilant celebrations in the streets but a resigned acceptance that young men and women would be called upon to make great sacrifices. Regardless, while the shadow of the Great War loomed large in Canada in 1939, the country still rose to the challenge and went beyond even its most optimistic expectations to sacrifice its youth on the altar of the goddess of war.

5

THE INTERWAR YEARS

The Canada that First World War veterans returned to was quite different from the one they left behind. Many were shocked and angered over the government recently passing prohibition, a decidedly unpopular measure among soldiers for whom alcohol had been a constant feature of daily life. Many veterans also came back carrying the deadly Spanish flu, which spread rapidly throughout Canada, eventually claiming upward of 50,000 Canadian lives and killing more globally than the war itself.

Canada was in serious economic trouble. The collapse of the wheat and munitions industries resulted in a punishing postwar recession. Workers across the country felt they had sacrificed their rights in the name of the war effort and now demanded the government return the favour by helping to increase wages and improve working conditions. Yet a recession meant unemployment and jobs became scarce. At the same time, the cost of living in Canada had risen by 64 percent thanks to near-runaway inflation during the war. Throw into this mix the return of hundreds of thousands of veterans expecting preferential treatment in what jobs were available and the tension was close to boiling over.

Strikes and riots had already been flaring up in 1918, but it was in Winnipeg in May 1919 that the anger and frustration over the postwar landscape in Canada reached a fever pitch. A city-wide general strike led to weeks of violent conflict between strikers, joined by recently returned veterans, and government forces, including a private strikebreaking force hired by the city elites and made up also of recently returned veterans. Several deaths, dozens of wounded, numerous arrests, deportations, and veterans fighting veterans characterized the Winnipeg General Strike.[1] The chaos finally subsided by late June with promises of a Royal Commission to investigate the causes of the strike and the violence that ensued. While the Canadian government and Winnipeg business elites feared a Bolshevik revolution, the Royal Commission found that the objectives of the strikers were not revolutionary, and the Canadian public was shocked when the commission laid bare the heavy-handedness of the government's response. The pandemonium of the Winnipeg General Strike led to the collapse of Borden's coalition Union government and characterized a tense and hostile mood in postwar Canada.[2]

Life for many veterans was difficult upon their return to Canada. Most received their hard-earned yet meagre pay along with a clothing allowance and a war service gratuity determined by where they served and the length of service. There were also preferential job-hiring programs within the civil service, as well as government help for the purchase of agricultural land. For those

Battle lines are drawn during the Winnipeg General Strike, June 21, 1919.

with physical injuries, a small pension was paid out. For those who were visible minorities or who were suffering from psychological trauma, their ability to be compensated was a longer and far more difficult road.

As the postwar economic crisis worsened, many veterans argued that the benefits available were simply not adequate. Physically disabled veterans engaged in a constant battle with the government for improvements to their disability pensions. Effectively, the pension amount was determined based on the percentage of disability — 5 percent up to 100 percent disabled — coupled with rank during service. Yet the pension program was fraught with problems, not the least of which was the low payment amounts. Extensive lobbying by veteran groups saw payments improve throughout the 1920s and 1930s.

For most veterans, the process of reintegration into civilian life relied on the support of the government and that assistance, they argued, was an ongoing process, not a one-time cash payout. The negotiations for support did not conclude in 1919, despite the government's attempts to make it so. Veteran calls for help were framed in terms of a contract between the government and its citizens who had expressed the utmost loyalty by going to war on its behalf. Effectively, veterans argued that they were in no way seeking handouts or charity but were owed social support services by the government as recognition of their sacrifices.[3]

The most powerful organization continuously lobbying for veteran rights was the Royal Canadian Legion, formed in 1925 from an amalgamation of a variety of veterans' associations. Efforts by the legion and other veterans' groups spearheaded several social welfare initiatives during the interwar period. By 1919, tens of thousands of soldiers were receiving free vocational training in over 150 different occupations. In 1920, the government passed legislation providing preferential rates for veterans purchasing life insurance. By the early 1920s, nearly 100,000 veterans were receiving free medical care. When the Great Depression struck in 1929, much of the rhetoric from veterans' advocacy groups revolved around the issue of unemployment. Veterans receiving "relief" from the government were able to successfully advocate for a change from the term "relief" to "unemployment assistance" and were given cash instead of vouchers.

While initially only for veterans or their dependents, some of these initiatives were eventually expanded to include all Canadians. Issues regarding pension payments, unemployment protection, health insurance, affordable housing, and access to education were all part of the veterans' agenda, and small yet notable gains were made in every category. The social reform advocacy of veterans during the interwar period played an important role in some of the early discussions and initial successes in changes to welfare state policy in Canada.[4]

The Royal Canadian Legion was also instrumental in helping to cement one of the most enduring myths from the First World War — that the Battle of Vimy Ridge was a nation-building moment. Among those communities affected by the war, there was widespread support for memorial activities. Across the land, cenotaphs and memorials were erected to the dead. From Victoria, British Columbia, to the colony of Newfoundland, cenotaphs became the recognized form to mourn the loss of so many, and many communities now shared in that collective grief embodied in November 11 — Armistice Day.

These commemoration efforts were a sombre yet poignant method by which the country collectively dealt with the trauma of the war. While this grassroots commemoration movement gained momentum, the Canadian government, the public, and veterans' organizations all clamoured for a European memorial to honour those Canadian soldiers killed in the war to end all wars. There were four locations considered: the area near Ypres, the battlefield close to Courcelette, Vimy Ridge, and, finally, Canal du Nord, Arthur Currie's personal preference for a national memorial.

Vimy, frankly, was a contested choice. In fact, Currie himself wrote about the possibility of placing a monument at Vimy Ridge and stated: "If they place the memorial at Vimy, it will confirm for all time the impression that Vimy was the greatest battle fought by the Canadians in France. In my mind that is very far from being a fact. Vimy was a set-piece for which we had trained and rehearsed for weeks. It did not call for the same degree of resource and initiative that were displayed in any of the three greatest battles of the last hundred days."[5] Currie did recognize, though, that the heights of Vimy Ridge would make an impressive setting for a Canadian memorial. He was not the only one who was unsure about Vimy being the appropriate site; many veterans and politicians agreed with him.

It was Prime Minister William Lyon Mackenzie King (who did not serve during the war and had never visited the battlefield) who believed that Vimy was, indeed, hallowed ground and spearheaded Vimy's transition into a myth-making moment.[6] Under King's direction, Vimy was officially chosen as the site of the great Canadian memorial in Europe. The Canadian government purchased some of the land that encompassed the battlefield, while the French government ceded 284 acres to Canada. This ensured Canadian control of the portion of the ridge that now bears the memorial, roughly the area of the 4th Division's attack. Walter Seymour Allward was selected to design and oversee the construction of the memorial, and by 1925, construction on the monument began. The stone chosen was, in fact, pulled from the same quarry used by Diocletian, the late third-century/early fourth-century Roman emperor, to construct his own palace.

By the early 1930s, as work on the monument continued, the Canadian Legion started to plan a massive pilgrimage to Vimy centred around the unveiling of Allward's memorial. The unveiling date was set for Dominion Day, July 1, 1936, despite the fact that no one consulted with Allward himself. The sculptor was now presented with a very real deadline, though the unveiling had to be moved to July 26 to accommodate all interested parties. Massive subsidies for travel as well as extensive organization by the Canadian government, the legion, charitable donations, and even the private sector (Eaton's was a major donor) allowed 6,200 veterans and their families to travel to Europe. The group included 50 nursing sisters, 70 French Canadians, and even a few Japanese-Canadian veterans. As well, in attendance would be Albert Lebrun, the French president, and none other than King Edward VIII. The unveiling went off without a hitch, but the pilgrimage for many veterans was not just about the Vimy unveiling; most sought to return to many of the spots they had fought at decades earlier. For the public, however, it was the Vimy unveiling that encapsulated the pilgrimage. The Battle of Vimy Ridge and its monument now stood as the key symbol of Canada's First World War experience.

While excitement over the Vimy pilgrimage temporarily shone the spotlight on Canada's military achievements, the interwar period witnessed the branches of Canada's armed forces decline to nearly an unusable state. Prime Minister King, who politically dominated much of the interwar period, had no love for the military, which was reflected in his government's budget priorities. During its first administration in the early 1920s, King's government merged the various military branches — the Air Board, the Department

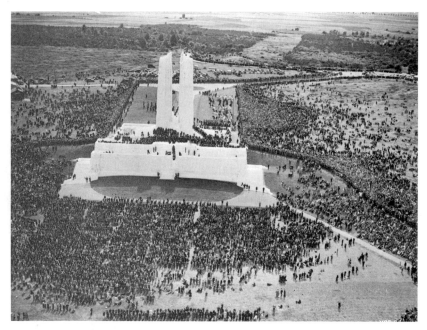

An aerial shot of the crowd gathered for the unveiling of the Vimy monument, July 1936.

of Militia and Defence, and the Department of Naval Services — into the Department of National Defence. And then King began making cuts. Defence spending fell from $30 million to as low as $13 million, and just as King began to open the coffers, the Great Depression hit. Even Prime Minister Bennett, the unlucky Conservative Party leader who beat King in 1930, found no room in his retrenchment policy for military spending.

The Permanent Force (PF) and the Non-Permanent Militia (NPM) were always the backbone of the Canadian military establishment, but there was little support after 1919 for any serious enlargement of the force beyond pre-war levels. The NPM returned to its pre-war status, underfunded, undertrained, under-equipped, and understaffed, yet with a plethora of new regimental battle honours. The General Staff had hoped for a PF 30,000 strong; it got permission to recruit 5,000 and failed to hit that mark. Most Canadians simply did not have the stomach for military spending in the aftermath of the terrible cost of the First World War. Even during the brief prosperity of the 1920s, King's Liberal government reduced the pay of PF personnel. There was some reorganization, however. Instead of one

PF regiment, there would now be three: the Royal Canadian Regiment, the French-speaking Royal 22nd Regiment (the Van Doos), and the Princess Patricia's Canadian Light Infantry. Regardless of this reorganization, the PF remained understrength for much of the 1920s, barely getting above 4,000 in all ranks.[7] Still, a use was found for the army. Units were called out to maintain law and order in labour disputes in Winnipeg, Manitoba; Cape Breton, Nova Scotia; and Stratford, Ontario. The PF operated the Northwest Territories and Yukon Radio System, which brought modern communication connections to the far corners of the country. The PF was also used to run labour camps during the Depression.

The brainchild of Andrew McNaughton, upward of 170,000 young men were recruited into these labour camps and paid 20 cents per day to work on public projects and defence infrastructure. The poor conditions of these camps coupled with the low pay and military-esque environment led to growing disgruntlement and an eventual protest trek to Ottawa. When the "trekkers," as they were called, arrived in Regina, they were prevented from going any farther. Riots broke out, violence ensued, and the whole fiasco became a blight on Prime Minister R.B. Bennett's Conservative administration. McNaughton was quietly removed as Chief of the General Staff, and King's Liberals returned to power championing the slogan "King not Chaos." Little changed for the military under the returned Liberals. Continual cuts to the defence budget meant the Permanent Force and Non-Permanent Militia were effectively reduced to just below their 1913 levels.

The Royal Canadian Air Force (RCAF) was the newest and arguably most exciting of the branches. During the First World War, more than 22,000 residents of Canada served in Britain's Royal Flying Corps and its successor, the Royal Air Force. That meant there was a body of skilled pilots who came back to Canada after the war from which a national air force could very well be created. A two-squadron Canadian Air Force was, in fact, formed in England in late 1918, disbanded in 1919, then reformed in 1920 as a non-permanent air force, the equivalent of a militia for the air. Two years later it achieved permanent status and was granted the royal honorific in 1923.

Air power had matured rapidly during the Great War, and many believed it would come to define the next conflict. Some, like McNaughton, believed the RCAF, not the Royal Canadian Navy (RCN), should be the first line of defence against attack. As well, the RCAF was given full responsibility for all aviation

"Trekkers" boarding freight cars to Ottawa, June 1935.

in Canada, including civil. This gave it a unique relevance among the branches of the military; RCAF pilots flew forest fire patrols, aerial surveying missions, anti-smuggling operations, and even crop-dusting.[8] Yet, like its sister services, it suffered from the ups and downs of Canada's economic fortunes, and while the 1930s saw the RCAF move from a civil-military function to a purely military one, abandoning its responsibility for civil aviation, it also witnessed the air force suffer under continual budget cuts.

However, no branch deteriorated like the RCN. By 1918, there was a Canadian fleet of 130 small coastal patrol vessels under the command of the British Admiralty. Almost all these ships were converted fishing vessels, primarily trawlers and drifters. But this navy of small ships was disbanded quickly after November 1918 and a Canadian navy struggled to survive after that.

The story of the Canadian navy's fight for survival in the interwar period was intimately connected to the work of Commodore Walter Hose. One of the more important figures in Canadian naval history, Hose was literally born at sea. He first served with the Royal Navy before seeking promotion within the newly established Royal Canadian Navy. Hose was appointed captain of the HMCS *Rainbow* in 1911 and eventually rose to the position of director of the Naval Service in 1921. That same year saw three Canadian vessels, nearly the entire RCN fleet, sail to Costa Rica to strong-arm that nation into giving in to the Royal Bank of Canada's oil concessions.[9] Later that year, King's Liberals won the federal election, and to deal with a global

The Canadian delegation at the London Naval Conference, 1930.
Left to right: Walter Hose, J.L. Ralston, Lester B. Pearson, and
Major H.W. Brown.

recession combined with the spirit of peace that emanated after the signing
of the 1921 Washington Treaty, King began to cut spending. The naval budget
dropped from its modest $2.5 million to $1.5 million where it remained for
years to come.

Hose's navy was reduced to two destroyers and four minesweepers, and
he was forced to cut personnel while closing both the Royal Naval College
and the Youth Training facility. To give the navy a national footprint, Hose
did create the Royal Canadian Naval Volunteer Reserve, though it struggled
to reach its full complement of 500 personnel. A late 1920s economic upsurge
combined with a Liberal majority in the 1926 federal election led to an increase in naval spending. Emboldened by this new confidence, Commodore
Hose was able to get the government to agree to Canada's first-ever national

naval policy. This was the first time Canadian naval policy was dictated by Ottawa and not London.[10] He also secured a small but modern fleet of six destroyers and four minesweepers. The late 1920s was a time of great optimism for the RCN: Hose's position was retitled Chief of the Naval Staff, he had secured for Canada its own national naval policy, and it seemed as if a small but modern fleet was on its way.

The first two destroyers sailed into Halifax in 1931 — HMCS *Saguenay* and *Skeena*. Canada even found itself sending two ships to El Salvador to protect British interests in the region when that country fell into political chaos. Yet the early 1930s saw Canada falling deeper into the throes of the Great Depression. This time it was the Conservative government under R.B. Bennett that looked to cut expenses, with Hose's navy at the top of the list. Hose was not helped by Andrew McNaughton, who believed that the future of coastal defence lay in air power, not sea power. With Bennett wanting to slash expenses, and McNaughton no friend of the navy, a proposal was put forward to scrap the RCN altogether! Hose fought tenaciously to save it and save it he did. Instead of the proposed $2 million cut, the navy's budget was reduced by $200,000. The navy survived but just barely.[11]

While Canada's military was reduced to pauperism, Canada's First World War achievements and sacrifices became a springboard to greater autonomy for Canada within the British Empire. No doubt political leaders such as King were loyal to the British Empire, but many questioned the nature by which Canada was automatically pulled into such a devastating conflict. For King in particular, the war had shattered communities and families across the land and nearly ripped the nation's "two solitudes" of English and French apart. Canada's war effort had to count for something in the postwar world. Certainly, the country's seat in the rather powerless League of Nations was part of this new postwar identity, but for King, Canada's role within the British Empire had to be reassessed.

King's predecessor, Robert Borden, had already started the process by securing London's acceptance of Resolution IX. In 1922, however, when Great Britain and the empire almost went to war with Turkey over the port city of Chanak, King shocked London when he declared Canada would not automatically send military support without approval from Canada's Parliament first. The crisis passed before Parliament had to make that unprecedented decision. In 1923, King once again asserted Canadian autonomy when he authorized the negotiation and signing of the Halibut Treaty with the United States, bypassing London and ignoring the protests of the British Foreign Office, which believed it was still Britain's prerogative to negotiate trade deals on behalf of Canada.

At the 1926 Imperial Conference, King led the way in securing London's recognition that the dominions were indeed autonomous, equal to one another, and in no way subordinate to the United Kingdom. This Balfour Declaration was followed up five years later with the signing of the Statute of Westminster, legally making Canada a fully autonomous nation within the newly titled British Commonwealth. This meant that Ottawa would now guide Canada's international relations in trade and diplomacy, and it would be the Canadian Parliament and people deciding when Canada would next go to war.

Prime Minister William Lyon Mackenzie King (far left) at the All-German Sports Competition in Berlin, June 27, 1937.

Sadly, it would not take long for the Canadian Parliament to be faced with that terrible decision. Adolf Hitler had come to power in Germany in 1933, and slowly the dark clouds of war gathered over Europe. By 1935, Hitler had effectively ripped up the Treaty of Versailles and begun a process of full re-militarization. At the same time, his ally, Italy's Benito Mussolini, sought to revive the imperial glories of ancient Rome and invaded Abyssinia (modern-day Ethiopia). In 1936, German forces were in Spain backing Francisco Franco's nationalists. Despite a few dissenting voices, however, Canada was not going to interfere, and the international community had little interest in Canada's opinions.

Canada also towed the British line and embraced appeasement. Jewish refugees fleeing the anti-Semitic Third Reich were turned away when they arrived on Canada's shores seeking asylum. Prime Minister King even visited Berlin in 1937 and was wooed by Hitler and his Nazi goons.[12] King returned to Canada convinced that Hitler was simply a patriot attempting to redress past wrongs. He was impressed by Germany's industrial turnaround and was certain that all Hitler wanted was peace. Events in Europe proved him and so many others wrong. Hitler remilitarized the Rhineland in 1936, annexed Austria in 1937, was foolishly given the Sudetenland at the Munich Agreement of 1938, and then simply took the rest of Czechoslovakia while defensive-minded France, tepid Britain, and the neutral United States looked on.

Despite the positive feelings from his Berlin trip, King slowly realized that Hitler wanted a war and was probably going to get it. The aggressive actions of Germany, Italy, and Japan led many within Canada to call for rearmament. However, King was very aware of the potential political problems he could face if Quebec were even to sniff the possibility of another war when that could mean conscription. For King and his government, the focus would be on the defence of Canada, not on an overseas expeditionary force that might draw Canada closer to conscription and King nearer to a national crisis like the one Borden had experienced.

But events continued to unfold rapidly, and more pressure was placed on the prime minister. King reluctantly gave in and authorized the Department of National Defence to begin slowly but surely rearming, though it would not be nearly enough to prepare Canada for war. The Permanent Force of 455 officers and 3,714 other ranks would once again make up the core of an expanded wartime army. The militia, at just below its 1913 level, saw 15 divisions consolidated into half that number, most equipped with First World War weapons. Some units were merged, others were turned into tank brigades without modern tanks or mobile units and often without armoured vehicles.

After the Munich Agreement of 1938, and despite King's emphasis on home defence, the General Staff under Major-General T.V. Anderson started secretly preparing to dispatch an oversees expeditionary force. The navy also benefited from the increase in defence spending. Several new destroyers were added, and the force doubled in size to nearly 200 officers and 1,800 other ranks. The RCAF profited the most, seeing its budget rise 10 times from 1935 to 1939. Nonetheless, when war broke out, the RCAF, like its sister services, was still wholly unprepared for the war to come. It contained 3,000 all ranks, flying mostly obsolete planes with a smattering of modern Hurricanes.

Canada, like so many other nations, had hoped for peace and gotten war. While some forward-thinking politicians and military personnel had prophesized the violent outcome of the 1930s, the country's prime minister and his inner circle demurred. When events unfolded rapidly in 1939 and 1940, this would come back to hurt the Canadian military as it embraced an ever-expanding role during the Second World War.

6

THE SECOND WORLD WAR: THE CONFLICT AT SEA AND IN AIR

Contrary to Prime Minister King's initial beliefs, Adolf Hitler proved to be desperately in search of war, and when Germany invaded Poland on September 1, 1939, he got just that. Despite a symbolic waiting period after Britain's own declaration of war, there was never any question whether Canada would enter it. The issue at hand was what type of contribution Canada was going to make. It was here that the shadow of the First World War loomed large over King. He was determined to avoid an infantry-heavy contribution like that of the last war, one that would lead to high casualties, the potential for conscription, and ultimately a national crisis like that in 1918.[1] King was not going to see the country split apart over the issue of conscription. This meant that the initial Canadian war effort would be directed toward roles that limited casualties, what King defined as "limited liability." One infantry division was authorized to head overseas under the command of General Andrew McNaughton, while another trained at home. The major military contribution for Canada was going to be at sea and in the air where casualties, it was thought, would remain light.

King also hoped that enhanced logistical support for Britain would make up for the limited land-based commitment. This assistance came in the form of the traditional wartime exports, munitions and wheat, as well as a variety of war *matériel*. Yet the project King hoped would satisfy as Canada's primary contribution was the British Commonwealth Air Training Plan.[2] Canada's Prairies and open skies were a perfect setting for the establishment of a massive pilot and aircrew training program. It was free from enemy attacks, contained plenty of room for manoeuvring and mistakes, and was also close enough to Britain to get trained airmen overseas and into the war as quickly as possible. Fairly tense negotiations between King and the British government occurred in October before the plan was agreed upon in December 1939. The initial costs were to be $600 million, with Canada paying just over half. Recruits came from Australia, New Zealand, Great Britain, South Africa, Poland, Czechoslovakia, and elsewhere, contributing to the international flavour of the program. Still, half of all the recruits came from Canada. Training consisted of flying machines that were relics of the last world war, but experience was gained and vital skills were developed. However, training was dangerous, and 3,000 trainees lost their lives before even graduating.

The young men in the program lived and trained at 231 different sites across the country. Flooded with hundreds, if not thousands, of eager young men were small towns such as Vulcan, Alberta; Abbotsford, British Columbia; Yorkton, Saskatchewan; Carberry, Manitoba; and numerous others. Money came with the young men, and the local towns and bars overflowed with "Acey-Deuceys" proudly wearing the uniform of an aircraftman second class. While tension certainly existed between the young men and the locals, especially over women, and not a few alcohol-fuelled brawls were the result, the training program was an unmitigated success. The budget eventually ballooned to $2.2 billion, with Canada paying most of it, while 131,500 airmen graduated from the program, most of them ending up in Bomber Command. The British Commonwealth Air Training Plan was one of the most important contributions Canada made toward the larger war effort.

When France fell in June 1940, Canada's position changed dramatically. The nation now ranked as Britain's number two ally, and King's attempt at a war of "limited liability" was simply not going to pan out. By the end of that year, the Canadian navy was embroiled in the pivotal Battle of the Atlantic, and Canadians in both the Royal Canadian Air Force (RCAF) and the Royal Air Force (RAF) were engaged in the air. The army, however, had yet to get involved.

Pilot trainees of the British Commonwealth Air Training Plan with Curtiss P-36 aircraft at the Little Norway training centre, Toronto Islands.

The first Canadians of what would eventually make up the First Canadian Army arrived in England in December 1939. This 20,000-strong division was commanded by General Andrew McNaughton. One brigade of McNaughton's division was sent to France briefly in early June but was quickly pulled back to England as France fell. After British and French soldiers were evacuated from the French town of Dunkirk, McNaughton's division became a mobile strike force, one of the few fully equipped and trained divisions left in Britain. All that summer the Canadians bounced around between anticipated invasion points, earning the moniker "McNaughton's Travelling Circus."

By the end of 1940, British Commonwealth forces were fighting a land war in North Africa, driving back an outmatched Italian Army. By early 1941, this was reversed. The Italians were reinforced by their German allies, and the British Commonwealth troops found themselves on the retreat.

Pressure was mounting on King to commit Canadians to the land war. In England, three Canadian divisions and a tank brigade were now training while spending most of their free time at the local pubs. The distance to North Africa meant it was an unlikely destination for these troops. Yet an opportunity to commit Canadians troops arrived in the summer of 1941. As

Canada's sea and air commitments expanded, the country took part in two military disasters on land: one in Hong Kong, the other in France at Dieppe.

Hong Kong

In August, Chief of the General Staff Harry Crerar and Defence Minister J.L. Ralston had lunch with Crerar's old Royal Military College buddy, A.E. Grasett, who had just recently returned from command of the garrison in Hong Kong. What was said at this meeting has been lost to history. However, Grasett did go back to London in early September and confidently inform the British that Canada would send reinforcements to Hong Kong if asked.[3] Thus, in late September, the official request for troops came from London. King felt that dispatching soldiers to Hong Kong would mollify English-Canadian demands for Canada to get into the ground war (demands also resonating from elements within his own Cabinet) while ensuring that it was not such a large commitment as to risk ire from French Canada. The prime minister thus reluctantly agreed to send Canadians to Hong Kong, a decision that led to disaster for those unlucky souls selected to go.

Hong Kong was a symbolically important piece of the British Empire in the Pacific. It was also a small part of a supply chain to the Chinese Nationalist leader Chiang Kai-shek, who was currently fighting the Japanese on the mainland. The island itself, however, was simply indefensible. British prime minister Winston Churchill had even openly stated that. Its defensive fortifications were decrepit, and the garrison suffered from poor leadership, particularly garrison commander Major-General Christopher Maltby, which would become apparent during the battle itself.[4] While the garrison troops were generally of good quality — a mixture of British, Indian, and local Hong Kong soldiers — they were up against an extremely skilled and experienced Imperial Japanese Army that had spent years fighting the Chinese on the mainland.

Joining this lost cause was C-Force under the command of Great War veteran Brigadier-General John K. Lawson, consisting of 1,973 soldiers in two battalions — the Royal Rifles of Canada and the Winnipeg Grenadiers — along with two nursing sisters. The battalions were chosen because of their experience performing garrison duty in Newfoundland and Jamaica as well as their proximity to the Pacific. While not as well trained as their Canadian counterparts currently in Britain, they were as well prepared as any other Canadian units then available. In fact, the Winnipeg Grenadiers had even conducted training exercises in the mountainous subtropical heat of Jamaica, terrain and climate similar to that of Hong Kong. There were still issues. Some of the units lacked modern equipment, some of the newer men had still to complete their full training, and a small number had yet to even fire their weapons. Most damning, however, was that the addition of nearly 2,000 Canadians was never going to make a difference, anyway.

The Canadians arrived in Hong Kong in November, and the Japanese launched their attack on December 8, mere hours after the attack on Pearl Harbor (the different calendar date being a result of different time zones). By December 10, British positions on the mainland had fallen, and by December 19, the Japanese were on the island. Because of poor pre-battle dispositions laid out by General Maltby, the Japanese were able to move behind the individual pockets of defenders and seize key strategic pieces of high ground. The battle quickly became desperate.

Despite the lack of combat experience, both Canadian and Japanese accounts suggest the Canadians put up a terrific fight. This was highlighted by

Infantrymen of C Company, Royal Rifles of Canada, aboard HMCS *Prince Robert*, en route to Hong Kong, November 15, 1941.

the action of John Osborn of the Winnipeg Grenadiers, a company sergeant-major. Osborn was born in England and came to Canada shortly after the end of the First World War. He farmed for a time in Saskatchewan and then worked on the Canadian Pacific Railway before enlisting in Winnipeg in 1939. On December 19, 1941, Osborn was helping to organize the Canadian defence at the base of Mount Butler. Already wounded, he continued to engage the Japanese in close-quarters fighting. When a Japanese grenade landed amid him and his men, Osborn threw himself onto the explosive and was killed, but his men were saved. His brave actions earned him the Victoria Cross. At the same time, Brigadier-General Lawson's headquarters became surrounded. His last message was that he was going outside to fight it out. Perhaps apocryphally, it is said he met the enemy with a pistol in each hand before being subsequently killed. Lawson's public bravery and death led to the Japanese giving him a full military burial, a rare show of respect by the Japanese for their enemy.

Canadian prisoners of war liberated from Sham Shui Po Camp, Kowloon, Hong Kong, September 1945.

By December 22, the island was effectively cut in half by the advancing Japanese. The defenders were running out of ammunition and food, and because Maltby had failed to post defenders around the island's main water tower, the men were running out of water. Despite this, fighting continued. On Christmas Day, hours before the surrender, a Canadian counterattack by the Royal Rifles drove the Japanese from a position known as Stanley Village, one of the few instances of the battle in which the Japanese were driven back. But that did little to change the outcome.

The defenders had been fighting continuously for days with little to no sleep and had stubbornly held on. With every position captured, the Japanese committed atrocious acts against civilian and soldier alike, including bayonetting patients at St. Stephen's College field hospital and raping the nurses. The horrific actions of the Japanese did not stop there. When Maltby ordered his soldiers to surrender on the afternoon of December 25, the Canadians and their allies who had fought so hard were subject to a lengthy period of brutal imprisonment under the Japanese. Two hundred and ninety Canadians died in the fighting; the rest were taken prisoner, while a further 264 died in the sadistic Japanese prisoner-of-war system. Tragically, this would not be the last Canadian disaster of the war.

Dieppe

The Hong Kong tragedy certainly resonated in both Ottawa and London, yet the Canadians training in Great Britain were still chomping at the bit to see action. The First Canadian Army was officially formed in England in April 1942. Its commander was General McNaughton, but he was on sick leave and his temporary replacement was Lieutenant-General Harry Crerar who, as the previous Chief of the General Staff in Ottawa, was a major advocate for Canadian participation at Hong Kong. Now in England, he sought an opportunity to get the First Canadian Army into the fight. His opportunity came at Dieppe.

The raid on Dieppe was the culmination of a variety of pressure points. The British had been launching small-scale raids on the German-defended coastline since the summer of 1940. Churchill wanted something more substantial, something that could provide a public-relations victory for the

Allies. At the same time, the British were desperate to capture German intelligence material — anything that could help them decipher German U-boat wireless communications in the Atlantic. While they had broken these codes briefly in 1941, the German communications were back in the dark by early 1942. This meant that the Allies could not direct their convoys away from the "wolf packs" and gave the German fleet the advantage in the crucial Battle of the Atlantic. Thus, attached to the raid would be a "pinch" operation conducted by a special commando unit that would use the main raid as a distraction so they could attack a German naval headquarters and capture one of the new German four-rotor Enigma machines, a device that would help them once again break the U-boat code.[5]

When Crerar got wind of this planned operation, he pushed successfully for the Canadians to lead it. Chosen for the raid was the 2nd Canadian Infantry Division (2 CID) under Major-General John Hamilton "Ham" Roberts, a 53-year-old professional soldier from Pipestone, Manitoba. Roberts played a very small role in the planning of this operation, since most of it was conceived at Combined Operations Headquarters under the ineptitudes of Vice-Admiral Lord Louis Mountbatten.

Mountbatten's scheme was for the Canadians to land at three beaches: the main assault at Dieppe, with supporting assaults on the flanks at Puys to the north and Pourville to the south. While the Canadians dealt with their objectives, small units of British commandos would knock out a series of coastal artillery batteries and raid several key objectives for the gathering of intelligence. The Canadians would hold the beaches for approximately six hours before they withdrew. The raid itself was to be supported by firepower from sea and air, including naval destroyers, bombers, and attack fighters. This firepower was intended to suppress enemy machine-gun, mortar, and sniper positions, while the surprise of the raid landing before sunrise would overwhelm what enemy was left.

On paper, this all appeared sound, but there were serious issues with the plan. Most egregious was the naive belief that supporting firepower would neutralize enemy guns on the cliffs overlooking the beaches. Common sense should have dictated that the naval guns, light bombers, and Spitfires in support were not going to be accurate enough to take out these well-camouflaged German positions flanking each beach.[6] If these were left intact, the Canadians would wade into a killing zone. As well, Mountbatten and his staff relied too much on the surprise factor to make up for any potential failure by the supporting arms. Even if the German guns were not neutralized, they hoped the surprise landings coupled with the speed of advance would get the Canadians through the killing zone.

Operation Rutter, as the Dieppe Raid was first named, was set for early July 1942. However, despite marshalling all his forces, Mountbatten was forced to cancel due to poor weather. Not one to be deterred, he pressed for another chance. In the aftermath of the cancellation of Rutter, Mountbatten found himself losing assets. Neither the navy nor the air force had wanted much to do with Mountbatten's plan in the first place. The navy's commitment was already quite small — only eight Hunt-class destroyers with their relatively weak four-inch guns being offered in support, hardly the heavies Mountbatten was hoping for from his friends in the navy. As well, in the weeks following Rutter's cancellation, the air force reduced its support. Instead of large numbers of heavy and medium bombers, Mountbatten was now to receive a few squadrons of medium and light bombers, three of which were RCAF squadrons, along with 48 squadrons of Spitfires, six of which were RCAF. Despite this reduction in firepower, Mountbatten pressed on, and Operation Jubilee, as the raid was now called, was officially set for August 19.

The raid was a complete disaster. The covering fire from the destroyers and bombers proved impotent. While more than 800 RAF and RCAF fighter pilots fought bravely above the beaches in one of the largest air battles to date, this gave little respite to the unfortunate souls landing that morning.

Even though 2 CID was one of the most well-trained divisions in all of England, nothing could have prepared it for the murderous wall of fire it encountered. At all three beaches, landing craft were destroyed by mines or German mortar fire while those soldiers who made it onto land at Puys, Pourville, and Dieppe were effectively pinned down within minutes. At Dieppe proper, German mortar explosions turned the beach shingle into screaming hot fragments of shrapnel while the same tiny stones damaged tank tracks, immobilizing upward of nine of the 27 tanks from the Calgary Tank Regiment. Those tanks that did make it to the seawall were trapped on the promenade by massive concrete barriers and were forced to simply travel back and forth, firing at German positions until they ran out of ammunition.

Just under an hour after the first wave hit the beach at Dieppe, General Roberts made his only serious command decision of the day, one that haunted

View looking east along the main beach at Dieppe, showing damaged Churchill tanks of the 14th Armoured Regiment (Calgary Regiment), August 20, 1942.

him afterward. He received a broken message indicating that the lead elements had, indeed, pushed into the town, so he authorized the Fusiliers Mont-Royal to launch and exploit this supposed success. The Fusiliers Mont-Royal landed at 7:00 a.m., and instead of a secure beach, advanced straight into a killing zone. For hours the Canadians were effectively stuck, absorbing punishing amounts of German fire. By 11:00 a.m., the first of the landing craft arrived on the beach to take the men home. Yet the landing craft proved easy targets and they, too, were blown out of the water by German mortar and artillery fire. Just over 30 landing craft were destroyed in their efforts to extract the men from the disaster and only 400 Canadians managed to get off the beach. One of the men who stayed behind was Captain J.W. Foote, chaplain for the Royal Hamilton Light Infantry. He worked tirelessly during the battle performing last rites, carrying wounded into cover, helping to staunch wounds, and eventually chose to remain behind, stating that the men on the beaches were going to need him more than those returning to England. For his bravery and sacrifice, Foote was one of two Canadians to receive a Victoria Cross that day.

Dieppe stands as one of the worst days in the history of the Canadian military. Nearly 5,000 Canadians left England to participate in the attack and just over 2,200 returned. Eight hundred and thirty-six Canadians were killed that morning. It would be the single most-costly day of the Second World War for the Canadian Army. While the Canadian government sold the operation to its public as a great success, the casualty lists told a different story. The narrative of the raid shifted from a brilliantly executed commando operation by 2 CID to one that provided valuable lessons for future amphibious attacks — anything, no matter how untrue, to justify the terrible costs of that day.[7]

While Crerar and McNaughton both deserve some of the blame for accepting the raid without giving any input into its design, most of the responsibility lay squarely at Mountbatten's feet. Yet his royal blood and connections meant he escaped reprimand, and incredibly, he ended up as supreme allied commander in Southeast Asia.

General Roberts was not so lucky. He became the scapegoat for the operation, and his career commanding men in combat was over. One more gaffe, however, dogged him in the decades after the war. In the days leading up to August 19, Roberts had naively commented that the operation would be a piece of cake, so every year on the anniversary of the raid until his death in 1962, a package showed up on his doorstep; inside was a stale piece of cake.[8]

The War at Sea

The Royal Canadian Navy of 1939 was wholly unprepared for the immense task it faced in what would be one of the most important battles of the entire war. When war broke out, the North Atlantic immediately became an essential supply line for the British Commonwealth war effort. The route through the North Atlantic was the shortest between North America and Great Britain. The Germans sought to apply a strategy similar to the one they used in the First World War in which their U-boats would seek to cut off this lifeline to Britain. When France fell in June 1940, the "North Atlantic Run," as it was called, suddenly became more accessible to Germany as its U-boats were now able to operate out of bases along the French coast. If Britain was to survive, and if the British Commonwealth was to defeat Nazi Germany, then the endless stream of merchant vessels carrying everything from food to munitions to people had to be protected. It proved to be one of the most challenging battles fought by Canada during the entire conflict and arguably became Canada's greatest contribution to victory.[9]

The primary tactic for defending merchant vessels was the convoy system. Much like a herd of sheep protected by a shepherd and his sheepdogs, a convoy contained dozens of merchant vessels guarded by an outer ring of warships. In the early years of the war, these convoys formed up in Sydney or Halifax, Nova Scotia, or in St. John's, Newfoundland, and then were escorted by the Royal Canadian Navy (RCN) to a pre-designated rendezvous point where the convoys were handed off to the Royal Navy and guided to their final destination.

The RCN faced significant challenges right from the beginning. First was the desperate need for more warships to protect the growing size of convoys as well as the increasing frequency of convoy travel. The corvette thus became the workhorse of the RCN convoy war. It was a ship design based on whaling vessels. Although not fast and certainly not comfortable for those on board, it was tough and durable and could be built quite quickly in Canada's domestic shipyards. Armed with a four-inch gun and high-explosive depth charges, the corvette had enough firepower to chase away the enemy. By the summer of 1940, 64 corvettes were built along

Convoy assembling in Bedford Basin, Halifax, April 1, 1940.

with 24 Bangor-class minesweepers, another cheap workhorse for the RCN. While destroyers were certainly preferred, the RCN had few of them and instead had to rely on corvettes and minesweepers for the bulk of its convoy protection.

Hunting these convoys were the dreaded U-boats. Armed with up to six torpedoes, the submarines could move at a top speed of 17 knots when surfaced, while the maximum velocity of the corvettes was 16 knots. The U-boats were vulnerable to attack when surfaced, though once threatened could submerge in under half a minute. Underwater, the U-boats were much slower but also much more difficult to detect by rudimentary Allied sonar. The trade-off was clearly speed for stealth. In 1939, most of the small U-boat fleet, no more than 57 vessels, patrolled the waters off Great Britain's coasts. With the fall of France, however, Admiral Karl Dönitz, commander of Germany's U-boat fleet, obtained new bases along the Bay of Biscay from which to launch his submarines deeper into the Atlantic. By the end of that summer, the U-boat fleet was operating 930 miles off the European coast and inflicting more and more damage on the Atlantic convoys. Still, even by the end of 1940, most of the shipping losses incurred by the Allies happened in British waters. With the realization that the German surface fleet was going to be no match for the Royal Navy, and with increasing U-boat successes, resources were directed toward expanding Germany's submarine fleet.

Port broadside view of Flower-class corvette HMCS *Hawkesbury*, July 11, 1944.

Like Germany's U-boat fleet, the RCN was also undergoing rapid expansion. By the end of 1940, nearly 90 vessels, all corvettes and minesweepers, were under construction in Canadian shipyards. Added to this were six obsolete American destroyers that had arrived in Canadian waters after a "destroyers-for-bases" deal between the British and the Americans. The rapid expansion by the RCN posed some serious problems in terms of finding trained personnel.[10] Most of those commanding the corvettes were drawn from the Merchant Marine or the RCN Reserve, while the lower-deck ratings were pulled from the RCN Volunteer Reserve, many of who had never been to sea. Training was rudimentary and quick, and most expectations were simply that the men would learn on the job.

As losses from U-boats increased, both the RCN and Royal Navy extended their convoy protection deeper into the Atlantic. It was very clear by the end of 1940 that a large weak spot existed in the North Atlantic known as the "black pit," which referred to the lengthy air gap at the mid-ocean point between eastern Canada and the western isles of Great Britain where the

Captured German U-boats outside their pen at Trondheim, Norway, May 19, 1945.

convoys lost their air protection due to limitations on fuel. Air cover was the most effective method of defence against U-boats, yet this 372-mile gap was simply too far for any planes to cover while still ensuring they had enough fuel to safely make it back to base. There were certainly long-range planes being developed early in the war, specifically the Halifax and Lancaster, but these were reserved for Bomber Command. The RCN and RCAF Coastal Command had to make do with shorter-range Lockheed Hudsons and

The mid-Atlantic "air gap," which left convoys unprotected by air cover.

Douglas Digbys and later PBY Cansos. While innovating with these planes allowed pilots to fly them deeper into the North Atlantic, none of them were able to close the air gap completely. Admiral Dönitz and his U-boats were well aware that this lack of air cover was a great advantage for his fleet and sought to exploit it for as long as possible.

The prime targets for Dönitz's U-boats were the slow convoys coming out of Sydney, Halifax, and later St. John's. These convoys travelled no faster than nine knots. A voyage across the ocean at that speed often took 14 to 16 days. In many ways, the convoys were sitting ducks for the faster and more elusive U-boat wolf packs that patrolled the vast ocean. The RCN had very little experience in anti-submarine warfare, and the tools at its disposal were rudimentary at best. Every ship was loaded with depth charges, giant barrels loaded with TNT that were rolled off the deck and exploded at a pre-set depth, ideally shattering the hull of a submerged U-boat. A more successful method of destroying an enemy U-boat, especially in the early years, was simply ramming it. Other than that, a ship could shadow a U-boat until it was forced to surface or run out of air. Finally, and most effectively, was air cover. Planes could rapidly dive and attack a surfaced U-boat before it could get underwater. Yet the air gap meant that large stretches of the North Atlantic Run were without this valuable anti-submarine weapon. Frankly, the ideal ways to ensure the survival of a convoy were choppy seas, good light, and completely avoiding contact with the enemy. When contact erupted, the advantage lay with the U-boats.

Part of the problem for the RCN was the poor quality of its equipment. Most RCN vessels were equipped with an underwater detection device known as ASDIC, which was extremely sensitive to changing water conditions and prone to false readings. To detect U-boats on the surface, the RCN employed a different piece of technology, the SW1C (Surface Warning, Model One, Canadian). But even these proved ineffective in the heavy swells of the North Atlantic, which scrambled its ability to make accurate readings.[11] The British, on the other hand, had the far more effective Type 271 radar set, yet these were not handed over to Canadians until 1942. Frankly, the RCN remained technologically behind the British for almost the entire war. While some blame certainly lay with the British Admiralty, some of it also rested with Admiral Percy Nelles, chief of the Canadian naval staff, who was ultimately responsible for ensuring the RCN received the newest technology for its desperate battle.[12]

With slow-moving convoys, barely trained recruits, resources stretched too thin, and a lack of modern weapons and technology, it is no surprise the RCN struggled. During the first half of 1941, the Germans sank over 1.6 million tons of Allied shipping, a large amount of that coming on the RCN's watch. Convoy SC 42 was one of those. Leaving Sydney, Nova Scotia, on August 30, it consisted of 67 ships protected by four RCN vessels — one destroyer and three corvettes. On September 9, the convoy was spotted by a German U-boat, and within 24 hours, 11 U-boats converged on the convoy. A fierce and desperate battle ensued.

Lieutenant-Commander James "Chummy" Prentice in HMCS *Chambly* arrived on the scene and in consort with HMCS *Moose Jaw* engaged *U-501*. *Chambly* hit *U-501* with depth charges, while the *Moose Jaw* rammed it, eventually sinking it. Despite this, the U-boats inflicted heavy damage on the convoy. Fifteen merchant ships carrying 70,000 tons of cargo were destroyed. The British convoy that sailed out to take over for the beleaguered Canadians presented a stark reminder of the disparity between the RCN and Royal Navy: it consisted of five destroyers, two sloops, and two corvettes, all armed with the most modern weapons and technology. The battered and exhausted RCN crews handed over what was left of their merchant vessels and returned home to do it all again. The fate of SC 42 raised eyebrows within the British Admiralty, which became concerned about the RCN's ability to effectively escort and defend convoys.[13]

By this point, the Canadian convoy war was being directed from St. John's, Newfoundland. In May 1941, the Newfoundland Escort Force was established under the command of Commodore Leonard W. Murray. Born in Pictou, Nova Scotia, he had served at sea almost all his life in both the Royal Navy and the RCN. He now found himself in command of almost three-quarters of all Canadian ships and the senior commander responsible for the Canadian convoy battle. Merchant ships were escorted from Halifax and Sydney (and later Boston and New York City) where they met with the RCN vessels of the Newfoundland Escort Force. From here the convoy made its way to Iceland where the eastbound merchant ships were transferred to the protection of the Royal Navy and westbound merchant ships shifted to the safeguarding of the RCN returning home. Murray was an excellent commander but was aware of the disadvantages his fleet faced compared to that of the British. Despite his continual warnings to Ottawa that his men and ships were being pushed too hard, there was simply no time to rest. While Nelles and others could have certainly done more to help Murray, the reality was that the convoy war demanded every asset possible, and the RCN had to continue to make do, which they did but barely.

Things got even more difficult for the RCN. In February 1942, the Newfoundland Escort Force was renamed the Mid-Ocean Escort Force, a change in title that also accompanied a modification in travel plans. The convoys would no longer head to Iceland, which added too many extra days to the journey and often involved far more problematic weather conditions. Now, Murray's vessels would take a more southerly approach right through the heart of the U-boat fleet. No mid-ocean handover would occur, either; the RCN vessels would escort the merchant ships right to Londonderry on

Rear-Admiral Leonard Murray, spring 1943.

the west coast of Northern Ireland. In March, the RCN was further stretched when it agreed to take over escort duties for ships sailing from Boston and New York City into Canadian waters. The Americans refused to reallocate naval resources from the Pacific and thus the RCN was forced to pick up the slack.[14] All of this happened at the very same time that Admiral Dönitz shifted even more U-boats into the North Atlantic, 200 by the summer of 1942, including a number that entered Canadian waters and in May began to wreak havoc on shipping in the St. Lawrence River.

With resources stretched thin and no time to rest, refit, train, or recuperate, and with more and more German U-boats arriving in theatre, 1942 would be the nadir of the Canadian convoy effort. When German U-boats began sinking merchant vessels in the St. Lawrence River, Prime Minister King was forced to close it to shipping. British confidence in the Canadians hit its lowest by the autumn of 1942. Imports to Britain had continually declined since 1940, and much of the blame fell on the RCN. The British Admiralty was not interested in the multitude of factors that contributed to this; it simply saw the RCN as outmatched. It was not as if the RCN could not fight against submarines. It had destroyed five U-boats that very summer, but the limited number of ships meant no time to be pulled out of the line for training or re-equipping, which in turn led to exhausted crews, overworked vessels, and minimal protection when compared to the far larger and far better equipped Royal Navy.

By mid-1942, the British Admiralty had little good to say about the RCN's part in the convoy war, a sentiment that made its way right to the top.[15] Winston Churchill opined to Prime Minister King that perhaps the RCN needed a proper break from the gruelling day-to-day commitment of the North Atlantic Run. King agreed. The RCN, which supplied just under half of all the escort vessels in the North Atlantic, would be pulled out of the line, with the Americans temporarily filling in. This was certainly the low point for the RCN. It was a battered and bruised navy — constantly at a technological disadvantage — that gave up control of the St. Lawrence River to its enemy and was now pulled from convoy duty for a rest. The rest would not be much, but it would be enough.

When the RCN began to trickle back into the North Atlantic by the spring of 1943, a turning point was about to take place. British cryptologists broke the German naval cipher codes, allowing for the convoys to avoid the prowling wolf packs. At the same time, the RCN, now with the same upgraded technology the Royal Navy enjoyed, took the war to the U-boats. Four RCN convoy support formations called C-Groups were unleashed into the North Atlantic. These would respond to convoys under attack and sail to the fight. Armed with the latest weapons, such as forward-firing depth charges called Hedgehogs, and the latest technology, such as Type 271 radar and HF/DF sets, they became very effective at destroying and chasing away U-boats.

Finally, and most importantly, the air gap was closed. The British had at last realized the precarious nature of the North Atlantic battle and agreed to divert long-range bombers to operate as part of Coastal Command, supplying air cover for the convoys. These very long-range Liberators were aptly named. The merchant vessels and warships of the RCN could now count on air cover throughout the entirety of their journeys across the ocean. As well, a reorganization of command resulted in Rear-Admiral Leonard Murray being appointed commander-in-chief, Canadian Northwest Atlantic. Murray would be the only Canadian theatre commander of the entire war and was responsible for air, sea, and land assets from New York City to Newfoundland and out deep into the North Atlantic.

The combination of Murray's consolidated command along with U-boat hunting groups, long-range bombers, technological modernization, and

A Consolidated B-24 Liberator in flight, 1942.

intelligence breakthroughs all culminated to make 1943 the turning point in the Battle of the Atlantic. In March 1943, as the RCN re-entered the conflict, 160 U-boats roamed the Atlantic. That month alone the submarines sank 108 merchant ships with 627,377 tons of Allied shipping lost. Only two months later, May saw Dönitz lose 35 U-boats, including one commanded by his son. For the last six months of 1943, total tonnage sunk by the U-boats was just over 500,000. The threat to one of the most vital logistic lines in the history of 20th-century warfare was now secured.

While U-boats continued to threaten convoys and merchant ships for the remainder of the war, never again did they pose as serious a threat to the supply chain across the cold Atlantic seas. An incredible 99 percent of all merchant vessels escorted across the Atlantic by the RCN made it to their destinations. Even in the dark days of 1942, this percentage remained consistent, despite the Royal Navy's belief otherwise. The lifeline remained open, and notwithstanding some very serious setbacks, the RCN was crucial in making this happen. The testament to this was D-Day when the *matériel* wealth of the western Allies poured onto the Normandy beaches in June 1944 to begin the liberation of Northwest Europe. By that time, the RCN controlled the entire western half of the North Atlantic and had achieved one of Canada's most important victories of the entire war.

While the Battle of the Atlantic was certainly the RCN's largest contribution to the war effort, that was not its only one. In fact, RCN ships and sailors were present in all corners of the aquatic world. A small number of RCN corvettes operated in the Caribbean providing escort protection for oil tankers carrying the lifeblood of the war effort. Hundreds of RCN personnel also served throughout the Royal Navy. For example, HMS *Belfast*, a light cruiser, included 60 Canadian ratings (i.e., naval personnel), just under 15 percent of the entire ship's complement, when it helped sink the German battleship *Scharnhorst* in late December 1943. Lieutenant-Commander Fred Sherwood, from Ottawa, commanded the British submarine HMS *Spiteful*, which operated in the Indian Ocean, sinking several Japanese vessels. Lieutenant Robert "Hammy" Gray, from Trail, British Columbia, flew Corsairs for the British Pacific Fleet and earned the Victoria Cross when his plane crashed after sinking the *Amakusa*, a Japanese destroyer-escort.

In the Pacific, a small RCN fleet protected Canada's West Coast by primarily patrolling key choke points in the Strait of Juan de Fuca and Queen Charlotte and Hecate Straits. Three passenger liners turned armed merchant cruisers worked to the south, capturing German vessels attempting to flee neutral South American ports. One of these, HMCS *Prince Robert*, spent 24 hours in port at Pearl Harbor on the island of Oahu, three days before the Japanese surprise attack on December 7, 1941. As well, several corvettes and armed merchant cruisers supported joint U.S.-Canadian operations in the Aleutian Islands, at first, harassing the Japanese who had taken the islands of Kiska and Attu in the spring of 1942, and later, supporting the recapture of those islands in the summer of 1943. Patrolling the inland waters of Vancouver's west coast, with its numerous islands, inlets, and hiding spots, was the Fishermen's Naval Reserve, nicknamed "The Gumboot Navy." A "navy within a navy," as the official history of the RCN writes, it also played an active role in assisting with the confiscation of the Japanese-Canadian fishing fleet, nearly 1,000 vessels, in the immediate aftermath of the attack on Pearl Harbor.[16] HMCS *Uganda*, a light cruiser that entered service in late 1944, participated briefly in the invasion of Okinawa before returning to Esquimalt after most of its crew elected not to continue to serve in the Pacific campaign.

As part of Lord Mountbatten's Combined Operations service, several RCN landing craft (formed in units of landing craft flotilla) were used to transport soldiers to and from the beaches during the Dieppe Raid in August 1942, the Operation Torch landings in North Africa in November 1942 (along with 17 RCN corvettes on escort duty), Operation Husky (the invasion of Sicily in July 1943), and Operation Baytown (the invasion of mainland Italy in September 1943).

Besides the Battle of the Atlantic, the RCN was busiest in and around Great Britain. Much of this activity was centred around the new Tribal-class destroyers entering service from late 1942 onward. These destroyers were intended to form the nucleus of a postwar Canadian surface fleet.[17] The first two destroyers to enter service, HMCS *Iroquois* and HMCS *Athabaskan*, cut their teeth in the Bay of Biscay hunting U-boats throughout the summer of 1943. When HMCS *Haida* entered service later that year, the three destroyers were

Starboard stern three-quarter view of HMCS *Prince Robert*, June 16, 1943.

sent north to Scapa Flow where they provided protection for the extremely dangerous "Murmansk Run," the Arctic convoy route from Great Britain to the Soviet Union's Murmansk port. In early 1944, now accompanied by HMCS *Huron*, the four destroyers returned to the English Channel as part of the Royal Navy's 10th Destroyer Flotilla. The RCN destroyers were now actively hunting German surface vessels, seeking to eliminate the German naval threat to Allied English Channel operations. There, targets were mainly destroyers and smaller torpedo boats. While the destroyers were clearly very effective in carrying out their tasks, it came at the cost of losing the *Athabaskan*, which was sunk in late April by a German torpedo. The next month, however, the RCN presence in the channel was further boosted by the arrival of the destroyers HMCS *Algonquin* and HMCS *Sioux*, just in time to participate in the D-Day landings on June 6, 1944.

The RCN contributed 110 ships to the 6,900 vessels taking part in Operation Neptune, the naval component of the D-Day operation. Canadian destroyers provided artillery support for landward operations and helped protect the fleet against German naval attacks. The *Haida* and *Huron*, for instance, were on the sharp end of a German attack when a small German surface fleet launched an assault against the western flank of the Allied fleet. The two Canadian destroyers responded magnificently, sinking one German destroyer on the night of June 8 and the next day forcing a second one to run aground. Of particular importance to the D-Day

Flower-class corvette HMCS *Regina*, circa 1942–43.

landings was the minesweeping work of 31st Canadian Minesweeping Flotilla, which on the night of June 5 cleared the mines blocking the approaches to Omaha, the American landing beach. As well, several Canadian landing craft flotilla helped ferry troops to shore in the early morning hours of June 6 and continued bringing reinforcements thereafter. In many ways, Operation Neptune was the high point of Canadian naval participation beyond the Battle of the Atlantic.

Once the Normandy landings were secured, RCN vessels focused on defending the seaward flank, ensuring that German vessels could not interrupt the all-important logistical chain that connected Allied soldiers on the continent to Great Britain. Two RCN motor torpedo boat flotillas — small, fast, surface vessels armed with torpedoes, machine guns, and even depth charges — operated along the flanks of the Allied fleet, engaging German vessels attempting to break into the beachhead area. By late June and early July, the Germans were throwing everything they had left at the Allied fleet protecting the growing Normandy beachhead, including destroyers, torpedo boats, E-boats (small fast-attack craft), and even minesweepers. RCN destroyers and several British vessels manned by RCN crews carried on with the hunt for German surface-fleet vessels in the English Channel while rotating in and out of the Murmansk Run, which continued to pose some of the greatest dangers to Allied vessels.[18] Canadian minesweepers stayed to clear mines throughout the channel, and Canadian landing craft flotilla were utilized in several amphibious operations, including work in the Scheldt Estuary.

While the RCN's role in the Battle of the Atlantic has often held prominence in the narrative of Canada's war at sea, Canadian naval personnel played a part in nearly every theatre and many of the major actions throughout the conflict. The war saw the Canadian surface fleet expand in an almost unbelievable fashion, and by the end of the war, Canada boasted the fifth-largest navy in the world.

The War in the Air

The Royal Canadian Air Force was in no condition to fight a modern war when hostilities erupted in September 1939. There were far too few planes, most of which were obsolete, and hundreds of eager Canadians ended up serving in the RAF while the RCAF played catch-up.[19] Eventually, enough Canadian pilots were overseas that three Canadian squadrons were formed: RAF 242 (Canadian) Squadron, 110 (RCAF) Squadron, and 1 (RCAF) Squadron. Soon, dozens of Canadian pilots found themselves in the thick of the fight when the Battle of Britain erupted in the summer of 1940. After the fall of France, Adolf Hitler turned his attention to a potential invasion of Great Britain, but to cross the English Channel in force he needed to control the skies. Thus, in July, the Luftwaffe began a sustained campaign to destroy the air capabilities of Britain and its allies. Three pilots from 1 (RCAF) Squadron received the Distinguished Flying Cross during this crucial period, and 242 (Canadian) Squadron suffered so many casualties that it could no longer be considered a "Canadian" squadron when the battle ended in October 1940. Twenty-three Canadians lost their lives defending Britain from the Luftwaffe, helping to end Hitler's plans to invade. More than 100 Canadians counted themselves as the brave "few" Winston Churchill famously referred to.[20]

By the summer of 1941, a dozen RCAF squadrons in Fighter Command were active in Britain and became part of an aggressive air offensive aimed at finding, engaging, and destroying the Luftwaffe. This "leaning into France" saw patrols ranging in size from a small number of fighter planes (known as "rodeos") to larger combinations of fighters and bombers (known as "circuses") entering French skies to draw the Luftwaffe out to fight. When the enemy obliged, the skies lit up as Hurricanes and Spitfires engaged German Messerschmitts and Focke-Wulf Fw190s. During this offensive, more Allied planes were shot down than German ones. However, the Allies replaced their lost aircraft much quicker, and thanks to the British Commonwealth Training Plan, trained pilots arrived in Britain in greater and greater numbers.

Canadian fighter pilots also fought in the Mediterranean. In fact, the only RCAF fighter squadron overseas to assist outside Northwest Europe was 417 Squadron, which served in North Africa with the Desert Air Force and then supported the Allied invasion of Sicily in July 1943 and mainland Italy in September of the same year. The 331 Wing, which included RCAF bomber squadrons 402, 424, and 425, also supported the Allied invasion of Sicily and mainland Italy until returning to Northwest Europe in October 1943.

Many Canadian pilots served in RAF squadrons, several of which were stationed on the island fortress of Malta, now utilized by the Allies as a

Unidentified crew member refuelling a Hawker Hurricane of 1 (RCAF) Squadron, October 1940.

base to harass and destroy Axis shipping into North Africa. Here several Canadian pilots obtained ace status, including Canada's top ace George "Buzz" Beurling from Verdun, Quebec, flying with the RAF 249 Squadron. Dubbed the "Knight of Malta" by the Canadian press, Beurling was certainly an oddball character — a loner with strange idiosyncrasies who preferred to fly solo as opposed to the accepted doctrine of in pairs. Regardless, he was an excellent fighter pilot, particularly adept at deflection shooting, and by the time his tour in Malta ended in late 1942, he had 29 confirmed kills and was a national celebrity.[21]

By 1943, over a dozen RCAF fighter squadrons — now all labelled between 400 and 449 — were being organized in Great Britain as preparations for the invasion of Northwest Europe commenced. In June 1943, Second Tactical Air Force was formed to provide the invasion force with a ready

George Beurling (left) meets Prime Minister King, November 1942.

call of fighters and bombers to support ground operations. Almost all RCAF squadrons that were once part of Fighter Command would serve at some point in Second Tactical Air Force. The RCAF was offered to fly in direct tactical support of the First Canadian Army, but if accepted it would have meant waiting until the First Canadian Army was operational in July.[22] This offer was declined, and the RCAF chose instead to lead the way into France where most of its squadrons ended up flying in support of the Second British Army.

As more and more of the European continent was liberated by the Allies, RCAF squadrons started to move from their long-time bases in Great Britain to new ones in France and later Belgium and the Netherlands. By 1944, there were 17 RCAF squadrons operating as part of Second Tactical Air Force in day-fighter, night-fighter, and fighter-bomber roles, with one squadron, RCAF 418, performing an intruder role, a highly dangerous one whereby 418's pilots, flying Boston Mark IIIs and later Mosquitoes, flew deep into enemy territory at night to strike targets. The pilots of 418 Squadron were highly effective in this role, and by 1945 were even conducting intruder raids during daytime. Theirs became the highest-scoring RCAF squadron of the entire war in terms of targets eliminated.[23]

By the time the Allies had established a strong foothold on the continent, the Luftwaffe had been decimated. The continual efforts by British, Commonwealth, and American pilots to engage the Luftwaffe since 1941, coupled with the ongoing effects of a sustained bomber offensive, meant the Allies had near-complete authority of the air by the summer of 1944, with an almost 10-to-1 ratio of Allied to Luftwaffe planes. The skies now belonged to the RCAF whenever it flew its missions, which it did aggressively. Spitfires generally escorted bombers and engaged what was left of the Luftwaffe's fighters. Typhoon fighter-bombers were often used to attack enemy trains and transportation lines and harass enemy ground forces, while Mosquitoes flew night-fighter and intruder missions and conducted valuable aerial reconnaissance. While the effects of aerial support were often overexaggerated by commanders, there was no question that dominating the skies played a major role in victory. Transportation routes were destroyed, hurting the enemy's ability to reinforce and resupply. Enemy ground forces were nearly stopped from moving in the daytime to avoid aerial attack, and undoubtedly Allied soldiers watching Allied planes strike enemy positions was good for morale.

A Mosquito of 418 Squadron.

Air support in the battle against U-boats also played a major role in victory, and the RCAF participated in that part of the war overseas with Coastal Command and at home with Canada's Eastern Air Command, responsible for air operations along Canada's Atlantic coast. Operating out of Halifax, St. John's, and later Gaspé, squadrons patrolled the western half of the North Atlantic and supported convoys heading into the unforgiving waters. In the first years, most Eastern Air Command squadrons flew obsolete aircraft and struggled to make any serious dent in the war against U-boats. However, by 1942, they began to receive modern Hudsons, Hurricanes, Cansos, Catalinas, Dakotas, and eventually game-changing Liberators that finally closed the air gap. With these aircraft, Eastern Air Command started to make a serious impact. By January 1943, 16 squadrons operated out of Nova Scotia and Newfoundland hunting U-boats and supporting the convoy war.

The most successful Eastern Air Command squadron was 162. While originally based out of Nova Scotia, it was seconded to Coastal Command in early 1944 and stationed first in Reykjavik, Iceland, and later in northeastern Scotland. While in Scotland, 162 Squadron enjoyed an incredible period of success, sinking four U-boats and sharing in the destruction of a fifth. It was during this time that one of its pilots, Flight Lieutenant David Hornell from Toronto, was awarded the Victoria Cross. On June 24, his Canso engaged *U-1225*, and despite his plane being hit by German fire and erupting into flames, he pressed home the attack, finally sinking the submarine with depth charges. Hornell's plane had taken so much damage, however, that he was forced to crash-land at sea. He and his crew then spent 21 hours in the freezing water before they were rescued. By that time, two of his crew had already perished from hypothermia, and shortly after being pulled out, Hornell succumbed, as well.

While Eastern Air Command registered only six confirmed U-boat kills (these did not include the ones successfully attacked by 162 Squadron, which were attributed to Coastal Command), the mere presence of effective air cover, especially from 1943 onward, became a significant deterrent to

Flight Lieutenant David Hornell, VC.

U-boats seeking to stray into the western half of the Atlantic Ocean and played a key part of the Allied victory in the Atlantic.

RCAF squadrons in Coastal Command also contributed to victory by providing air cover for convoys in the eastern half of the Atlantic while sinking nine U-boats. Operating primarily out of Great Britain, eight RCAF squadrons served with Coastal Command, including the temporary secondment of 162 Squadron, with an RCAF bomber squadron (405) serving briefly, while 413 Squadron, one of the earliest RCAF Coastal Command units to be formed, was transferred to Ceylon (modern-day Sri Lanka) in 1942. Although anti-submarine work was their primary objective, the RCAF squadrons in Coastal Command also contributed to anti-shipping activities, helped protect the western flank of the D-Day invasion fleet, and even conducted mine-dropping operations in the approaches to German-held ports.

Canada's greatest assistance in the air war, and one of the most controversial aspects of the country's entire war experience, was its role in Bomber Command. After the fall of France, Bomber Command was almost the only tool at the Allies' disposal that could strike at Axis targets, yet bombers were notoriously inaccurate. Even in daylight, bomber crews rarely hit their targets. At that time, British High Command was quite reluctant to shift from precision bombing of specific enemy targets to area bombing of German cities for fear of causing civilian casualties. All that began to change, however, in the summer of 1940 when the Luftwaffe started to target British cities. More and more senior British commanders and politicians came to accept that the bombing of German cities was appropriate retribution while also hoping the bombers could hurt Germany's war industry.

However, because of their notorious inaccuracy, the only effective method was to blanket German cities in bombs to best ensure that important industrial and military targets were destroyed, even though it meant civilian casualties would occur. By the time Bomber Command received its new commander-in-chief, Sir Arthur "Bomber" Harris, in February 1942, area bombing was generally accepted. While Harris came to embody the bomber offensive, he was a product of widely held beliefs that area bombing could be a major factor in helping to win the war through the destruction of German industry and the erosion of German civilian morale.[24]

Flying in Bomber Command was one of the most dangerous jobs anyone could do. Casualty rates were incredibly high, so much so that early in the war the British were forced to switch from daytime to nighttime bombing runs to mitigate what was seen as unsustainable losses. But even operating at night, bomber squadrons continued to suffer horrendous casualty rates. From March 1941 to March 1942, Bomber Command lost 1,000 crewmen with little to show for the effort. Despite optimistic beliefs by Harris and others in the efficacy of bombing, the bomber offensive had yet to really show anything for itself by the early spring of 1942. For Harris, the answer was to step up operations and conduct larger and larger raids on German cities. On May 31, 1942, 1,047 bombers were dispatched to bomb the city of Cologne — the first 1,000-bomber raid — with 78 RCAF bombers taking part.

Canadian pilots served in RAF bomber squadrons right from the beginning of the war and not just in Europe but all over the world. It wasn't until the spring of 1941, however, that the first RCAF bomber squadrons were activated in Great Britain. Eventually, there were 15 RCAF bomber squadrons, which allowed for the formation of 6 (RCAF) Bomber Group, activated in January 1943. A bomber group was the air force equivalent of an army formation, and thus 6 Group became one of the largest Canadian formations of the war.

The aircrews of 6 Bomber Group got off to a very difficult start. Most of the pilots were inexperienced, since the crews were only recently put together. The 6 Group was equipped at first with outdated bombers (Wellingtons), which were much slower than the Halifax or Lancaster bombers currently in use by most of Bomber Command. The combination of inexperience and obsolete equipment meant that casualties in 6 Group for the first six months of operation were shockingly higher than the average for their peers. Casualty rates began to drop, however, as pilots gained experience and the Wellington was replaced with the far-better Lancaster and Halifax. Nonetheless, the toll on the men of 6 Group was immense, as seen in the higher-than-average numbers of planes that returned without completing their missions, known as the "turnback rate."[25]

The debate surrounding the bomber offensive both during the war and ever since has been focused on its effects. It was clear that the bomber offensive did not destroy German morale, nor did it make any dramatic impact on decreasing German industry, though it did place a ceiling on its potential. Even though bombers did not win the war as men like Harris and to a lesser extent Churchill believed it did, the bomber offensive contributed in many ways to the eventual victory. The intensity of the offensive helped somewhat

THE SECOND WORLD WAR: THE CONFLICT AT SEA AND IN AIR

to placate the Soviets who demanded a second front be opened in the west while the Red Army was taking the brunt of Allied casualties in the east. Much of the bomber offensive was focused on the Ruhr region, Germany's industrial heartland, and the incessant attacks against this region and its cities effectively capped the output of the German war economy. As well, to combat the bomber offensive, Hitler was forced to pull valuable resources from the front lines.[26]

Hundreds of German fighter planes were withdrawn from the Mediterranean and the Eastern Front to defend German skies. Thousands of guns, especially the 88 mm, perhaps one of the most effective anti-tank guns of the war, were moved back into Germany to be placed in an anti-aircraft role. This meant that Soviet tanks in the east, and later Allied tanks in the west, were facing far fewer of these feared weapons. Even the German war economy was forced to shift in response to the continual Allied air attacks, with more and more resources devoted to the production of aircraft and anti-aircraft guns at the expense of tank production. Thus, despite the high casualties, 6 Group was part of a campaign that slowly but surely wore down Nazi Germany's war machine.

The same year that 6 Group was activated, the bomber offensive increased in intensity. In late July, 81 RCAF bombers were part of the nearly 800-bomber stream that attacked Hamburg. Particularly dry conditions, coupled with the dropping of thousands of high-explosive and incendiary bombs, turned Hamburg into a blazing firestorm with temperatures rising to nearly 1,292 degrees Fahrenheit (700 degrees Celsius). The city was utterly destroyed and its population, at the time the second largest in Germany, was decimated, with nearly 43,000 killed and just under a million forced to flee to the countryside.

The punishment did not stop. By late 1943, bomber streams were directed against Berlin itself, not surprisingly the most well-defended city in the Reich. On November 22, 764 bombers, of which 110 were from 6 Group, pummelled Hitler's capital. Fifteen more major raids were launched against Berlin into 1944, and while the people and infrastructure of the city suffered, the attacks against this extremely fortified objective took its toll on Bomber Command in dangerously mounting casualties.

The bomber crews got a break in April 1944, however, when General Dwight D. Eisenhower took control of Bomber Command in the lead-up to

A district in Hamburg, Germany, in the aftermath of bombing during the Allies' Operation Gomorrah, July 24 to August 3, 1943.

D-Day. Now the objectives changed from heavily defended German cities to lightly defended railways, bridges, canals, and road networks in France — anything that could hinder German troop movement in response to the eventual invasion.[27] Suddenly, losses, which peaked at 7.3 percent in January 1944, dropped to less than 2 percent, a desperately needed reprieve.

Yet Harris, bristling at the loss of his bombers, reclaimed them in the autumn of 1944. By this point, the German war machine was collapsing. The Luftwaffe had been all but destroyed and the Allies began mercilessly punishing the German home front with unprecedented numbers of bombs. In the first three months of 1945, Bomber Command dropped as many bombs as it had in all of 1943.[28] This included the firebombing of Dresden on the night of February 13, 1945. Sixty-seven RCAF bombers were part of a stream of 796 bombers that delivered hell to the citizens of that city along the Elbe River. Like Hamburg, tens of thousands of civilians were killed and the city was nearly completely destroyed.

Despite the ferocity and frequency of bomber attacks in late 1944 and 1945, casualty rates remained much lower than during the dark days of the Berlin battles. In fact, by war's end, 6 Bomber Group boasted the lowest percentage of losses out of any of the bomber groups.[29] This was a fitting conclusion for a country that proved to be the largest dominion contributor to Bomber Command. Out of 125,000 airmen, 40,000 were Canadian, while 10,000 Canadians lost their lives. It is estimated that nearly 600,000 German civilians were killed because of the bomber offensive, most of them women, children, and the elderly.[30] It was a chilling cost to the bomber offensive's contribution to final victory, but as Lord Kitchener once said in 1915, "Unfortunately we have to make war as we must, and not as we should like."

The contribution of the RCAF during the Second World War would have almost been unbelievable on the eve of war. On September 1, 1939, the RCAF boasted 4,061 officers and men, and a smattering of obsolete or soon-to-be-obsolete aircraft. By the end of the war, it had grown to over 263,000 men and women in a variety of roles, including operating radar stations, intelligence gathering, transporting Allied goods, defending coastlines, hunting U-boats, engaging enemy fighters, and bombing enemy targets. Seventeen thousand one hundred and one Canadians lost their lives, while Canadian aircrew and ground crew were found in every theatre of action and in the skies over most of the world.

The War at Home

Prime Minister King faced immense challenges in gearing Canada toward a total war effort. Despite a resounding victory in the 1940 federal election, his hopes for "limited liability" were dashed by the summer of that year, and King had to not only ensure that Canadians enlisted in the rapidly expanding military but also that Canada's resources were organized in an efficient and effective manner to withstand the pressures of a long total war. While Canada enjoyed a bounty of natural resources that would help in the war effort for both Canada and its allies, the country's key resource was human power. But how was King going to mobilize a country of 11 million people to support the continued conflict?

Two key pieces in this mobilization were the National Resources Mobilization Act and the National Selective Service. The National Resources Mobilization Act was passed by King's government in June 1940, just as

France was collapsing, and gave the government wide-ranging powers to conscript soldiers for home defence (later in the war these conscripts were derogatively referred to as "zombies"). It also established controls over Canada's workforce. To better organize Canada's war industry, however, the National Selective Service was established in March 1942 and sought to solve a growing labour shortage in industries deemed essential to the war effort. With the National Resources Mobilization Act and the National Selective Service, the government managed Canadian labour in unprecedented ways. For instance, one could not transfer out of a job considered high priority to the war effort without permission. As well, under the National Selective Service the government had the power to order striking workers back to work. By 1943, just over 13 percent of all Canadians were working in a war industry heavily regulated by the federal government, and by war's end, 1.2 million people were employed by Canada's war industry.

A large percentage of these workers were women. As the war progressed, it became quite clear that women were going to play a far more important role than anyone had thought in 1939. At first women were asked to contribute to the war effort in ways that fit within the traditional gender roles of the time, which viewed women as caretakers of the home whose natural roles fell within the domestic sphere. Much of this early support thus included participating in any of the numerous volunteer organizations springing up across the country. As well, women were encouraged to grow "victory gardens," converting any available green spaces, including lawns, into gardens to help limit the burden on national food stocks. There were also expectations that women would help bolster the morale of the men overseas by mailing care packages and writing letters.

By 1942, as the nation began to impose food rationing, women were expected to help ensure that people obeyed ration limits. All of these efforts were seen as acceptable means of female support within the traditional gender roles of the time. Yet things began to change quite dramatically. As more and more men entered military service, a labour crisis emerged, particularly in essential war industries. It was quickly accepted that women were a solution to this labour shortage. In fact, in May 1942, a Women's Division of the National Selective Service was created to help coordinate female recruitment. Within that year, a record number of women, particularly married ones with children, entered the job market. Traditionally all-male jobs were now being performed

Women workers at Burrard Inlet dry dock, North Vancouver, British Columbia, circa 1942–44.

more and more by women. From instrument mechanics to power machine operators, women were helping to build airplanes, tanks, ships, and other weapons of war. By war's end, 33 percent of all Canadian women were in the workforce, nearly an 11 percent increase from 1939.[31]

There was very clear anxiety, however, over women entering roles that challenged traditional ideas of gender. The government attempted to assuage these concerns by constantly touting the temporary nature of the work, a necessary measure that would cease upon the war's conclusion. As well, media and advertising attempted to forge a delicate balance between celebrating women's efforts while also reaffirming traditional ideas about Canadian femininity. For instance, the iconic photo of Veronica Foster, nicknamed "Ronnie the Bren Gun Girl," shows an attractive woman — Veronica was, in fact, a model — garbed in factory clothes while daintily, or even seductively, caressing the barrel of a Bren gun with a cigarette in her hand. This photograph, and others like it, were widely distributed. It was a reminder to Canadians that industrial work, while important for the

Veronica Foster, aka "Ronnie the Bren Gun Girl," May 10, 1941.

war effort, in no way affected a woman's feminine qualities.[32] Regardless of general anxieties over changing gender norms, thousands of women entered jobs that would have been inaccessible in 1939. They proved their worth alongside their male colleagues and made a significant contribution to Canada's domestic war effort.

Adding to the general anxiety over changing gender roles was the growing number of women entering the armed services. Canada already had a history of women participating in its military conflicts going back as far as 1885 when a small detachment of women nurses accompanied a Canadian military force into the District of Saskatchewan. There were small numbers of Canadian nursing sisters in South Africa during the Second Boer War, and 3,100 served during the First World War with 2,500 going overseas. Military nursing was the least controversial of all the roles women played within the military. It fit perfectly with contemporary ideas about women's roles in society as Christian maternal nurturers. Almost 4,500 Canadian nurses served during the Second World War in all three military branches with most of them overseas in Britain. Smaller numbers of Canadian nurses served with field hospitals and casualty clearing centres in the Mediterranean and throughout Northwest Europe, and many of those overseas were exposed to immense hardship and danger, not to mention gruelling periods of unrelenting work.

While nursing received very little pushback from Canadian society at large, the recruitment of women into other military roles was far more contentious.[33] British women had already served in auxiliary roles during the First World War and were being called into service as early as September 1939. Buoyed by the example of Joan Kennedy, a British-born accountant living in Victoria, British Columbia, and others inspired by Joan's work, paramilitary volunteer organizations were established across the country. By 1941, 40 of these groups were in existence, and Kennedy and others were able to successfully lobby the Canadian government to finally allow women into the military.

The majority of women went into the Canadian Women's Army Corps, which at its peak numbered nearly 22,000. Just over 17,000 women entered the Royal Canadian Air Force Women's Division, and a further 6,781 joined the Women's Royal Canadian Naval Service, often called the "Wrens." There was significant anxiety from both the Canadian public and military over women enlisting in the services, particularly focused around perceived threats to traditional Canadian views of femininity. To mollify these worries, women were put into trades that still fit within prescribed gender roles such as cooks, clerks, laundresses, dental assistants, switchboard operators, et cetera. As well, policies were put in place that heavily regulated how women could behave and how they looked, including the use of cosmetics, hairstyles, and clothing, all with an eye to ensure that normative feminine ideals were prescribed when women entered the military.[34]

Yet unease continued over the ever-increasing numbers of women flowing into the armed services, and malicious gossip spread throughout the country exaggerating reports of drunkenness, pregnancy, venereal disease, sexual immorality, and even prostitution. This "whispering campaign," which also had parallels in Britain and the United States, hurt recruitment efforts in Canada.[35] Yet, as the war progressed, far more opportunities to serve made themselves available to Canadian women. By the end of the war, small numbers of women were mechanics, photographic technicians, air traffic controllers, and drivers. As well, they could be found working in signals intelligence and operating radar stations. While they were paid less than men, suffered harassment and discrimination, and had their behaviour heavily regulated, most women who served, even in the more mundane roles, spoke positively about their time in the military.[36] The 50,000

Personnel of the Canadian Women's Army Corps take a smoke break during a firefighting exercise in London, England, February 1943.

women who served freed up men for service closer to the front line and took a small but important step in the changing nature of women's roles in Canadian society.

As the Canadian military grew rapidly in size, significant pressure was placed on the various services to do away with both formal and informal barriers to the enlistment of persons of colour. The Royal Canadian Navy's strict "colour line" required that personnel be white and of European descent. This racial barrier reflected a similar policy within the Royal Navy, and maintaining a common recruitment policy with its parent organization was a priority for senior Canadian naval officers. Similarly, at the outbreak of war, the RCAF also imposed strict barriers for recruitment, echoing that of its parent organization, the Royal Air Force. Not only were candidates to be white, but specifically British subjects or immediate descendants of British subjects. As well, within the RCAF, higher health and education requirements created a tangible systemic barrier for many non-whites to enlist. Canada's army, with the largest demand for personnel, was the branch where most persons of colour were able to enlist. There were, of course, many examples of recruiting stations refusing prospective enlistees based on their skin colour, but there was no formal "colour line" as there was in the navy or air force. Yet a racial hierarchy certainly existed.

Indigenous men found they were more readily accepted into the army than those of Chinese, Japanese, or Indian descent. Despite very clear racial barriers to enlistment as the war progressed, casualties mounted, and the Canadian military expanded, many restrictions were removed or loosened. The RCAF abandoned its "colour line" in 1942 and the RCN followed suit a year later, though both these services continued to see very limited numbers of non-white personnel.[37]

William K. Lore was one of the first Canadians to benefit from this change in recruitment policy. Born in Victoria, British Columbia, Lore was the son of Chinese immigrants, and while his application to the RCN was rejected three times, after March 1943, he was finally accepted. When he was commissioned a sub-lieutenant in June 1943, Lore became not only the first Chinese Canadian to serve in the RCN but the first officer of Chinese descent in any navy in all the British Commonwealth. Lore worked in Ottawa, then London, then Ceylon (modern-day Sri Lanka), and was eventually attached to the U.S. Seventh Fleet under Douglas MacArthur to become one of the first Allied officers to step foot in newly liberated Hong Kong.

Traditional ideas about gender and race were not the only ideas being challenged, either, as the war saw impressive and fairly radical economic measures taken that pushed Canada down the path toward a welfare state. Driving these economic measures during the war was the fear of repeating the mistakes made in the First World War in which rampant inflation and an uncontrolled rise in the cost of living collided with a postwar recession that created vast unemployment and culminated in serious labour unrest. The wartime demand for labour saw the 1939 unemployment rate of 11.4 percent decline steadily to nearly zero by 1943. Canada's gross national product doubled in size. Spending power dramatically increased, and while the cost of living started to rise at an alarming rate once again, by October 1941, government controls on wages and prices flattened the curve. The key to all this was the Wartime Prices and Trade Board, which set the prices of consumer goods, controlled wages, implemented rent controls, and was given the power to prosecute anyone contravening its orders. It was a powerful economic force and was highly successful; Canada did not experience the runaway inflation and untenable rise in the cost of living that stained the

First World War domestic experience. At the same time, Canadians benefited from steadily increasing wages. The average annual wage in 1939 was $956, by 1943 it was $1,525.[38]

Another immense challenge for the government was how to pay for the war. By the late summer of 1940, this did not just mean Canada's war effort but also how to financially support Great Britain, which was desperate for money, food, and *matériel* in the aftermath of its retreat from the continent. Trying to meet this urgent need, coupled with Canada's own expanding military commitments, meant Canada's war expenditures ballooned in cost. A key source of revenue was taxes. Property, income, and corporate taxes all increased substantially, while new taxes were introduced on luxury items and excess profits of companies that benefited financially from wartime demand. The government also fell back on the time-honoured tradition of loans and war bonds.

However, in its efforts to provide the supplies requested by Great Britain, Canada dramatically increased its imports from the United States. Effectively, one-third of the value of every tank, ship, or vehicle constructed in Canada was built with imported materials from the United States.[39] Because the sterling was useless to Canada outside the British Empire, Canada was, in effect, financing a large chunk of Britain's purchases while spending more and more money in the United States on meeting those purchase orders. It was estimated that by the summer of 1941 Canada was spending $400 million more per year on U.S. imports.

The Lend-Lease Act passed by the U.S. Congress in March 1941 further complicated this financial picture. Great Britain could now potentially go straight to the United States for its war *matériel*, thus seriously damaging Canada's expanding war economy, which relied so heavily on exports to Great Britain. This was a precarious trade imbalance. How could Canada keep its British orders while continuing to drive the nation's war economy and still avoid a total trade imbalance with the United States? The answer was the incredible Hyde Park Declaration signed between Prime Minister King and President Franklin D. Roosevelt in April 1941. In this superb moment of Canadian-American diplomatic relations, the Americans agreed to increase their imports of raw materials from Canada, effectively matching the financial amount Canada was spending in the United States. Of note, the U.S. goods Canada was importing specifically to make war *matériel* for

Britain were now to be charged to Britain's Lend-Lease account. With this agreement, the growing trade deficit was dealt a mighty blow and Canada's war industry continued to expand. By 1943, government defence spending peaked at $4.3 billion and the economy became so strong that the Canadian government gifted Britain $1 billion. By the end of the war, Canada provided nearly $3.5 billion in aid to Great Britain. This amounted to roughly one-fifth of the war's total cost to Canada, estimated at $18 billion.[40]

Not only was King able to secure an important economic agreement with the United States but he also passed a series of social welfare measures, much of which formed the building blocks for Canada's move toward a social welfare state. It was clear in the years leading up to the war that the new political party emerging from the Prairies, the Co-operative Commonwealth Federation (the forerunner of the New Democratic Party), was gaining significant political support advocating for a wide range of social welfare measures. King hoped that the implementation of some similar measures could curb that party's growing popularity. As well, with government coffers filling up, King was able to spend on such measures. Finally, King's government embraced a Keynesian strategy whereby the expected postwar recession could be mitigated by giving Canadians greater economic support. Some of the major initiatives by King's government included unemployment insurance, passed in 1940, and family allowances, initiated in 1945. Topping all this off was the ambitious Veterans Charter, which gave cash bonuses to returning veterans, offered them vocational training and land grants for farms, implemented preferential hiring, and provided tuition for post-secondary education.

This vision for a postwar Canada was further chiselled out by the Committee on Reconstruction, established by King in February 1941 and put under the leadership of Cyril James, a noted economist and president of McGill University. The committee's job was to recommend steps to ensure the healthy reconstruction of the postwar Canadian economy, culminating in the committee's 1943 *Report on Social Security for Canada*. This document has since become known as the Marsh Report, named for its author, Leonard Marsh, an economist working on the committee. The Marsh Report, inspired by the Beveridge Report in Great Britain a year before, called for wide-ranging social security measures such as government-sponsored employment programs, expanded benefits for the unemployed and workers' compensation, increases in old-age pensions, greater financial support for retirees, and health insurance for Canadians. For many in the Liberal government, the Marsh Report was too radical for the time, and King only acted on a small number of recommendations. Many of the recommendations in the report, however, were implemented in the postwar years by a variety of different governments, so in many ways the Marsh Report became an accidental blueprint for the Canadian social welfare state.

When the war ended in 1945, Canada's economy did not collapse as it had in 1918. In fact, it kept on growing, helped by Europe's desperate need for resources to rebuild itself. By war's end, the Canadian economy was stronger than it had ever been. Average Canadians had more opportunities for work, more money in their pockets, and far more spending power than ever before in the country's history.[41]

Not all benefited from this incredible economic growth. Some, in fact, felt the sting of a government that held unprecedented power over its people and sought to use it in the name of national defence. In 1939 there were 22,000 Japanese Canadians living in British Columbia, accounting for 98 percent of all people of Japanese descent in the country. They were a thriving and law-abiding population, particularly successful in British Columbia's fishing industry. Yet the population faced very serious discrimination from within the province. British Columbia had a long history of racism toward Asian immigrants, rooted in the widely held belief that the province should consist of only white Anglo-Saxon stock. When Imperial Japan launched its surprise attacks on Pearl Harbor and Hong Kong, the Japanese-Canadian population became an immediate threat in the eyes of B.C. nativists.

Security measures were taken right away. By the end of December 1941, 38 suspected Japanese loyalists were arrested, all persons of Japanese descent were ordered to register with local authorities, and the Japanese-Canadian fishing fleet was confiscated. For many within King's circle that was enough. The navy, the Royal Canadian Mounted Police, and even King's military ad-visers felt that any security threat had been neutralized. Yet pressure mount-ed, particularly from white supremacist circles within British Columbia. No voice was more powerful than that of Ian Mackenzie, a B.C. politician who by 1941 sat in King's Cabinet as the minister of pensions and national health.

As the Imperial Japanese forces continued to win in the Pacific, King and his government eventually bowed to the pressure. In late February 1942, a total evacuation of Japanese Canadians was ordered, and by the end of that

A Japanese-Canadian family awaits transportation to an internment camp, 1942.

year, thousands of men, women, and children were living in internment camps where most of them spent the remainder of the war. Their property and goods were confiscated by the government and auctioned off to provide funds for the war effort. Out of the 22,000 interned, 13,000 had been born in Canada. Thousands of others had become the equivalent of *modern* naturalized Canadian citizens. One of these was Masumi Mitsui, the decorated First World War veteran. After the war, he became the branch president of the local Royal Canadian Legion Hall in Port Coquitlam, British Columbia. When registering with the local authorities, Mitsui threw down his First World War medals in disgust. When the war ended, many like Mitsui were forced to simply start over. The internment of Japanese Canadians was a stark reminder that even Canada was not immune to the dark consequences when prejudice and fear came together during times of war.[42]

One of the human-power concerns that challenged King was the issue of conscription. When war began, King was firmly against conscription. He hoped that Canada's military force, whether on land, in air, or at sea, would be entirely volunteer-based. When France fell, the Canadian government passed the National Resources Mobilization Act, but those conscripted were only to serve within Canada. By 1942, almost all the major Allied countries had imposed conscription except Canada. King still prevaricated, the spectre of the conscription riots of the First World War haunting him.

As the Liberal prime minister, a significant portion of his support came from Quebec, and King feared that conscription would not only rip the country apart, as it nearly had in 1918, but also that it would destroy the Liberals' chance at victory in the next federal election. Yet, by 1942, Canada's military commitments were growing faster than ever anticipated, and King was forced to issue a plebiscite to gauge the public's reaction to the possibility of conscription for overseas service. The plebiscite showed that most Canadians supported conscription for overseas service, but it also revealed that the majority of people in Quebec were largely opposed. Despite this, King's government now had a national public mandate to conscript for service overseas.

It was not until the summer of 1944 that the conscription issue really reared its head. By then, Canada's military commitments included a bomber group, a navy controlling the western half of the Atlantic, and an army that was engaged in both Italy and France. Casualties were mounting and a reinforcement crisis was emerging. The issue was specifically noticeable among front-line units. Canadian military planners, working with British predictions, underestimated the casualties that combat units would sustain once Canada's army was fully engaged.[43] By the end of the summer of 1944, the First Canadian Army in Northwest Europe and I Canadian Corps in Italy were both suffering shortages in their combat units while having a surplus of men working in other areas.

In the fall of 1944, Minister of Defence J.L. Ralston, a veteran of the First World War, visited France and Italy and became convinced that the only solution to the manpower shortage was to send National Resources Mobilization Act men overseas. It was estimated that 16,000 more infantrymen were needed. There were 60,000 conscripts defending Canadian territory. King resisted Ralston's pleas, hoping the desperately needed reinforcements could be made up of volunteers from this group. Ralston continued to press his case, and King, concerned about a coup within his own Cabinet, slyly accepted Ralston's resignation (a resignation he had offered in 1942!). His replacement was none other than Andrew McNaughton, the man Ralston removed from command of the First Canadian Army.

King hoped McNaughton could lead a publicity campaign to persuade volunteers to go overseas. McNaughton believed he could do just that. He was wrong. By early November, as the Canadians were wrapping up the Battle of the Scheldt Estuary, even McNaughton had come to the realization that volunteerism was not going to provide the bodies needed. At the same time, King's Cabinet was in near-revolt. A number of pro-conscription Cabinet members threatened resignation. Faced with the collapse of his Cabinet and McNaughton's failure to increase volunteer numbers, King enforced overseas conscription on November 23, 1944.[44] The only serious resistance came not from Quebec but from a small garrison in Terrace, British Columbia, whose brief mutiny was quickly diffused and quietly swept under the rug. While all this was going on, however, Canada's army overseas took steps to fill the gaps in its ranks by pulling soldiers from the "tail" (i.e., cooks, drivers, office staff, rear-area personnel, et cetera) and putting them in the "teeth" (i.e., front-line combat units). In the end, 16,000 National Resources Mobilization Act men were ordered overseas, with 13,000 eventually being sent. King had deftly avoided another conscription crisis.

7

THE SECOND WORLD WAR: THE CONFLICT ON LAND

Italy

The British Commonwealth victory at the railway junction of El Alamein followed by Operation Torch landings in late 1942 put the Axis powers squarely on the run in North Africa. By May 1943, the last of German and Italian troops retreated from Tunis, and the Allies were now faced with a serious strategic choice. Where to attack next? While the Americans wanted resources focused on the invasion of Northwest Europe, Winston Churchill was able to successfully push for an invasion of Sicily. By capturing that island, the Allies could establish air bases closer to Axis-dominated Europe and extend control over Mediterranean shipping lanes while even potentially knocking Italy out of the war. Thus, President Roosevelt agreed that Sicily would be the next target, while resources continued to be built up in Britain for the eventual liberation of Northwest Europe.

Besides Hong Kong, Dieppe, and a few hundred Canadians who had served with the British First Army in Tunisia, the Canadian contingent in Britain was largely untested when it came to fighting on land. When news of the proposed Sicilian invasion got back to Ottawa, Defence Minister J.L. Ralston lobbied hard to have the Canadians included. General McNaughton was reluctant but was eventually willing to send a division to Sicily. He did, however, want a guarantee it would be returned to his army when Northwest Europe was invaded. Prime Minister King, however, was still wary about getting Canada into a high-casualty ground war, but Ralston won out.

The choice for Sicily was the 1st Canadian Infantry Division (1 CID), commanded by Major-General H.L. Salmon, and the 1st Canadian Army Tank Brigade (soon renamed the 1st Canadian Armoured Brigade), led by Brigadier-General R.A. Wyman. Both units were extremely well trained, well equipped, and despite having no battle experience, eager for combat. When General Salmon was killed in a plane crash in April 1943, command of 1 CID went to 40-year-old Major-General Guy Simonds, who had gained experience in North Africa and whom British General Bernard "Monty" Montgomery pinned as one of Canada's most promising officers. While not very endearing to his men, he was a disciple of Monty's, promoting a tactical doctrine of well-planned battles utilizing Allied superiority in firepower. This could at times be a rigid command doctrine and would face challenges in Sicily.

Sicily was a defender's dream and an attacker's nightmare. While the coastline provided some open ground, the interior was extremely mountainous, criss-crossed with numerous rivers and narrow roads running through steep valleys. The Axis plan was to hold off the Allies as long as possible, and the terrain of Sicily was perfect for such an approach. Axis forces could set up a series of ambushes utilizing the mountainous terrain to their advantage, inflicting casualties on the advancing Allied troops before pulling back to the next position. Defending the island were two crack German divisions numbering around 40,000 soldiers at its peak, along with about 200,000 Italians of mixed quality.

Operation Husky was the name given to the Sicilian invasion, the largest amphibious operation ever launched to that date. The plan called for the landing of seven divisions backed by significant air and naval assets. General George Patton's U.S. Seventh Army would take the western half of the island, while Montgomery's British Eighth Army would seize the eastern half. The 1 CID would operate as the left flank of Monty's army, and this junior formation was not intended to be used in any heavy fighting on account of its inexperience. The Allies landed in the early morning of July 10, with the Canadians arriving at the southern tip of the Pachino Peninsula. And while there was sporadic fighting, after a few cursory shots the Italians generally surrendered. It quickly became clear that only a small number of Italians were willing to fight, and the bulk of the island's defence fell on the shoulders of the Germans.

By mid-July, a strategic shift catapulted the Canadians into the spotlight. Montgomery's advance along the eastern coast was bogging down as his vanguard approached Catania. Instead of breaking through in the east, Monty sought to shatter the German defensive line via a left hook that would effectively punch through the centre of Axis defences.[1] To lead this left hook, Monty chose the division best in position to carry out the assault, none other than 1 CID. Simonds's division suddenly went from a supporting role to spearheading the British Eighth Army's attack directly into the German centre. The Canadians thus encountered fierce resistance the farther they

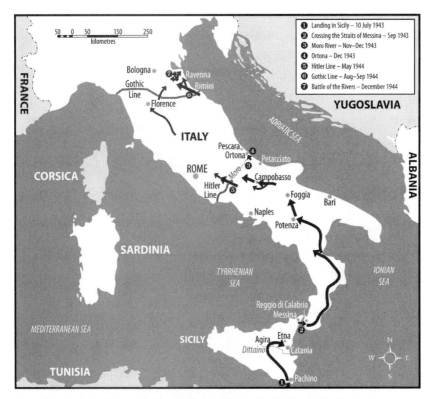

Map of major Canadian operations in Sicily and mainland Italy, 1943–45.

advanced, frequently meeting German ambushes. A frustrating pattern developed whereby a firefight would ensue until the German defenders deemed their position lost, at which point they retreated. The Germans engaged in this fighting withdrawal all the way back to interconnected defensive positions known as the Etna Line.

However, the Canadians became very effective at dealing with German defensive tactics. At Grammichele, the Canadians faced their first serious opposition and overcame it by showing initiative in moving around the enemy flanks and converging on the town from multiple sides. Elements of the powerful Hermann Göring Division and an elite Italian division were forced to pull back in the face of these Canadian manoeuvres.

Excellence in small-unit tactics continued to define Canadian attacks, and by July 20, the Canadians were in the heart of the Etna Line facing stout German defensive positions anchored along the hilltop towns of Leonforte and Assoro. The latter was captured after a brilliant night march by the Hastings and Prince Edward Regiment that took it up the extremely steep rear slope of Castle Hill overlooking the town. Despite German efforts, the Canadians could not be dislodged from this position. From Castle Hill, the Canadians called in deadly artillery fire on the enemy embedded within the town. The

Canadian soldiers utilizing donkeys to help transport weapons and supplies in Sicily, 1943.

Germans were finally forced to retreat the next day when the 48th Highlanders of Canada conducted its own steep climb up the other side of Assoro.

Leonforte would prove more costly. Perched 656 yards above sea level, it was one of the most heavily defended positions in the area. The Canadians were forced to advance in spurts, slowly but surely pushing into and then around the town. The Canadians showed initiative and determination, finally breaking the German resistance when the Princess Patricia's Canadian Light Infantry, backed by tanks from the Three Rivers Regiment, fought their way through the town and closed off any avenues of reinforcement. Leonforte fell on July 22 at the cost of 161 casualties, including 56 Canadian dead. Assoro, which fell on the same day, cost the Canadians 37 casualties.

By this point, 1 CID was displaying veteran initiative in its battles. The capture of Leonforte and Assoro had destabilized the German defensive line. The Canadians now shifted their attention to the last key defensive position at Agira. Here, Simonds sought to impose a more ordered and structured battle doctrine onto 1 CID. Gone was the speedy, impulsive, initiative-based tactics, and instead, with Monty watching, the Canadians sacrificed speed for a more rigid attack plan utilizing the Eighth Army's immense firepower.

Starting on July 24, the Canadians launched a series of frontal assaults backed by extensive artillery support along with tactical air support from the Desert Air Force. The Royal Canadian Regiment, supported by the Three

The imposing heights of Mount Assoro in Italy today.

Rivers Regiment, went first to no avail. This was followed by an attack from the Hastings and Prince Edward Regiment, which pushed closer to Agira but was also eventually stopped. The Patricia's jumped into the fray on July 26, followed by the Seaforth Highlanders from British Columbia and then the Loyal Edmonton Regiment. By July 28, the Canadians had Agira nearly cut off and the Germans finally withdrew. The battle for Agira was costly, with 438 Canadian casualties, yet this crucial defensive position had been broken and the Etna Line was now cracked.

By early August, the Americans executed a series of amphibious flanking assaults, advancing eastward along the northern Sicilian coast toward Messina. The rest of Britain's Eighth Army was still moving up the east coast dealing with stubborn German defenders. On August 17, Messina finally fell to the Americans, only hours before the first British troops arrived. Yet Messina would be remembered not for Patton beating Monty, but for the failure by the Allies to prevent Axis forces from withdrawing to the Italian mainland.[2] Tens of thousands of Axis soldiers and their equipment that could

Seaforth Highlanders pipe band in Agira, Italy, July 1943.

have potentially been trapped on the island had crossed and were now preparing to defend the mainland. Yet those units that did escape to the mainland were so battered from the fighting that many had to be rebuilt, requiring extensive German reinforcements to do so.

Sicily was a clear-cut strategic victory. The Mediterranean Sea lanes could now be controlled by the Allies, Mussolini's government had fallen, and tens of thousands of Italian prisoners-of-war had been captured. On top of it, 1 CID had now been bloodied in combat. The "Red Patch" had not only gained valuable combat experience but had proven itself a first-class fighting formation, one that would be tested in the difficult tasks that lay ahead on the Italian mainland.

Britain's Eighth Army hit the shores of mainland Italy on September 3. The U.S. Fifth Army, commanded by Lieutenant General Mark Clark, was on the beaches of Salerno six days later. The general strategic plan for Italy was much the same as for Sicily: a continued push northward engaging the enemy when battle was offered. Montgomery and his Eighth Army were given the task of advancing up the east coast of the Italian boot, while Clark's army took the west. The more northward the Allies could advance, the closer their bombers could get to targeting the resource-rich areas within the Reich's southern sphere of control. The closer the Allies got to these resource-rich areas, the more the Germans might divert troops from other theatres to stop them. This was, indeed, what happened.

The Germans, led by the same man who had commanded the defence of Sicily, Field Marshal "Smiling" Albert Kesselring, saw this 16 divisions eventually reinforced to 23 in October. That was all they would be able to rely on, however, as the Italians officially surrendered on September 8, 1943 (Benito Mussolini having been deposed back in July in the aftermath of the Allied invasion of Sicily). From then on, the German-controlled areas of Italy were now officially occupied by the Third Reich. Kesselring's plan, much as in Sicily, was to conduct a fighting retreat, wearing down the Allied advance, then stopping them at a series of reinforced defensive lines.

The Canadians encountered light resistance as they spearheaded the Eighth Army's march northward from Calabria. Mines, booby traps, and brief firefights on narrow and dangerous roads made the going slow, but steady progress continued. The weather worsened, however, and the memories of hot days in the Sicilian sun were replaced by the cold, wet winter realities of the Italian mainland. Sickness began to take hold by early October as the men suffered from malaria and jaundice, causing more casualties than enemy bullets and shells. Morale plummeted.[3]

By late October, the Canadians were finally pulled out of the line to spend some much-needed time resting and recuperating in the Italian town of Campobasso. Nicknamed "Canada Town," Campobasso was overrun by Canadians seeking entertainment of all sorts. Alcohol, fresh food, music, films, clean clothes, hot showers, and restful sleep were all crucial to reviving the men's spirits. But Canada Town posed some other challenges, specifically venereal disease. Despite the free distribution of prophylactics and a focused campaign warning of the dangers of unprotected sex, venereal disease rates skyrocketed alarmingly, and the Royal Army Medical Corps had its hands full in returning men to fighting health. In early December, the party was over and the Canadians were put back in the line facing the Moro River and the Adriatic port town of Ortona, which occupied the eastern flank of the Winter Line, a complex series of German defensive positions stretching from the west coast to the east. Here Kesselring intended to make a major stand.

All eyes, however, were on Mark Clark's Fifth Army operating along the west coast and heading straight for Rome. Monty, hoping to avoid another Messina, wanted to beat the Americans to the Eternal City. In fact, he planned to punch through the Winter Line at Ortona and then seize a key east–west highway that would allow his Eighth Army to do just that.

The attack on Ortona was led by Major-General Chris Vokes who had replaced the jaundiced Guy Simonds at the end of September. Leading the 2nd Canadian Infantry Brigade (2 CIB) in Sicily, Vokes had developed a reputation as an aggressive commander. He would have his hands full. Ortona was not just going to be a difficult town to fight in; it was going to be hard even to get there in the first place. South of the town were two natural obstacles that posed immense problems for the Canadians: the Moro River and then "The Gully" to its north, a three-mile trench that ran across the entire Canadian front.

The attacks on the Moro River and The Gully degenerated into brutal, slow-moving, slogging matches in which both sides blanketed the battlefield with extensive artillery and mortar fire. Many Canadians never even saw the enemy as they probed and prodded, inching forward to seek some sort of safe ground to cross. From December 6 to 13, Vokes threw everything he had at the Germans in a piecemeal fashion, and his division was pummelled for it. By the

Canadian soldiers looking at the "Canada Town" sign in Campobasso, Italy, October 21, 1943.

morning of December 14, the Canadians finally crossed The Gully, with every single combat battalion in the division used in the week-long push. Everyone was exhausted, casualties were high, and some were now referring to Vokes as "The Butcher."[4] Yet the Canadians were on the outskirts of Ortona and the fighting had so worn out the German division facing them that it had to be withdrawn and replaced by the elite 1st Parachute Division.

Ortona was an ancient town whose founding myth dated back to the Trojan War. Its narrow streets and four-storey buildings, often sharing the same wall, meant a dense, packed, urban fighting space. The town itself was organized around three key piazzas, all of which needed to be captured. The experienced German paratroopers had turned Ortona into a killing ground. The Germans had blocked off streets with massive rubble mounds where booby traps, tanks, and machine guns lay in wait in perfect urban camouflage. The few streets that were not blocked off were covered by deadly accurate mortar, machine-gun, and sniper fire. Deep cellars and underground tunnels facilitated enemy movement and allowed for ambushes. Never had the men of 1 CID faced such a battlefield challenge. The task for capturing Ortona fell to the 1st Canadian Infantry Brigade (1 CIB) led by Brigadier-General Bert Hoffmeister, one of Canada's finest battlefield commanders.

On the morning of December 21, 1943, Hoffmeister ordered the attack. The Loyal Edmonton Regiment carefully advanced into the eastern half while the Seaforth Highlanders moved into the western. It was not long before all hell broke loose. Entire rows of houses were brought down on the advancing Canadians, and sniper and machine-gun fire picked off any soldiers exposed in the streets. Hidden in carefully constructed piles of rubble, the enemy fired their highly effective *Panzerfausts*, hand-held anti-tank weapons. The close proximity of the well-concealed enemy led to the incapacitation of tank after tank from the Three Rivers Regiment. Booby traps exploded when Canadians tripped wires or picked up objects purposefully left by the Germans.

Despite the horrific nature of this combat, the small-unit initiative and flexibility that was so well developed in Sicily quickly emerged. Because the streets were covered by enemy fire, the Canadians switched to moving through the densely packed buildings. Sometimes they simply blew up a building, collapsing it on top of the enemy. Other times, Canadians leaped from balcony to balcony. The Canadians also implemented a tactic that became the hallmark of the fighting for Ortona — "mouse-holing." Beginning in the upstairs of one building, they placed an explosive charge against the wall connected to the adjacent structure and then detonated the charge, killing or incapacitating any Germans caught on the other side. The Canadians then rapidly pushed through this mouse hole and cleared the upstairs before dropping grenades down the stairs to the bottom floor. Because of the narrow nature of the stairways, the Germans were unable to throw their larger "potato masher" grenades back up. Each room on each floor was methodically cleared before the next wall was blown open and the Canadians rushed through to repeat the procedure. Despite continual losses, the Canadians drove the Germans back house by house, block by block, piazza by piazza.

As Christmas approached, the Battle of Ortona became something of a media sensation. Travelling with 1 CIB were personnel from the Canadian Army Film and Photo Unit. These war correspondents and videographers captured the brutality of the battle, and soon Ortona was given the nick-name "Little Stalingrad," which stuck. The voices of Matthew Halton and Ralph Allen were heard all over the English-speaking world as they re-ported from the front lines and their cameramen sent back footage of the intense urban battle.

When Christmas arrived, one of the most iconic moments in Canada's Second World War experience occurred. Captain D.B. Cameron, the regi-mental quartermaster for the Seaforth Highlanders, was never going to let something like one of the most ferocious urban battles in the entire Italian theatre stop his men from getting a Christmas Eve dinner. Despite ongoing fighting, he organized a large meal in the nearly destroyed Church of Santa Maria di Costantinopoli behind the front lines where pork, nuts, fruit, beer, candies, and cigarettes were handed out over a white tablecloth in dishes with proper cutlery. Small groups of Seaforths were rotated in and out of the front line to accommodate everyone in the regiment and almost all were fed, an incredible logistic achievement in the midst of pure carnage. The Christmas Eve dinner became a tradition with the Seaforths, and D.B. Cameron was eventually invested as a Member of the Order of the British Empire.

As the Germans were pushed back in Ortona, the 2nd Canadian Infantry Brigade fought its own difficult battle over mud-soaked terrain as it advanced to the west of the town, attempting to outflank the Germans and trap them in Ortona. By December 28, the Germans realized they were at risk of being completely encircled, so the paratroopers finally withdrew. They had been so badly mauled in the defence of the town that the division was close to total collapse.[5] The Canadians, too, had suffered greatly. Since the first attacks on the Moro River in early December, 1 CID had sustained nearly 2,400 cas-ualties with another 1,600 sick. Every rifle company was depleted by half its original strength. Yet Ortona was now in Canadian hands. Before the men of 1 CIB were ordered to move on, they made sure that any follow-up troops knew exactly who had captured this ancient coastal village. A sign was left behind that read: THIS IS ORTONA, A WEST CANADIAN TOWN.

With the closing of the battle for Ortona, the Canadians hunkered down for the remainder of winter. The Germans were not gone, however, and the battlefield turned into a static First World War type of environment, with the Canadians holding a series of positions a mile or so north of Ortona, separated from the Germans by a shell-pocked no man's land. Montgomery's

A wounded Canadian soldier (Lance Corporal Roy Boyd) is evacuated in Ortona, Italy, December 30, 1943.

ambitious hope that the breakthrough from Ortona would allow him to move west to capture Rome never materialized.

In January, the Canadian presence in Italy underwent significant expansion when the 5th Canadian Armoured Division (5 CAD) arrived, commanded by newly promoted Brigadier-General Bert Hoffmeister, along with headquarters for I Canadian Corps under the command of Lieutenant-General E.L.M. Burns.

On the west coast, a dramatic turn of events had changed the strategic situation quite a bit. General Clark's U.S. Fifth Army attempted an audacious landing at Anzio to get behind the Germans defending the western half of the Winter Line. This failed and Clark's army found itself bottled up and nearly pushed back into the ocean. Helping to desperately defend the perimeter were Canadian soldiers of the 1st Special Service Force, a joint American-Canadian commando unit.

It was clear that Britain's Eighth Army, now commanded by General Oliver Leese, would have to come to Clark's rescue.[6] By April 1944, Leese's forces had completed the move to the west coast. They now faced the German Tenth Army. Leese was ordered by his superior, General Harold Alexander, commander of the 15th Army Group in Italy, to punch through two extremely well-built German defensive lines via the Liri Valley. This valley was the gateway to Rome, and if Leese could break through the Gustav Line and then the Hitler Line behind it, he could capture the key highway running straight to the capital. To do this, Britain's Eighth Army would have to fight over nearly six miles of German-held territory, dealing with an entrenched enemy while crossing four major rivers with mountains flanking both sides of the valley. Ideally, Leese would be able to break through and capture Rome. However, if he could not, Alexander hoped that enough pressure could be placed on the Germans that Clark could then break out from his Anzio beachhead.

On May 11, the multinational units that made up Britain's Eighth Army launched their attack behind a barrage of nearly 2,000 guns. Britons, Indians, French, and Poles led the way, while the Canadians remained in reserve. The going was slow, the cost heavy, but eventually the Gustav Line fell. While 1 CID relieved the 8th Indian Division to help continue driving the Germans back, it was the Polish capture of the monastery fortress on the heights of Monte Cassino that finally forced a German withdrawal of nearly five miles back to the Hitler Line. At this point, Leese ordered a pause in operations, and preparations began for a massive set-piece assault on the Hitler Line that would finally shatter the last Winter Line resistance and open the way to Rome. The Canadian role in this attack was given the name Operation Chesterfield.

The plan, as laid out by Lieutenant-General Burns, was for 1 CID to punch into the Hitler Line defences followed by 5 CAD, which would exploit this breach and complete the breakthrough. Facing the Canadians were the battered German divisions of the 90th Grenadier Division and remnants of the 1st Parachute Division, so recently mauled at Ortona. Despite not being at full strength, these two divisions were well entrenched within an expertly designed defensive system.

Operation Chesterfield was launched the morning of May 23, 1944, with the Canadians advancing under the cover of a massive rolling artillery barrage and extensive tactical air support. Despite this firepower, the going was slow. General Vokes was reluctant to use the full weight of his division to crack into the German defences. The attack further stalled when the Canadian right flank was exposed after the British failed to capture the key town of Aquino. Canadian infantry and armour were met with withering fire. Mortars, machine guns, artillery, tanks, and the teeth-rattling screams of *Nebelwerfers*, multi-barrelled rocket launchers, punished the advancing

The ruined abbey at Monte Cassino after the German surrender, May 1944.

Canadians as they struggled through dense barbed wire and minefields in an attack eerily reminiscent of the First World War. By the end of that day, however, 1 CID captured its objectives, losing almost 900 men in the process. Now it was 5 CAD's turn to complete the victory.

"Hoff's Mighty Maroon Machine," as the men affectionately called Hoffmeister's division, was sluggish in forming up and this, coupled with terrible roads, created a delay in launching its attack. Yet when the assault finally got underway, early in the morning of May 24, the division crashed into the Melfa River, carving out a bridgehead on the other side and finally breaking out by the end of the day.

Despite heavy losses, the Canadians were now poised to break through the Hitler Line until General Leese, who held a low view of the Canadians, stepped in. He ordered the British 6th Armoured Division to push through the Canadians, adding an entire division's worth of vehicles to an already extremely crowded battlefield. A traffic jam of monumental proportions was the result. The Canadians and British were lucky the Germans were in no position to launch a serious counterattack, since the densely packed columns of vehicles were dangerously vulnerable.[7] Because of this, it wasn't until May

26 that the Canadians finally broke out from the bottleneck and once again began to close the distance with the retreating enemy. Fighting continued, but by the end of the month the Canadians were withdrawn from the battle-field. Operation Chesterfield was over.

At the same time, a strategic error of epic proportions was played out when General Clark's Fifth Army finally broke out from their Anzio beach-head. Instead of moving east to trap the Germans retreating from the Liri Valley, Clark went straight north to capture Rome, seeking the glory of lib-erating the capital as opposed to dealing what could have been a death blow to the German Tenth Army. Clark's decision allowed the Germans to escape, and as Tim Cook, one of Canada's most prolific military historians, writes, "He should have been tried by court martial for gross dereliction of duty."[8]

Breaking through the Hitler Line was incredibly difficult: 800 Canadians killed, 2,500 wounded, 4,000 sick, and hundreds evacuated due to battle exhaustion, the Second World War equivalent to shell shock. Yet the fight for the Liri Valley was a victory, and the Canadians had played a central part. The Germans had been badly mauled, their defensive positions broken, the Allies now had more air bases to launch attacks deep into German-held Europe, and Rome was liberated. Perhaps these battles would have received greater atten-tion had the Allies not launched the invasion of France two days after Rome's liberation — the battle for Normandy had begun. Despite all eyes now on Northwest Europe, the Canadians, and their allies in Italy, continued fighting northward toward the dark shadow of the Gothic Line.

More imposing than the Winter Line, the Gothic Line was another heavily fortified defence-in-depth network. It was built along the spine of the north-ern Apennine Mountains to a depth of nearly 12 miles and criss-crossed by numerous rivers, with dozens of villages, towns, and cities, as well as a series of predesignated killing zones. German artillery, mortars, and machine guns were sighted on the narrow roadways and open fields. A series of riverbeds and fortified hilltops created deadly obstacles, while most villages were razed and forests cut down to ensure the Canadians had nowhere to hide. Tens of thousands of mines were laid, extensive networks of anti-tank ditches had been built by Italian slave labour, and over 93 miles of barbed wire made the objective look like something out of a First World War nightmare.

The Germans intended to hold here and prevent Allied access into the Po Valley and the industrial heartland of the Italian north. Even though

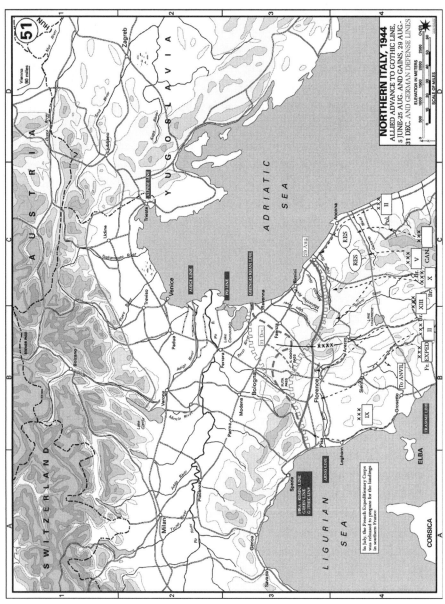

Allied advance to the Gothic Line, June 5 to December 31, 1944.

the German Tenth and Fourteenth Armies had been badly mangled at the Winter Line, they had escaped potential encirclement and had time to rebuild enough to present a daunting defensive front to the approaching Allies.

The Allied war effort in Italy was very much a sideshow at this point. Both the U.S. Fifth and British Eighth Armies were at the bottom of the list when it came to reinforcements or supply.[9] In fact, seven divisions and nearly half the air power were transferred out of the Italian theatre in August to support Operation Dragoon, the invasion of southern France. Effectively, both armies were now weaker than they had been at the Winter Line yet were expected to continue the push north and keep German forces tied down as much as possible. Hitler, however, played right into their hands and continued to send divisions to reinforce the Italian defences. Despite what felt like a never-ending slog up the Italian boot, the Allied strategy in Italy was working.

For several weeks, I Canadian Corps had rested and recuperated after the vicious battles in the spring, but in late summer it was put back in the line. By this point, the corps was not just an experienced fighting formation but one that had even earned the respect of its enemy, so much so that Field Marshal Albert Kesselring believed the Allied attack on the Gothic Line would come from wherever in the line the Canadians were positioned.[10]

The Allied plan for breaking the Gothic Line was focused on penetrating its eastern half along the Adriatic coast near the town of Pesaro where it was felt the flatter ground was more suitable to utilizing Allied advantages in armour. Leese's Eighth Army would spearhead the thrust into the Gothic Line, while Clark's Fifth Army would exploit that with a follow-up attack near Venice. While some optimistic planners hoped the Germans would be thrown back into the Alps, far more expected another slow, attritional advance.

Even though Leese had very little faith in Burns, the Canadian Corps commander who was a convenient scapegoat for Leese's own failings in the Liri Valley, he curiously settled on a plan that put I Canadian Corps centre stage in the Eighth Army's attempt to break the Gothic Line. Leese placed the Polish II Corps on the Canadian right and the much larger V British Corps on the left, the corps that in hindsight was probably better suited to spearhead the attack.[11] Regardless, the Canadians did their job and did it well. Burns's plan called for Vokes's 1 CID to advance and break into the Gothic Line followed by Hoffmeister's 5 CAD, which would complete the breakthrough and push on to Rimini. The capture of Rimini would entail I Canadian Corps advancing over 30 miles from its starting point.

The attack was launched on the night of August 25 and ultimately proved to be the corps's most challenging and difficult fight of the entire Italian campaign. Initially, the Germans fought a delaying action, inflicting a steady stream of casualties on 1 CID as it fell back to the safety of the Gothic Line proper. Once he understood he was facing the Canadians, Kesselring became convinced that this was, indeed, the spearhead of the Eighth Army's major assault and reinforced the region with the 26th Panzer and 29th Panzer Grenadier Divisions. German resistance was brutally and effectively stubborn, and Burns's corps didn't reach the Gothic Line until August 29, at which point Burns had already sent 5 CAD into action to support Vokes and his division. Both divisions were now operating side by side.

The Canadian battle to penetrate and then shatter the Gothic Line was essentially a series of hammer blows by both divisions, supported by artillery and air assets. The attacks were directed against a series of heavily fortified hilltops. Every hilltop became its own brutal mini-battle, and with each one captured, a part of the Gothic Line crumbled. Often, waiting for artillery support proved deadly, and opportunities to seize objectives were carried out by the daring small-unit skill of individual sections of Canadian soldiers. With the capture of Point 111 on the night of August 30 by the Perth Regiment (11 CIB, 5 CAD), the Gothic Line was officially pierced, though with the loss of that regiment's commanding officer, Lieutenant-Colonel Fred Vokes, brother of Chris Vokes.

More hammer blows were still needed to widen the small gap created in the German defensive line to penetrate deeper into the enemy's heart. The British Columbia Dragoons (5 CAB, 5 CAD) captured Point 204 on August 31 and held on for dear life against vicious German counterattacks as their comrades in the 4th Princess Louise Dragoon Guards (Royal Canadian Armoured Corps, 5 CAD) carried out a textbook assault utilizing fire and movement with the support of a creeping barrage to take the final key German position, Point 253, standing 312 yards above sea level. Out of 200 Perths attacking, only 15 made it to the top. However, this secured the Canadian hold on the vital hilltop, and the Gothic Line was officially broken.

The Germans, however, were not defeated just yet, and the nearly exhausted Canadians had to continue pushing forward, this time in co-operation with V British Corps, to capture the final objective of Rimini. The Germans were experts at using Italy's terrain to their advantage, and coupled with heavy rain that began to fall in early September, the Anglo-Canadian push to Rimini bogged down. Leese then ordered a general pause. Naval artillery and air assets from the Desert Air Force continued to pound the Germans while the Eighth Army recuperated, and attacks were launched once again on September 12, 1944. By the next day, Hoffmeister's division held the all-important Coriano Ridge dominating the approaches to Rimini. The 5 CAD, having lost 320 tanks in its three weeks of fighting, was now pulled from the line, while Vokes's division pushed forward alongside Greek, New Zealander, and British soldiers.

The 1 CID's combat units were dangerously undermanned as they inched closer and closer to the San Fortunato Ridge, the final key piece of terrain. The ridge was at last captured on September 20 after a well-executed assault by four different Canadian regiments capped off with a desperate charge to seize the summit. With this ridge in Canadian hands, the Germans were forced to pull back from the region and eventually abandoned Rimini itself on September 22. The battle for the Gothic Line was finally over. Out of the Eighth Army's 14,000 casualties, I Canadian Corps suffered 3,900 in some of the toughest fighting for any Canadian soldier in any theatre of the war.

Even though all signs in Northwest Europe indicated an eventual Allied victory, the orders were to continue pushing north. The weather turned poor, the objectives appeared more and more meaningless, and morale plummeted. Battle exhaustion, crime, and desertion all rose at alarming rates as Canadian soldiers slogged forward and engaged the enemy.[12] Even Burns could not escape this winter of dissension. After a public standoff between Burns and Hoffmeister, the new Eighth Army commander, Richard McCreery, dismissed Burns. His replacement was the British-born Charles Foulkes, and while Foulkes led the corps in some tough fighting through the winter, by February 1945, it was pulled out of Italy and sent to Northwest Europe to finally rejoin the First Canadian Army.

Strategically, the Italian theatre was a clear Allied success. Fifty-five German divisions were eventually tied down in their efforts to defend Sicily and mainland Italy. The fighting was incredibly difficult, and the costs were high. The Eighth Army suffered just over 123,000 casualties, with the Canadians counting for 21 percent of those, including 5,399 killed. Close to 93,000 Canadians served in the Italian theatre, and by the end of the campaign, it was apparent that Canadian soldiers were some of the most experienced and effective there. From the Etna Line all the way past the Gothic Line, Canadian soldiers overcame stiff resistance, and while they certainly enjoyed a *matériel* advantage over their opponents, the nature of the Italian terrain, the weather, and priorities elsewhere meant the Canadians and their Allied brethren often fought with serious handicaps. They prevailed time and time again. When, from the floor of the British Parliament, Lady Nancy Astor labelled the soldiers in Italy the "D-Day dodgers," what was meant as a careless slight toward those who did not participate in the D-Day landings quickly turned into a badge of honour and those Canadians who fought there wore it proudly.

Normandy

The D-Day landings on June 6, 1944, witnessed the Canadian army, navy, and air force come together as an important part of the largest combined-arms military operation in history. Planning for it had begun in 1943, and in early 1944, U.S. General Dwight D. Eisenhower was chosen as the man to command the Allied forces in Northwest Europe. The man selected to command the actual invasion force was Bernard Montgomery, who would then take command of the 21st Army Group once a sufficient beachhead was established and Eisenhower's Supreme Headquarters Allied Expeditionary Force (SHAEF) could cross the English Channel and assume control.

There was immense anxiety about the task ahead of them. For four years, the Germans had been fortifying the coastline of Northwest Europe: 2,800 miles of concrete bunkers, machine-gun emplacements, artillery encasements, millions of mines, tens of thousands of soldiers all made up Hitler's imposing "Atlantic Wall." In charge of defending the French coast was General Erwin Rommel, commander of Army Group B, which consisted of the German Seventh and Fifteenth Armies. Yet the German strength of 60 divisions was spread out along the long coast with most of the Fifteenth Army in the Pas-de-Calais region where the Allied invasion was expected to land. This expectation was further reinforced by a brilliantly executed deception plan known as Operation Fortitude, which had the Germans believing an army led by General George Patton (and at one point a Canadian army) would land there.[13] Hitler also complicated issues when he ordered the inland reserve of 10 crack divisions to be split between three different commands, with Rommel only getting authority over three of these, a poor decision becoming all too common for the Führer by this point in the war.

While the Germans thought the invasion would come at Pas-de-Calais, the Allies were planning to land in Normandy, whose terrain and roads offered several good routes from the beaches into the French interior. The landing itself was divided into five beaches: Omaha and Utah to be captured by three American divisions, Gold and Sword to be seized by two British divisions, and Juno for the Canadians, specifically the highly trained yet almost totally combat-inexperienced 3rd Canadian Infantry Division (3 CID) commanded by Major-General Rod Keller. Yet Keller would have support. His division was backed by the Sherman and Firefly tanks of the 2nd Canadian Armoured Brigade as well as an incredible amount of artillery from both land and sea. It was expected that the main German armoured counterattack would come directly at the Canadians and the 3rd British Division on their left. The doubling of 3 CID's artillery and the access to extensive naval fire support was meant to even the odds against the elite German panzers they would be facing. In fact, 3 CID could call on more artillery than any other division landing in Normandy.[14]

Between 1:00 and 1:30 a.m. on June 6, the first Canadian soldiers touched down in France when the 1st Canadian Parachute Battalion dropped into Normandy to destroy several bridges over the Dives River and secure a number of key crossroads. Four hours later, the combined might of the Allied navies opened fire. Not long after, Allied pilots from over half a dozen nations were in the skies directing their bombs, rockets, and machine-gun fire against transportation routes, defensive installations, and any enemy foolish enough to emerge from cover.

While all this contributed to an absolute cacophony of chaos in the battle space, the German defences along the beaches themselves were relatively unscathed. This meant that the Canadian infantry about to land at Juno would enter a murderous wall of fire. Between 7:50 and 8:15 a.m., the lead elements of 3 CID left the safety of their landing craft and attacked this deadly wall of steel. On the division's right, the 7th Brigade was given the task of capturing the coastal village of Courseulles-sur-Mer, while the 8th Brigade was tasked with Bernières-sur-Mer in the centre and Saint-Aubin-sur-Mer on the

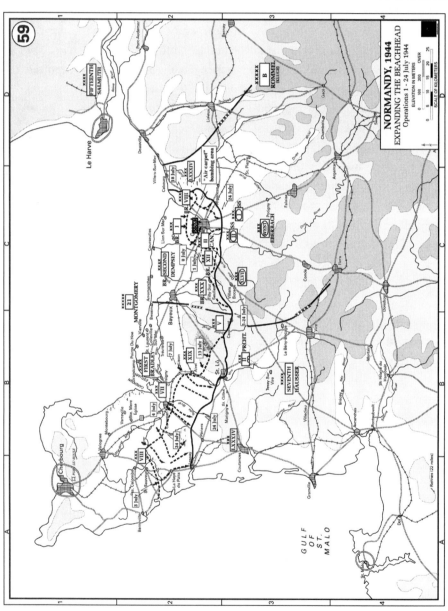

Map showing the extent of the Normandy beachhead as of July 24, 1944.

division's left. Within minutes of disembarking from their landing craft, men who had trained together for years watched as their friends and comrades fell at an alarming rate. At Bernières-sur-Mer, one platoon of the Queen's Own Rifles (a platoon at full strength normally had 37 men) lost 19 soldiers when the landing craft lowered its ramp directly in front of a waiting German machine gun. Despite bodies dropping everywhere, the years of intense training took over and the Canadians, almost unbelievably, continued forward, even though many had never even seen a dead body before that morning.

By 10:30 a.m., Canada's 3 CID had cleared Juno and began moving inland toward its ultimate objective of Carpiquet Airfield, almost nine miles from the beach. The seizure of the airfield would mean Canadian control of the key railway line and highway between the Norman cities of Caen and Bayeux. It would also provide a crucial air base on French soil for the Allies. By 8:00 p.m., however, the Canadians were ordered to halt two miles short of Carpiquet Airfield. At this point, the 3rd British Division to its left, had beaten back a counterattack by the 21st Panzer Division, yet the 12th SS Hitler Youth Division and Panzer Lehr Division were on the move and the Canadians and British had to prepare to defend against them. The importance of capturing the airfield had now been superseded by the absolute necessity of destroying these incoming counterattacks.[15]

By the end of June 6, the Canadians had advanced the farthest inland of any Allied troops. It had cost the landing force 359 killed and 715 wounded, half the predicted casualties. Nineteen paratroopers and another 22 Canadian airmen had also died. The beaches had been secured: 150,000 Allied soldiers, and thousands of guns and vehicles, including nearly 1,000 tanks, were now on French soil, and more kept arriving. It would all be needed. Meanwhile, the Canadians prepared to meet a German panzer thrust by the fanatical teenagers of the 12th SS Hitler Youth, who were confident they were going to drive the Canadians right back into the ocean.

The 12th SS Hitler Youth consisted of teenage boys who had grown up in the Nazi state and were wholly indoctrinated in the belief of Aryan superiority, the supremacy of the Nazi Reich, and the godlike status of Adolf Hitler. They were well equipped and well trained and were commanded by veteran officers of the Eastern Front. Yet they were disastrously overconfident and poorly managed and were fed piecemeal into the meat grinder that became the Canadian defensive front. From the day after the Allied invasion onward, Canadian soldiers and tank crews backed by naval artillery and air support punished wave after wave of the attacking Hitler Youth. While historically the Germans were presented as possessing an edge in the quality of their tanks, specifically the feared Panther, the Canadian Shermans, the up-gunned Fireflys, anti-tank guns, and self-propelled artillery were able to match the German onslaught. Day after day, the 12th SS Hitler Youth recklessly threw itself against pockets of 3 CID defenders in tiny villages such as Authie, Buron, and Putot, which became vicious scenes of battle. Time and time again, the Hitler Youth was thrown back and its casualties mounted rapidly, as did those of the Canadians. Most poignant, 156 of the Canadian dead were executed while prisoners of the increasingly frustrated fanatical teenage soldiers.

By the end of June 11, the two sides were dug in and faced each other across a no man's land of villages and fields. However, the counterattacks had been stopped. Shelling and sporadic fighting continued, of course, but the sword that was the 12th SS Hitler Youth had been blunted; the Canadians were not going to be driven back into the sea. At this point, 3 CID had

Allied *matériel* on Normandy beaches after D-Day, June 1944.

suffered nearly 3,000 casualties, with most of these in front-line infantry units. Replacements were coming, but the drain on experienced and trained manpower was alarming.

At the same time, frustration mounted back at SHAEF at what was seen as slow moving by Montgomery's forces in the Caen region. Increasing pressure was placed on Monty to break out of the bridgehead and capture Caen. Yet, over the course of June, the Germans had sent more and more of their best troops into the Caen region to face the Canadians and British. Effectively, Montgomery's forces were siphoning off German reserves that could have been used against the Americans farther to the west.[16] This left the Americans with a better potential opportunity for a breakout. Still, Monty had to move forward, and that meant capturing Caen and bursting out from the bridgehead. The Canadians were now going to go on the offensive.

The 3 CID's first major push out of the bridgehead began on July 4 with Operation Windsor, a large set-piece limited objective attack on Carpiquet Airfield by the 8th Brigade that would not have been out of place at the First World War's Vimy Ridge or Hill 70. Like those battles, most of the objectives were in Canadian hands by the end of the first day. Because the position so

Captured soldiers of the 12th SS Hitler Youth Division, July 1944.

threatened the flanks of German-held villages just north of Caen, the enemy made numerous failed attempts to dislodge the Canadians.

While Operation Windsor was taking place, the rest of the division prepared for a major Anglo-Canadian drive to capture Caen and the bridges over the Orne River. Launched on July 8, this push was called Operation Charnwood. The two remaining brigades in 3 CID, the 7th and 9th, cleared out the key fortified villages of Buron and Authie and eventually secured the Abbaye d'Ardenne, the former headquarters for the 12th SS Hitler Youth. The pressure of Charnwood forced the Germans in front of the 8th Brigade to finally retreat, allowing Carpiquet Airfield to fall to the Canadians by the end of that first day. While this was going on, the 7th Brigade fought its way into the centre of Caen where it erected the Canadian flag over the rubble of the destroyed city of William the Conqueror.

On July 11, only days after the capture of Caen, II Canadian Corps was activated. It was commanded by Guy Simonds, Montgomery's favourite Canadian general. Included in II Corps was 3 CID and the newly arrived 2 CID commanded by Major-General Charles Foulkes, the man who eventually took over Canada's I Corps in Italy. Temporarily, II Corps was part of the

Riflemen of the Regina Rifle Regiment hold a position in the rubble of Caen, France, July 10, 1944.

Second British Army, since the First Canadian Army would not be activated for a couple of weeks.

Simonds was eager to get into the fight and got his first chance with Operation Atlantic on July 18. Simonds's task was to drive his corps through Caen toward the heights south of the city. This would protect the British right flank as the rest of the Second British Army drove south to capture Falaise in Operation Goodwood. Despite the use of heavy bombers, extensive artillery, and hundreds of tanks, the British push toward Falaise failed; the Germans were simply too well dug in. On the Canadian front, the first day saw some strong gains, including some well-executed attacks by 2 CID, which experienced its first combat since Dieppe. The Canadians ran into difficulty, however, advancing up the gently rising slope of Verrières Ridge where German mortar and machine-gun fire dominated the ground. Simonds allowed a brief pause before launching a second effort up the ridge, though without tank support. It failed and only small gains were made before the attack was called off on July 21.

By this point, the Anglo-Canadian front was facing five more divisions and nearly 500 more tanks than the Americans.[17] It was clear that the bulk of the German Army had been thrust into the Caen sector, and Monty needed to keep them there because the American attempt at a breakout, Operation Cobra, was coming in only a few days. The Germans in front of the Second British Army suspected another offensive was on its way and were particularly focused on defending the heights of Verrières Ridge from which they could seriously disrupt any further British thrust south toward Falaise. In fact, Field Marshal Günther von Kluge, who had taken command of the German forces in the west in mid-July, believed that the main Allied breakout attempt would come from the Anglo-Canadians, so he further reinforced that sector, playing directly into the hands of the Allies.

The Canadian attempt to dislodge the Germans from Verrières Ridge did not go smoothly. Operation Spring was launched in the early morning of July 25, several hours before the Americans commenced Cobra from the west. The infantry of 2 and 3 CID were met with a wall of enemy fire. While some villages were captured, chaos was the order of the day as the Germans turned wheat fields into killing zones. The operation was capped off by a disastrous attack by the Black Watch that saw the regiment suffer over 300 casualties in less than an hour. Operation Spring failed to deliver the promised ridge.

In fact, the Canadians suffered 1,500 casualties in the assault, making it the second-worst single day of losses behind Dieppe.

Despite Canadian difficulties, by the end of July, the broader Allied strategy was working. The stubborn attempts to hold back the Anglo-Canadian advance had reduced the German forces in the region to nearly unsustainable levels. As well, the Americans had taken advantage of the German focus on the Anglo-Canadians, and by the end of that month broke free of the Norman *bocage*.[18] So, despite a furious attempt by the Germans to stop them at Mortain, the Americans continued to advance rapidly. The Germans were now faced with a potential encirclement, helped immensely by Hitler's foolish order to his generals to hold their ground at all costs.

As well, by the end of that month, the First Canadian Army was activated under the command of Lieutenant-General Harry Crerar. While the army contained Simonds's II Canadian Corps, it also consisted of British and Polish troops and was far more of a multinational force than Canadian politicians and senior commanders had originally envisioned. In early August, this multinational force led by II Canadian Corps advanced south toward Falaise.

Operation Totalize, the first attempt at this advance, was to be Simonds's magnum opus. He created a complex plan that called for his men to make a daring night attack supported by 1,000 heavy bombers. The assault was to be heavily motorized, highlighted by Kangaroos, which were M7 self-propelled artillery converted into armoured personal carriers that would not only rush the infantry forward but protect it from small-arms fire. If the operation was successful, Verrières Ridge would fall within hours and two days after that Falaise would be captured by the 1st Polish Armoured Division. The offensive was launched at midnight on August 7, and within hours the heavily defended ridge was in Canadian hands. By the next morning, however, the operation began to fall apart.

The inflexible and complicated schedule of attack, as well as major traffic congestion from so many vehicles, slowed things down once the ridge was secured. A minor delay grew into a major one that in turn gave the Germans time to adjust their defences. When the attack resumed, a wave of American B-17 bombers dropped their bombs short, right on the heads of Canadian and Polish troops, causing hundreds of casualties. Still, II Canadian Corps continued its advance and captured a series of key high points before the assault was called off on August 11. While a breakthrough did not occur, and 600 Canadians died in the operation, the corps had advanced nine miles and inflicted irreparable damage on the German defences in the region.[19]

The capture of Falaise was achieved by Operation Tractable, the final operation for the Canadians in the Battle of Normandy. Operation Tractable mirrored Operation Totalize in many ways. The attack was to be highly motorized and spearheaded by tanks and vehicles, including the Wasp, a universal carrier fitted with a flame-thrower, which would prove very effective in convincing Germans to surrender. As well, Simonds intended to utilize bomber support again, this time from the RAF and RCAF, and once more a wave of bombers dropped their payloads short, causing friendly-fire casualties.

The Germans were in trouble when Tractable was launched on August 14. The Americans came in hard from the west and south, while the Anglo-Canadians drove from the north and moved to block any eastern escape routes. Falaise fell to the Canadians on August 18. The next day, Field Marshal von Kluge committed suicide, and his replacement, Field Marshal Walter Model, realized there was no option except to flee the tightening noose of what came to be known as the Falaise Pocket; 100,000 Germans now frantically retreated eastward over the few remaining bridges of the Dives River. It was Polish and Canadian troops who finally closed the pocket. A battle group led by Major David Currie secured control of Saint-Lambert-sur-Dive and the final bridge over the river. Operation Tractable was a success, Currie was awarded the Victoria Cross for his leadership, and the Battle of Normandy was over.

The German defeat in Normandy was absolutely crushing. Two German armies were effectively destroyed with more than 300,000 casualties. The much-hated 12th SS Hitler Youth was wiped out. The 40,000 Axis soldiers who successfully escaped now made their way east to set up along the Seine River. The Canadians had clearly played a central role in the victory, suffering 18,444 casualties with over 5,000 killed. In any Canadian division, the front-line infantry made up just under half of all divisional troops, yet front-line infantry suffered 76 percent of all casualties.[20]

The Scheldt Estuary

As the Germans retreated to the Seine River, General Eisenhower came over from England and established SHAEF's headquarters. Montgomery's 21st Army Group, made up of the First Canadian Army and the Second British Army, now began pushing east. Logistics quickly became Montgomery's primary concern. Each division needed about 500 tons of supplies per day, and the farther the 21st Army Group got from the Normandy beaches, the harder it was going to be to keep the forces supplied. At the same time, Montgomery started to advocate for a concentrated narrow thrust across the Rhine River and into Germany that could potentially shorten the war but would need serious logistical support. Thus, the First Canadian Army was ordered to advance along the left flank of the 21st Army Group, effectively the long left flank of the entire western Allied offensive. The Canadian task was to capture a series of coastal towns, all of which had working port facilities that would help alleviate some of the logistical strain.

Crerar ordered I British Corps to capture Le Havre, which it did on September 12, nearly destroying the city in the process. Then II Canadian Corps was ordered to focus on Dieppe, Dunkirk, Boulogne, and Calais. The Germans abandoned Dieppe to Foulkes's 2 CID, and the Canadians proudly entered the city that had cast such a traumatic shadow since August 1942. The German garrison in Dunkirk was screened by the Canadians and eventually passed over to the Belgians who kept the Germans bottled up in the city until the war's end. The 3 CID, under newly appointed commander Major-General Dan Spry, was given the task of capturing Boulogne and Calais. Both operations were carried out with similar precision. Thousands of French civilians were evacuated from the battle space by Canadian Civil Affairs officers prior to full-scale assaults that saw the Canadians fight effectively in urban space.[21] By the end of September, both cities were in Canadian hands and their ports now functioned on behalf of the Allied war effort.

However, Antwerp was the real jewel in the logistical crown. It was one of the largest port facilities in all of Europe, and its ability to handle 100,000 tons per day would effectively solve much of the logistical issues facing the Allies. Amazingly, the city and its port were captured intact by the British on September 4. The problem was the approaches into Antwerp via the Scheldt Estuary were still occupied by the Germans, particularly German artillery, which meant that despite the city and docks being in Allied hands, no Allied shipping could get in. The task for clearing the Scheldt was given to II Canadian Corps and would prove to be one of the most important campaigns for Canada's army in the entire war.

Hamstringing the Canadians was the fact that Montgomery was prioritizing the Second British Army's continued fight along the Ruhr after Operation Market Garden in the Netherlands fell short of its final objective to achieve a bridgehead over the Rhine River and establish an Allied invasion route into Germany. Monty even directed some of the First Canadian Army to be used in support of the Second British Army's operations while keeping the 4th Canadian Armoured Division (4 CAD) out of most of the fighting. Despite Eisenhower's repeated requests that Antwerp be made the priority, Montgomery balked. A tense back-and-forth ensued until an explicit order from Eisenhower arrived at Monty's headquarters on October 13 (one week into the Battle of the Scheldt Estuary), and that settled the matter.[22] After this, the strategic focus finally shifted to Antwerp, and elements of the Second British Army were now ordered to support the First Canadian Army's operations.

The Battle of the Scheldt Estuary began with 3 CID's attack on the Breskens Pocket, a region along the Belgian-Dutch border that dominated the southern shore of the approach into the West Scheldt Estuary. As with most of the terrain the Canadians would be fighting in during the Battle of the Scheldt, the pocket was heavily flooded and criss-crossed with tall dikes, low-lying polders, and canals.

General Simonds took an active role in planning the assault on the Scheldt Estuary and devised a good plan for 3 CID's attack on the Breskens Pocket. The 7th Brigade would make a daring frontal attack across the Leopold Canal, the southern defensive line for the Germans, supported by over two dozen flame-throwing Wasps. With the Germans focused on the 7th Brigade, the 9th Brigade would launch an amphibious flanking assault to the east a couple of days later and crash through the German defences.

Brigadier-General J.G. Spragge's 7th Brigade launched its assault across the Leopold Canal in the early morning of October 6. Silhouetted by streaming jets of flame, Canadian soldiers established a bridgehead but could barely push beyond it. For three days, the Canadians stubbornly defended against relentless German counterattacks. On October 9, a fleet of Buffalos — amphibious

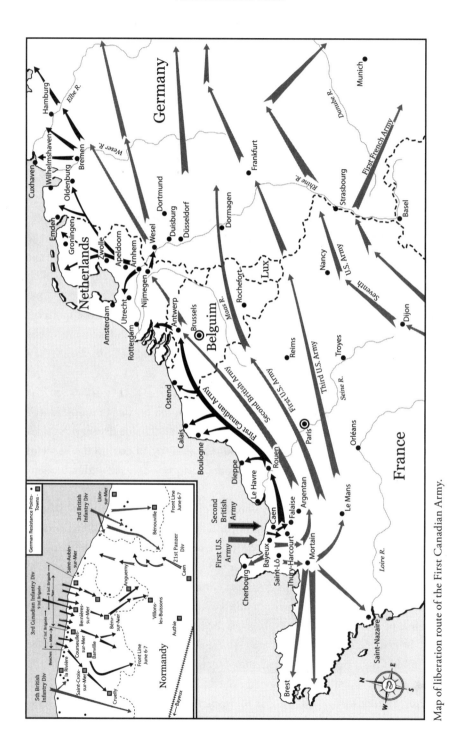

Map of liberation route of the First Canadian Army.

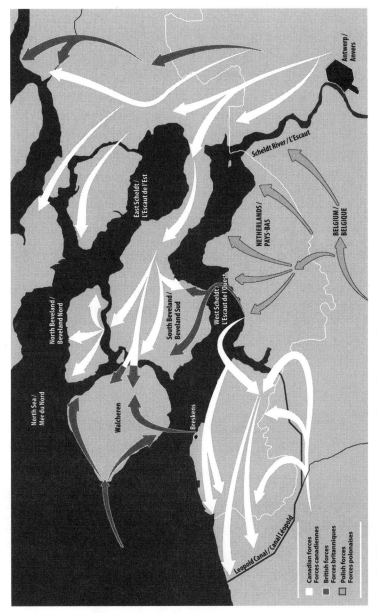

Map of Scheldt operations, October 2 to November 8, 1944.

transport vehicles — delivered the 9th Brigade right into the German eastern flank. Led by Canada's most effective brigade commander, Brigadier-General John Rockingham, the amphibious assault caught the Germans by surprise, and ever predictable in their response, their waves of counterattacks were chewed to pieces by the Canadians and supporting artillery. For all the obsession over German tactical prowess, by this point in the war the Canadians were well accustomed to the German doctrine of counterattack and used it against them with deadly effectiveness. Nonetheless, the terrain still favoured the defenders, and it took the support of the 8th Brigade as well as elements from 4 CAD and the British 52nd Division to finally force the Germans to surrender on November 3.

While 3 CID was scrapping its way through the mud-soaked fields north of the Leopold Canal, 2 CID was moving toward the Beveland Peninsula to clear the north bank of the Scheldt Estuary. The division spent most of October fighting its way north from Antwerp before finally assaulting the Beveland Peninsula, which it did on October 24 with Operation Vitality. Like 3 CID, Foulkes's 2 CID had to contend with flooded terrain, thick mud, and dikes as high as 13 feet, creating natural defensive barriers. Infantry companies battled

The 4th Canadian Armoured Division conducting a flame-thrower demonstration across a canal in Belgium, October 1944.

through the muck, driving the Germans back despite growing Canadian casualties. By the end of October, the Beveland Peninsula was cleared and all that was left were the Germans holding out on Walcheren Island.

The plan now was for 2 CID to launch an attack along the narrow causeway connecting the island to the peninsula. The causeway was no more than 44 yards wide and a little less than a mile long. As at the battle of the Breskens Pocket, still raging as 2 CID approached Walcheren Island, the Canadian attack was intended to draw German troops toward it while an amphibious assault finished them off.

Much of Walcheren Island sat below sea level and was protected from the ocean by an extensive series of dikes. General Simonds wanted to breach these dikes and flood the island in order to restrict German movement. Concern over the 30,000 civilians still on the island meant that permission for the bombing attack went all the way to the top, and it was Winston Churchill who approved the plan. On October 3, nearly 250 bombers breached the dikes at Westkapelle, followed by successful bomber runs on October 7 at Flushing and October 11 at Veere, which left the island almost totally submerged.

On October 31, the Canadian attack on the causeway went in. Infantry from the Black Watch, the Calgary Highlanders, and Le Régiment de

Buffalo amphibious vehicles in the Scheldt Estuary, October 13, 1944.

Maisonneuve, supported by artillery, skillfully manoeuvred themselves down the causeway. The fighting for the causeway was fierce but drew German counterattacks while British amphibious assaults landed in the German rear. By November 8, the last of the Germans defending the island surrendered. The Scheldt Estuary was now in Allied hands, and the first Allied ships arrived in Antwerp less than three weeks later.

The battle for the Scheldt was one of the most important operations fought by the Canadian Army in the entire war. It also pushed 2 and 3 CID to near breaking point. The intensity and duration of the fighting meant the infantry companies were whittled down. Despite a continual supply of partially trained reinforcements, most infantry battalions struggled to return to even 80 percent of their authorized strength, with casualties falling heavily on the front-line combat infantry. This attrition also occurred at the same time that the acrimonious issue of conscription was tearing Prime Minister King's Cabinet apart.

The dramatic rise in battle exhaustion was one of the major indicators of how tough the fighting was. While prolonged exposure to combat was certainly a primary factor in determining battle exhaustion, the weather and battlefield conditions were important secondary factors contributing to spikes in

A flooded village on Walcheren Island, Netherlands, March 10, 1945.

combat stress injuries. During the battle for the Scheldt, Canadian infantry lived and fought in cold, wet, muddy conditions. Slit trenches were filled with water. Sleep was obtainable only in small spurts. Uniforms remained caked in mud and grime. Hot food and hot showers were rare. Disease spread, morale dropped, cases of desertion and self-inflicted wounds, while still quite rare, rose. From the newest recruits to the ablest veterans, to commanding officers of platoons and even battalions, battle exhaustion afflicted all levels and only began to subside once combat ended.[23]

After the Battle of the Scheldt, the battered Canadians received a well-earned break when the First Canadian Army was placed in reserve at the end of November. While Canadian soldiers were still active along the front, patrolling and raiding, the tempo of combat had subsided significantly. For most soldiers, this period provided an opportunity for rest and relaxation — and/or intercourse and intoxication — in the various towns and communities throughout Belgium and southern Holland. In an eerie parallel to the First World War, the Canadians sidestepped a last-ditch German offensive to try to alter the balance of the war when Hitler launched an assault through the Ardennes Forest in December 1944. While the Battle of the Bulge certainly sent shock waves throughout the Allied command, it failed in the end and only served to decimate what was left of Germany's offensive capabilities in the west.

The Push into Germany

By early February 1945, the First Canadian Army was back in the line and preparing to take its first steps into Germany in what would become known as the Battle for the Rhineland. Crerar was ordered by Montgomery to spearhead an Anglo-British assault from Nijmegen in the Netherlands southward, coinciding with an American push northward that would trap the Germans in a massive pincer and eventually push them back across the Rhine.

For this attack, codenamed Operation Veritable, General Crerar's army was much more powerful than the one that had cleared the Scheldt. Thirteen divisions — 3,400 tanks, 1,200 guns, and 470,000 soldiers — made up the incredible striking power of the army.[24] It was up against the Siegfried Line, a wide belt of defensive positions, anti-tank ditches, minefields, and flooded terrain anchored on two dense forests. When Veritable was launched on the morning of February 8, English, Welsh, Scottish, and Canadian soldiers were protected by tactical air support above and backed by the largest Canadian artillery barrage of the war. While German defensive operations had always been conducted with a high degree of stubbornness, resistance took on a fanatical edge as the Germans were now defending their homeland. Nonetheless, within two days, the First Canadian Army broke into the Siegfried Line. Then problems arose. The American attack never came. The Germans had opened two large dams, swamping the terrain in front of the Americans and delaying the southern pincer, which allowed the Germans to shift their reserves to the Anglo-Canadian front.

Assigned to protect the left flank, II Canadian Corps advanced over dense minefields, thick forest, and flooded terrain toward the town of Cleve. While 2 CID on the corps's right progressed along a relatively intact highway and captured the town, 3 CID on the left faced a formidable yet recognizable enemy: flooded terrain. The men of Major-General Dan Spry's division, nicknamed the "water rats" because of their operations in the inundated Breskens Pocket, were now very effective at fighting over waterlogged ground. The going was tough and pressure to keep moving was building. On February 20, for instance, Simonds relieved the exhausted Brigadier-General Spragge, the man who had led the 7th Brigade since August 1944.

At this point, Crerar ordered the First Canadian Army to pause as a second operation was organized to coordinate with the American assault that had finally started on February 23. Because so many German reserves had been moved to the Anglo-Canadian front, the American advance was swift and merciless. Three days after the Americans attacked, the First Canadian Army launched one of its own, Operation Blockbuster, designed to push through the Hochwald Forest and capture the rail junction of Xanten, completing the northern pincer.

The attack was carried out on the morning of February 26, with the XXX British Corps on the right where they would link up with American units near Geldern, and 2 and 3 CID spearheading II Canadian Corps's attack on the left toward Xanten. While making good progress at first, Canadian infantry companies were worn down in the attritional combat, and the Canadian assault began to slow. One company of the Queen's Own Rifles, operating along 3 CID's left flank, were down to just five soldiers fighting on the front

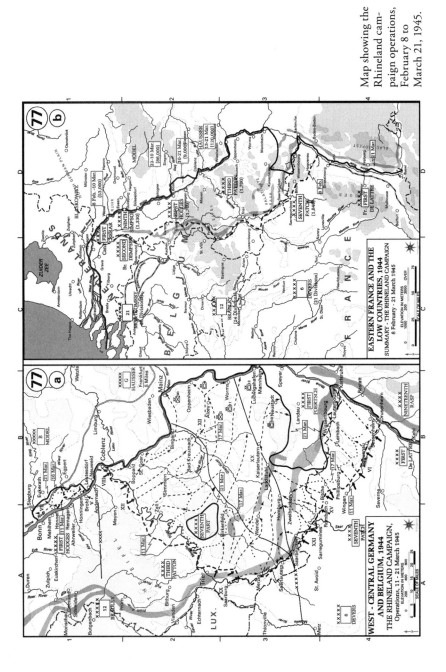

Map showing the Rhineland campaign operations, February 8 to March 21, 1945.

line.[25] One of these was Sergeant Aubrey Cosens from Port Junction, Ontario, who almost single-handedly knocked out the last of the German resistance around the village of Mooshof. Cosens, who was shot and killed later that day, was awarded the Victoria Cross.

By the next day, 4 CAD had joined in the assault as three Canadian divisions now punched their way into the Hochwald Forest. Ferocious armoured battles erupted as 4 CAD tried to rush through a narrow gap that ran through the Hochwald. The gap was heavily defended, and the dense woods on either side funnelled the Canadian tanks into a killing zone. German resistance was brutally obstinate. By March 2, the three Canadian divisions had been joined by two more British divisions, supported by the planes of the Second Tactical Air Force. Two days later this massive co-operative effort finally broke through. At this point enemy resistance was collapsing all along the front and the battered Germans were pulling back across the Rhine. The U.S. First Army crossed the mighty river on March 7, while Xanten finally fell to the Canadians the next day.

Although Blockbuster was over, Canadian operations in the Rhineland were not done quite yet. In late March, the 21st Army Group launched Operation Plunder and followed this up a day later with Operation Varsity. Plunder was the landward crossing of the Rhine and included John Rockingham's 9th Brigade, which crossed at Rees. Varsity, the largest airborne operation in history, involved more than 16,000 paratroopers, including the 1st Canadian Parachute Battalion, which dropped near Wesel on March 24. The battles in the Rhineland cost the Canadians dearly: 5,304 killed, wounded, or taken prisoner. Some units suffered their highest losses of the entire war. A small number of these casualties even included recently arrived conscripts.

The Germans facing the Canadian thrust suffered worse. Over 22,000 were killed and wounded with an almost equal number taken prisoner, a sign that morale in the German Army was beginning to flag. There was reason for it. By the end of March 1945, the Reich that was supposed to last 1,000 years was collapsing. Hitler, mentally and physically unwell, was holed up in his bunker in Berlin, ordering around non-existent armies while the Soviets were 37 miles from the capital and closing.

At this point, the First Canadian Army was ordered northward to liberate the rest of the Netherlands still under German occupation and then to move

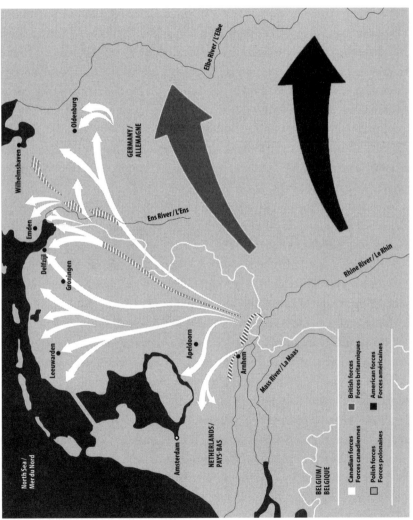

Map of the First Canadian Army's advance into the Netherlands.

into northwestern Germany. While the thrust into the Netherlands lacked the media-grabbing headlines that the advance into Germany held, it was still a crucial element of the 21st Army Group's northern advance. Success meant opening a critical supply route north through Arnhem, ridding the Dutch of their German occupiers, and finally clearing the German coastal belt toward the Elbe River. This advance was important in other ways. For the first time in history, two Canadian corps formations would be fighting alongside each other, since I Canadian Corps had completed its move from Italy into Northwest Europe by April. I Canadian Corps was ordered to force a crossing of the Lower Rhine near Arnhem, then swing west to liberate the most densely populated regions of the country. II Canadian Corps was commanded to continue its drive north.

Some tough battles were still ahead for Canadian troops, particularly II Canadian Corps. The 2 CID carried out an extremely effective attack on the city of Groningen where a mixture of German, Dutch, and Belgian SS held on tenaciously until defeated on April 16. After this battle, 5 CAD launched an attack against the port city of Delfzijl where the enemy seemed willing to fight nearly to the last man until the city fell on May 2. In the two battles, the Canadians lost over 400 killed and wounded while showcasing extremely effective combined-arms tactics with infantry and armour working closely to support each other within the urban space. Compounding the dangers was the fact that the Canadians were very careful to avoid civilian casualties, which meant reduced use of artillery and air power.

While I Canadian Corps was not engaged in combat as heavily as II Canadian Corps, it was faced with a crisis of a very different nature. The Dutch were starving. The German occupiers had stripped the country bare of its resources, and by the end of 1944, the daily caloric intake for civilians fell to dangerous levels. The winter of 1944–45 was particularly hard on the Dutch, earning it the moniker "The Hunger Winter" as the civilian body count began to rise at an alarming rate. Things were so bad that even Wilhelmina, the Dutch queen, wrote personally to President Roosevelt pleading for intervention, which eventually came. A truce was negotiated with the *Reichskommissar* of the Netherlands, Arthur Seyss-Inquart, and a massive airdrop program was initiated. American and British bombers flew non-stop into occupied territory and dropped more than 10,000 tons of supplies. At the same time, officers from I Canadian Corps Civil Affairs planned and implemented a ground supply operation known as Operation Faust.[26] Three hundred lorries drove continually into German-occupied territory for a week to deliver nearly 5,500 tons of supplies. To this day, the grateful Dutch have never forgotten their liberation by Canadians, nor the relief that helped stave off a potential humanitarian disaster.

By this point, the Axis powers in Europe were done. Mussolini was executed on April 28 and two days later Hitler committed suicide. In Italy, the German armies surrendered on May 2, and various German formations throughout Europe began to surrender in the days following. While most major fighting had subsided by early May, small skirmishes continued right up to May 7 when 12 Canadians were killed on the very same day of the final and unconditional surrender of the Nazi state. The war in Europe was finally over.

+ + +

While most Canadian personnel were now eager to return home, there was still work to be done. Half of the First Canadian Army was in the Netherlands where they were celebrated as liberators and were helping to rebuild a country shattered by war and occupation. The other half was in northwestern Germany where they were occupiers and conquerors of a defeated people. As an occupation force, the Canadian soldiers were there to enforce the authority of the Allied military government, which meant ensuring the demobilization of the German military, the arrest and capture of key Nazi officials, and even the protection of German civilians from groups of recently liberated prisoners of war (many of who were from eastern Europe) carrying out brutal reprisal attacks against their hated enemy.[27] Both the friendly occupation of the Dutch and the military occupation of the Germans would not last long. The Dutch grew tired of the Canadians, and the Canadian government grew weary of keeping a large force overseas. By May 1946, only a few hundred Canadians remained in Europe.

The Canadian government also prepared to send an official force to join the attack on Japan, one composed entirely of volunteers. HMCS *Uganda* was already in theatre when its crew refused to "volunteer" to serve in the war against Japan. Embarrassingly, the ship had to return home. An RCAF and army contingent were also being organized, but it never went; the Americans

Infantry of the West Nova Scotia Regiment surrounded by liberated Dutch civilians, May 9, 1945.

dropped the atomic bombs in early August and the Second World War soon came completely to an end.

Hundreds of thousands of Canadian veterans returned home to a country far different from the one they had left. Canada in 1939 had been reeling from years of economic depression, while Canada in 1945 was one of the strongest economies on the planet. The nation financially propped up an economically devasted Britain while moving deeper into the American economic orbit. The efficient though unglamorous leadership of Prime Minister King had not only allowed Canada to survive the war but thrive by the end of it. While tens of thousands of Canadians grieved the loss of loved ones, so many were better off economically than ever before.

Support for veterans was certainly top of the government's list, but with 1.1 million people in uniform, some were going to slip through the cracks. Many of the 4,300 Indigenous veterans were unable to get access to the benefits afforded them and returned to a country where they continued to be marginalized. The irony was that many felt they were treated as equals to whites while serving, and it was only upon returning home that they once again experienced the prejudice of a white supremacist nation.[28] Merchant seaman were not even considered veterans, despite suffering casualties and being crucial to victory in the Battle of the Atlantic. As well, of the 54,000 wounded soldiers, 29,000 were seriously so, and many of these spent months and years rehabilitating. Thousands of others struggled with mental trauma, of which there was very little support. Many more dealt with survivor's guilt, wondering how they lived while 45,000 of their comrades did not.

Nonetheless, Canada's contribution to victory was immense — far and above what anyone could have thought possible in 1939. Its men and women had fought on land, in the air, and at sea with incredible courage and tenacity, and despite setbacks, played a key role in the defeat of Hitler and the Nazi Reich.

8

INTERNATIONAL CHALLENGES: THE COLD WAR AND KOREA

The Cold War Begins

By the end of the Second World War, Canada had one of the 10 largest armies on the planet, the fourth-largest air force, and the third-largest navy. Yet its postwar demobilization was almost as impressive in rapidity as its growth only six years earlier. This was despite widespread optimism among the service chiefs that Canada would continue to maintain a large military force in the postwar world, a confidence that was quickly dashed. The navy asked for a fleet based around two aircraft carriers, four cruisers, and 20,000 sailors. They were given half that: one carrier, one cruiser, a few destroyers, and a number of smaller vessels with 10,000 sailors. Royal Canadian Air Force (RCAF) planners asked for 16 squadrons and 30,000 personnel. Instead, it got eight squadrons and 16,000 personnel. The army wanted 55,000 regulars, 177,000 reservists, and peacetime conscription for one year to create a permanent training force of 48,500. There was absolutely no way King's government was going to permit any kind of peacetime conscription, and the army was told it could prepare for a regular force of 27,000. On paper, Canada's military was now the largest peacetime force the country had ever fielded, yet fiscal restraint until 1948 meant that each branch rarely exceeded 75 percent of its total strength.

The primary role of Canada's peacetime military was home defence. In the postwar world, the new enemy was the Soviet Union. The belief was that if the Soviets were to attack, they would come through the Arctic and Canada's regular force would be able to react rapidly to defend against any Soviet incursion. They would then be reinforced by the Americans and supplemented by Canadian reservists.[1]

In terms of Europe, similar to the feeling in the First and Second World Wars, the thinking was that if war broke out there then the regular force would become the nucleus of an expanded overseas military contingent. With this in mind, the army was fashioned into a flexible mobile strike force that could deploy quickly in the face of any threat. The RCAF, which was only at 85 percent strength by 1948, contained a Mobile Tactical Wing, created to support the army and consisting of a fighter-reconnaissance squadron, an Air Observation Post squadron, tactical bomber support, and air transport. It also had air-sea rescue capabilities and a sizable air transportation fleet backed by a number of auxiliary squadrons flying Mustangs and the more modern Vampires. The navy had 12 ships in commission based around a light aircraft carrier on loan from the Royal Navy. Two Tribal-class destroyers were still under construction, while 42 vessels were in reserve requiring all levels of repair and maintenance.

Much of Canada's immediate postwar defence decisions fell at the feet of Brooke Claxton. A veteran of the First World War, Claxton became minister of national defence under King in late 1946 and stayed under his successor, Louis St. Laurent. Claxton oversaw some important changes in the Canadian military landscape. The Royal Military College in Kingston, Ontario, was reopened along with a National Defence College where military personnel from Canada, the United States, and Britain, as well as civil servants and the odd civilian, were given a broad education on the strategic challenges facing the nation. Royal Roads, a naval cadet college, was established in Victoria, British Columbia, and Claxton's department also opened a military college in Saint-Jean, Quebec, the Collège militaire royal, intended to increase francophone enlistment. This investment in education meant that Canadian officers no longer had to travel to Britain to receive such training, further weakening the Canadian military's imperial link to Britain.[2]

Mirroring the national experience, the Canadian military began to separate itself from the British sphere of influence and move cautiously but inexorably into the American one. The Second World War certainly accelerated that process. Back in August 1940 at Ogdensburg, New York, King and President Roosevelt had agreed to establish the Permanent Joint Board on Defence, a body of military and civilian personnel from both countries that advised on bilateral defence matters pertaining to North America. This was a major step in defence co-operation, and the postwar period saw this relationship deepen further. In February 1947, an accepted recommendation from the Permanent Joint Board on Defence saw Canada commit to transitioning to American weapons, equipment, training methods, and communication, increasing the military integration of the two countries.

While unprecedented co-operation occurred on the surface, Canadian leaders were still very cautious regarding the Americans. There was general anxiety about Canada's ability to act in a sovereign fashion if it could not withstand the pressure of its superpower ally and neighbour. An international body such as the United Nations (U.N.) was seen as one way to resist American influence and so was the creation of the North Atlantic Treaty Organization (NATO).[3]

By 1948, Canada, the United States, Britain, and the nations of Western Europe were concerned with the expansionist polices of the Soviet Union. In February of that year, the Soviet Red Army had effectively forced Czechoslovakia into the Soviet sphere. In Western Europe, a European Defence Union was formed in response. Meanwhile, Canada, the United States, and Britain were already privately discussing a formal alliance of the North Atlantic triangle. For Canada, a multilateral alliance would not only pose a deterrent to the Soviet Union but would provide a counterbalance to Canada's growing military partnership with the United States. Canadian diplomats caustically joked that "12 in the bed meant no rape" and worked hard behind the scenes to convince the Americans that a broader alliance was needed.[4] It did not take much, since even the most diehard American isolationists agreed that the absence of multilateral co-operation had played a role in the start of the last world war. In Paris in April 1949, Canada, the United States, Britain, and nine other European nations formed NATO. This was the first-ever peacetime military alliance for Canada and was predicated on the key principle enshrined in Article 5, which was that an attack against one member was an attack against all.

The formation of NATO certainly meant a commitment to greater defence spending. The total defence budget for 1946 was $172 million. A year later it was $195 million. By the time NATO was formed, it was $360 million. The problem was that most of the equipment being used was outdated and all the branches suffered from personnel shortages. Yet Canada's postwar military would be put to the test when war broke out in Korea in 1950.

The Korean War

When Japan was defeated in August 1945, the Korean Peninsula was divided into a northern half controlled by the Soviet Union and a southern half dominated by the United States. In the north, the Soviets handed power over to a Communist Party under Kim Il Sung, while in the south the Americans supported the quasi-democratic Syngman Rhee. In December 1945, the Soviets and Americans agreed that after a period of trusteeship the two Koreas would be united into an independent Korea. When Cold War hostility increased, unification became less and less likely and tension between the two Koreas continued to grow. The 38th parallel that divided the Koreas thus became the front line of the Cold War in Asia.

Then, on June 25, 1950, a large and experienced North Korean army — the Korean People's Army, supported by Moscow and the newly victorious Communist Party in Beijing — launched a surprise offensive into South Korea. Within two days, the poorly equipped and badly trained South Korean forces were in full retreat and the southern capital of Seoul was captured. That same day the U.N. Security Council, minus the boycotting Soviet Union, passed a resolution authorizing U.N. intervention. The Americans, who were already mobilizing, landed on the peninsula on July 1. Things did not go well, and by August, the Americans and their South Korean allies were trapped in a pocket around the port city of Pusan (Busan). There were very real fears at this point that the defenders would be driven into the sea and the Korean Peninsula would fall to the communists.

The Canadian government hesitated even when it seemed as if the south was doomed. Louis St. Laurent, Brooke Claxton, and others in the Cabinet felt that Canada's priorities should be continental defence and the protection of Western Europe. External Affairs Minister Lester B. Pearson was one of the strongest dissenting voices in the Cabinet, arguing that the conflict in Korea was an important test for the newly formed Cold War alliances.[5] The Canadian government relented slightly and authorized the dispatch of three Royal Canadian Navy (RCN) destroyers, the *Cayuga*, *Athabaskan*, and *Sioux*, to Korea to support the U.N. fleet. The ships arrived in Korean waters by the end of July and immediately set to work as part of the British task force already operating in theatre.

Canada's first military contributions to the Korean War carried out a variety of different roles: running routine patrols, enforcing the U.N. naval blockade, and protecting convoys of troops and supplies funnelling into the Pusan perimeter. In mid-August, the *Cayuga* became the first RCN ship to engage the enemy when it bombarded the North Korean–held port of Yosu (Yeosu).

As the Pusan perimeter seemed on the brink of collapse, the Americans were not happy with what they saw as a "token" show of Canadian support and asked for more, specifically a ground contribution. Dean Acheson, the U.S. secretary of state, even reached out to Pearson personally to hammer home the importance of this request. St. Laurent's Cabinet prevaricated and continued to meet through late July and early August debating this issue. The only soldiers capable of being sent overseas were part of the regular force, but there were real fears in Ottawa that if they were sent there would be no force left to defend Canada. It was Pearson, arguing that a strong U.N. showing would send a clear

Tribal-class destroyer HMCS *Cayuga*, 1954.

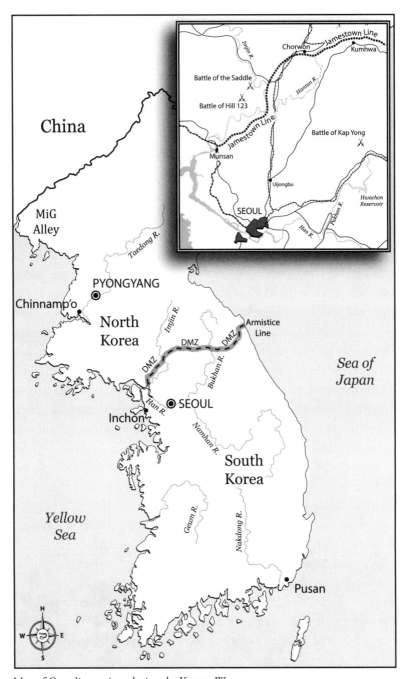

Map of Canadian actions during the Korean War.

message to the international community, who was able to convince the Cabinet and the prime minister to agree to send a brigade of volunteers 5,000 strong. Thus, on August 7, 1950, the Canadian Army Special Force was born.

Selected to command the brigade was Brigadier-General John "Rocky" Rockingham, one of Canada's finest officers from the Second World War. Rocky had commanded the 9th Canadian Infantry Brigade through some of its toughest scraps in Northwest Europe. By 1950, he was working in Vancouver as a superintendent for the BC Electric Company while still holding an officer rank in the local militia. Although there were Permanent Force officers who could have certainly led the Canadian Army Special Force, the appointment of Rockingham was meant to inspire other ex-servicemen to rejoin. That strategy worked — half of the original volunteers were Second World War veterans. Even though these volunteers were technically joining the Canadian Army, the conditions of their enlistment stipulated that they would only serve with the Canadian Army Special Force wherever it might be sent and only for 18 months.

The raising and training of the Canadian Army Special Force, soon to be called the 25th Canadian Infantry Brigade Group (25 CIBG), was haphazard. In a rush to get the brigade up and running, corners were cut. Under pressure from Brooke Claxton, the army began accepting volunteers before giving them their preliminary tests. Hundreds of accepted volunteers eventually had to be dismissed due to their unfitness to serve, and this constant departure of individuals had a deteriorating effect on morale. As well, to speed up officer training, the unusual step was taken to separate them from the other ranks and train them all at different facilities. This meant that for crucial periods of training in which battalion cohesion would normally be formed, the officers were not with the men they would command, and their men were not training with the officers who would lead them into battle.[6]

Even equipping the brigade proved challenging. Despite the Canadian Army moving toward adopting American kit, there simply were not enough American weapons to go around and most of the volunteers were already accustomed to British equipment from the Second World War. This meant the brigade would go overseas with a mix of Canadian, British, and American weapons and gear. Regardless of this chaotic system, by August, elements of 25 CIBG were training in British Columbia, Alberta, Manitoba, Ontario, and Quebec.

In the next month, events in Korea changed dramatically. General Douglas MacArthur, supreme commander of U.N. forces in Korea, staged a daring and successful amphibious assault at Inchon along the west coast in September 1950. The attack caught the North Koreans by surprise, and by the end of the month, its army was retreating rapidly. The U.N. forces were not just driving them back across the 38th parallel but pushing them even farther north, closer and closer to the border with China. At this point, it seemed as if the war was all but won. General Foulkes, Canada's Chief of the General Staff, was informed by the Americans that only a battalion would be needed, and this simply for occupation duties.[7] The battalion chosen was the second of the Princess Patricia's Canadian Light Infantry (2 PPCLI) under the command of Second World War veteran Lieutenant-Colonel Jim Stone. While the battalion still had weeks of training left, it was the closest to Canada's West Coast, and Brigadier-General Rockingham believed it was the farthest along in terms of preparation. Thus, in late November, the battalion shipped out, arriving in Pusan in mid-December. Once again, though, the strategic situation shifted dramatically.

With the U.N. forces approaching the northern border with China, the communist government in Beijing feared the U.N. offensive might be carried across the Yalu River and into China itself. In response, the Chinese government mobilized hundreds of thousands of Chinese troops, the People's Volunteer Army, who swarmed south to support the dissolving North Korean forces. Now it was the United Nations that found itself on the run, retreating south in the face of the overwhelming Chinese offensive.

Despite the desperate situation, Stone refused to commit his regiment to action until it had completed training. This was an incredibly brave move, considering the dire situation that faced U.N. forces as they sought to establish a solid defensive line around the Imjin River, just north of Seoul. While U.N. forces fell back, 2 PPCLI continued its training near Pusan and by mid-February was finally ready to enter the line. By this point, Seoul had once again fallen to the north, and 2 PPCLI was put into action 45 miles southeast of the destroyed capital as part of the 27th British Commonwealth Infantry Brigade. This brigade consisted of British, New Zealander, Australian, and Indian components and was part of the U.S. 2nd Infantry Division, attached to IX Corps as part of General Matthew Ridgway's U.S. Eighth Army.

Several weeks of smaller actions followed, and while 2 PPCLI suffered its first casualties, 14 dead by the time it was pulled out of the line on March 13, it allowed the Canadians to become acclimated to their new life at the front, operating in fog, rain, snow, and bitterly cold temperatures over rocky, shrub-covered hillsides where one misstep could send a soldier plunging to his death. Many of these early fights were small-unit attacks to occupy or defend key high points as the U.N. forces crawled their way back toward the 38th parallel. Although generally outnumbered, the U.N. forces benefited from far more artillery as well as domination of the air, which meant the use of overwhelming firepower against enemy troops before U.N. infantry closed the gap. These meat-grinder tactics, as they were described, worked. Seoul was recaptured on March 16, and it seemed as if the U.N. forces were building momentum as the enemy began to retreat in front of them. The Canadians were part of this general advance, and by mid-April found themselves in the Kapyong Valley, just north of the 38th parallel. And then the Chinese struck.

The People's Volunteer Army retreat had been designed to lure the U.N. forces into exposed positions, and on April 22, the Chinese launched their counterattack with the hope of driving a wedge between IX Corps and I Corps on its left in order to push onto Seoul. Fifteen miles north of the Canadians, two South Korean regiments collapsed in front of the attacking People's Volunteer Army, and the 27th British Commonwealth Infantry Brigade suddenly found itself no longer in reserve but facing the main thrust of the Chinese attack pouring down the valley along a key north–south road.

To slow the advance and give time for the U.N. forces to set up a stronger defensive line to the south, the Royal Australian Regiment and 2 PPCLI were ordered to occupy two key high points overlooking the valley floor: the Royal Australian Regiment to the east on Hill 504 and 2 PPCLI on the western side on Hill 677. Stone ordered his company commanders to set up defensive positions in a semicircle along the roughly 1.5-mile hill. As the Canadians were putting the finishing touches on their defensive positions, the Chinese hit the Australians with a late-night attack on April 23. Despite a stubborn defence, by late the next day, the Australians had been overrun and were forced to withdraw. The Patricia's were the only ones left holding the valley, and the Chinese turned their focus on them.

The first wave of attackers hit B Company on the Canadian right flank at around 10:00 p.m. on April 24. Machine-gun fire inflicted heavy casualties on

Soldiers of the 2nd Princess Patricia's Canadian Light Infantry crossing the Imjin River in South Korea, June 6, 1951.

the waves of attackers, but Canadian soldiers were shocked at how the enemy kept coming. Soon, they were into the Canadian positions. Bren and Vickers machine-gun fire ripped into the enemy at close range. Hand-to-hand combat ensued, bayonets piercing flesh. At 1:30 a.m., as things became desperate on the Canadian right flank, the Canadian left flank, held by D Company, was hit with a second Chinese assault. One platoon was forced to retreat in the face of such overwhelming numbers, and the western flank risked collapse. As a second platoon was close to being overrun, its commander, Lieutenant Mike Levy, called down close-range artillery and mortar fire onto the company's own position. U.N. artillery struck within 55 yards of the well-dug-in Canadians. Accurate New Zealand gunners lobbed 2,300 shrapnel burst shells into this maelstrom. The Chinese, above ground and thus exposed to the artillery fire, were ripped apart as the Canadians huddled in their slit trenches. This brave move by Lieutenant Levy worked, and by daylight, the intensity of the Chinese attacks subsided. D Company had held.

While sporadic fighting continued, the momentum of the Chinese attack had been blunted. A supply drop by American Flying Boxcars[8] ensured the Canadians replenished their dwindling stocks of food, water, and ammunition, and by April 26, the battalion was pulled out of the front line. The stubborn defence of the Kapyong Valley by the Canadians and Australians against a force three times their size had given IX Corps time to bring up reinforcements and effectively block the valley. This, in turn, allowed the Eighth Army to set up a stronger defensive line just to the south protecting the capital and eventually allowed U.N. forces to push back to the 38th parallel. In the fighting, the Canadians lost 10 killed and 23 wounded. Both the Royal Australian Regiment and 2 PPCLI were awarded the U.S. Presidential Unit Citation. The PPCLI is the only battalion in Canadian history to receive such a distinction.[9]

A decoration controversy did arise, however, in the aftermath of the battle. While Lieutenant Levy was the one who had requested the artillery fire, it was company commander Captain John Mills who conveyed Levy's request and was thus awarded a Military Cross, much to the frustration of many from Levy's platoon. After years of lobbying by Levy's peers and several Canadian historians, Levy was eventually recognized with a decoration from Adrienne Clarkson, Canada's governor general, in 2004, and posthumously received a decoration from the South Korean government in 2017.

By this point in the Korean War, Canadians were fighting at sea, on land, and in the air, though Canada's largest contribution to the air war effort is often left out of the narrative due to the fact that its servicemen did not technically serve in Korea itself. Less than a month after Canada's first three destroyers were sailing to the peninsula, the Canadian government authorized the transfer of RCAF 426 Squadron to the U.S. Military Air Transport Service. The squadron and its dozen North Star aircraft operated out of McChord Air Force Base near Tacoma, Washington, where it conducted round-trip air supply lifts between Washington and Haneda Airfield in Tokyo for the entirety of the conflict. Eight hundred RCAF personnel served with 426 Squadron, which flew just under 600 round trips during the conflict, providing much-needed airlift support for the U.S. Air Force.

By 1951, the RCAF began training its fighter pilots to fly the new Canadair Sabre, the Canadian-made version of the F-86 Sabre in use in the U.S. Air Force. It made sense for some Canadian pilots to get experience flying actual Sabres in combat, and the U.S. Air Force obliged. Twenty-four RCAF fighter pilots eventually went to Korea to serve with the U.S. Air Force, flying combat missions in the infamous "MiG Alley," the name given to the northwest portion of North Korea where fighter pilots engaged MiG-15s flown by Communist forces. While a MiG was only spotted in 10 percent of all missions, RCAF pilots flew nearly 900 combat missions and accounted for nine MiGs shot down. Most of the Canadian pilots were Second World War veterans such as Flight Lieutenant Ernest Glover from Niagara Falls, Ontario. Glover flew Typhoons over Europe before being shot down and taken prisoner by the Germans in 1943. In 1952, he was posted to Korea where he flew 58 combat missions and shot down three MiGs. He was awarded the U.S. Distinguished Flying Cross and the Commonwealth Distinguished Service Cross. A fellow Second World War veteran, Squadron Leader Andy Mackenzie from Montreal, had to eject from his Sabre in early December 1952 and was taken prisoner once on the ground. He lost 70 pounds while enduring interrogation, torture, and long stretches of isolation and was not released until late 1954, nearly 18 months after the armistice was signed.

Squadron Leader Andy Mackenzie in front of his F-86 Sabre, September 1952.

A total of 1,000 RCAF personnel served in the conflict, including 40 RCAF flight nurses stationed in Honolulu. These nurses flew in long-range four-engine aircraft that were converted into flying field hospitals to airlift wounded soldiers. The wounded were first transported from Korea to Japan, then Japan to Honolulu, and from there back to mainland United States.

Canada's commitment to the war at sea continued, as well. In November 1950, all three RCN destroyers were operating along Korea's west coast as part of a six-vessel task element under the command of Captain Jeffrey Brock of HMCS *Cayuga* when the Chinese counterattack stormed across the Yalu River and changed the nature of the Korean War. As events on land became more and more dire for U.N. forces, who by the beginning of December were in full retreat, Brock was ordered to lead his group into the Daido-ko Estuary to provide cover for transport ships evacuating friendly forces from Chinnamp'o, the primary port for the North Korean capital of Pyongyang. The estuary was a treacherous waterway with narrow, shallow stretches still quite unfamiliar to U.N. naval forces in the area. Because of the desperately unfolding strategic situation and the fact that several U.N. vessels were lying exposed in the harbour of Chinnamp'o, Brock made the risky decision to lead the group into the estuary the night of December 4 instead of waiting until the next day. Two of Brock's ships, one being the *Sioux*, temporarily ran aground during this passage, yet Brock's force was able to successfully sail in and cover the withdrawal from the harbour while inflicting damage on enemy infrastructure. For his leadership in what was Canada's most important naval operation of the Korean War, Brock was awarded the Distinguished Service Cross and went on to become a rear-admiral in the RCN.[10]

By January 1951, RCN destroyers began rotating out of theatre, though all would return for a second and some even a third tour. The *Sioux* was replaced by HMCS *Nootka*. Not long after it arrived in Korean waters, it and the *Cayuga* were fired upon while operating near Inchon. Despite this brief exposure to enemy fire, most of the first months of 1951 saw RCN destroyers devoted to protecting carriers from air or submarine attacks, what was known as "screening." In March, the *Cayuga* sailed home and was replaced by HMCS *Huron*.

Eventually, the *Haida*, *Crusader*, and *Iroquois* all rotated through Korean waters. The roles varied for all RCN destroyers, but generally they switched between carrier screening and blockade patrols. However, in October 1952, HMCS *Iroquois*, which had been in theatre for four months, was part of a two-vessel "train-busting" operation with USS *Marsh*. They were bombarding enemy rail lines along the east coast when a North Korean shore battery got a lucky hit, killing three of the *Iroquois*'s sailors and wounding 11 others. Out of the eight vessels and 3,621 RCN personnel to serve in Korea, these were the only casualties. The final RCN destroyer to leave Korean waters for good was the *Sioux*, which did so in 1955.

✦ ✦ ✦

The 25th Canadian Infantry Brigade Group arrived in Pusan in May 1951, and after a bit of equipment swapping with the Americans, particularly the brigade's M10 tank destroyers for American M4A3 Shermans, it set out north toward the front. By the end of the month, the brigade was joined by the 2 PPCLI and received its initial tastes of combat and first casualties, dealing with Chinese fire teams protecting the rearguard of a withdrawing Chinese army. By July 25, 25 CIBG linked up with the 28th British Commonwealth Infantry Brigade and the 29th British Infantry Brigade to form the 1st Commonwealth Division, a multinational one with British, New Zealander, Australian, Indian, and even Belgian troops. The division was attached to I Corps, commanded by Lieutenant-General John "Iron Mike" O'Daniel, which held the western flank of the U.S. Eighth Army, now under General James A. Van Fleet.[11]

By the summer of 1951, international calls for peace talks persuaded the two sides to discuss a potential armistice. Despite these talks, which began on July 8, the armies remained aggressive all along the front, and though casualties for the Canadian brigade were light, they were nonetheless a constant drain on manpower. The 1st Commonwealth Division under the command of Major-General A.J.H. Cassels occupied a six-mile front along the Imjin River north of Seoul and continued to actively patrol and conduct "reconnaissance-in-force" operations across the river. To eliminate the river as an obstacle, the entire division pushed across the Imjin in September. By October, a new defensive line, the Jamestown, was established, now 30 miles north of Seoul and just above the 38th parallel. This was an area of the front the Canadians were going to become very accustomed to, since they occupied portions of it until the ceasefire in July 1953. Once on the Jamestown Line, the Canadians continued aggressive patrolling, engaging Chinese ambush teams and conducting raids to gather intelligence and capture prisoners.

By the end of October, the front had entered into a "static" phase while peace talks resumed. U.N. commanders were ordered to stop any major operations, yet small-scale skirmishes, patrolling, and raids continued. By this point, 111 Canadians had died fighting in Korea.

One of the features of service in Korea that distinguished it from Canadians participating in the Second World War was the policy of rotation. During the Second World War, Canadian soldiers usually served for the duration of the conflict. In Korea, however, it was decided by Guy Simonds, the new Chief of the General Staff, that units were to serve for one year before being rotated out and replaced by a new battalion. Simonds wanted the personnel from the regular force to gain experience in theatre and not be lulled into a "home-defence" mindset.[12] Rotation allowed him to do this. By the time the strategic situation in Korea had settled into the static phase in late 1951, the first rotation was taking place, with 2 PPCLI replaced by elements of 1 PPCLI.

While U.N. forces were told not to launch any major operations, the Chinese were not afraid to initiate some of their own. On November 2, the Royal Canadian Regiment (RCR) beat back a concentrated attack. Three days later, elements of both the incoming 1 PPCLI and outgoing 2 PPCLI defended against an even stronger attacking force. By the morning of November 6, over 30 Chinese corpses could be spotted within 55 yards of the wire protecting the PPCLI positions. Perhaps twice as many corpses had been carried away by the Chinese, while the PPCLI counted three killed and 15 wounded. Although these were short, vicious scraps, the PPCLI faced one of its toughest tests later that month in defence of the position known as "The Saddle."

To strengthen the divisions' position in the face of unrelenting Chinese attacks, Cassels ordered 25 CIBG to occupy a saddle connecting the eastern foot of Hill 227 with the western slopes of Hill 355, a dominating high point roughly 2.5 miles west of the Imjin River. It had been fought over numerous times already, earning the sobriquet "Little Gibraltar." At the time, it was held by elements of the U.S. 7th Infantry Regiment. The Saddle itself was roughly a mile in length, and the defence of it was assigned to the Royal 22nd Regiment (the Van Doos) under Lieutenant-Colonel Jacques Dextraze.

The Van Doos had barely a day to improve its defences before the Chinese struck. On the afternoon of November 23, after 24 hours of intermittent shelling, the Chinese smashed into the Americans holding the top of Hill 355 while a smaller force hit the Van Doos on the American left. Within an hour and a half, the Americans had been pushed off Hill 355, and suddenly, the entire right flank of the Van Doos was exposed. Throughout the night, the regiment beat back four separate attacks, almost all of these falling on D Company, which held the front of the regiment's perimeter. Seesaw battles erupted as the Chinese occupied parts of D Company's line and then were pushed off. At one point, Corporal Léo Major from Montreal, a decorated veteran of the Second World War, personally led his scout platoon in a successful bid to recapture a lost position. As the Chinese counterattacked in force, Major refused an order to withdraw and instead called down mortar and artillery fire right in front of his own position. The Chinese attack was stopped. For his bravery, Major went on to receive a bar to his Distinguished Conduct Medal, effectively meaning he was awarded it for the second time, after first winning it in 1945.

With the Van Doos now taking the brunt of the Chinese attack, the Americans were able to regain their hold on Hill 355. Fighting then shifted to the left where the Chinese, attacking from the heights of Hill 227, further threatened the Van Doos, but again the regiment held firm. On November 26, the much-battered D Company was replaced by B Company, but by then the Chinese attacks had subsided. The Canadians had fought incredibly well, but it had cost the Van Doos 16 killed and 44 wounded. Seven hundred and forty-two enemy dead were counted in the area between the two hills, but estimates have enemy dead at upward of 2,000. Despite the Van Doos being rushed into their positions without much time to prepare, they had fought one of the finest defensive actions in the history of the Canadian Army.[13]

By this point in the war, the average Canadian soldier was kitted out in a mishmash of gear. Surprisingly, the Canadian-made winter gear the men originally came over with was not sufficient for the Korean winter, and soon the men were swapping for better British- or American-made kit. The weapons they had were a hodgepodge of British- and U.S.-made. While some continued with the same bolt-action Lee-Enfield rifle Canadians had used in the Second World War, others discarded theirs for the American-made M1 Garand or the Winchester M2 Carbine. The Sten gun, the British-made sub-machine gun that had been only slightly improved since the Second World War, was universally despised, and many preferred the American Thompson submachine gun so famous in gangster movies as the Tommy gun. Even when it came to field rations, Canadian soldiers often preferred American C-rations, with chicken stew or spaghetti and meatballs options as opposed to the British compo-packs, rumoured to be the unused rations from the Second World War.

There was no question that life at the front was tough, and while decent hot food was a key to good morale, so was the ability to get away from the fighting for periods of rest and relaxation. There were rear-area rest camps such as "Pete's Paradise" in the rear echelon of the RCR, which provided comforts that included a shave and a haircut, some good hot food, cold beer, a movie, and free time to write home. Farther back were divisional rest centres in Seoul and Inchon, though both these cities were so bombed out that they were shells of their former selves.

While alcohol and companionship seemed to be the objectives for many Canadian soldiers on leave, one of the safer ways in which Canadian officers sought to occupy the minds of their men was through sports. With winters in Korea similar to those in much of Canada, two hockey rinks were eventually built on the Imjin River with spectator stands and a concession hut. Nicknamed the "Imjin Gardens," the rinks hosted competitive hockey between the various battalions and even saw some of the warm-weather Commonwealth troops give a go at learning the game.

After three months served, Canadian soldiers were eligible for leave to Tokyo where alcohol was cheap and sex could be bought. For many Canadians there, excessive drinking and the frequenting of prostitutes were commonplace, and many returned to the front line with a "souvenir," soldiers' slang for venereal disease.[14] Just as in the Second World War, venereal disease was a serious problem for the Canadian rank and file. Some Canadians also broke the law. Away without leave, theft, and drunkenness were more commonplace, while there were also a small number of cases of assault, rape, and even murder. The Canadian military justice system never failed to prosecute those soldiers who had committed crimes, but the sad truth was that for crimes

Soldiers of the 3rd Battalion Princess Patricia's Canadian Light Infantry clean their weapons outside a bunker, December 16, 1952.

committed against Koreans an incredible and disturbing level of leniency was shown toward the felons.[15]

One of the distinguishing features of fighting in Korea was the vastly improved battlefield medical care. Perhaps the two most well-recognized symbols of which were the Mobile Army Surgical Hospital (MASH) and the helicopter, which had only just started being produced for the American military by the end of the Second World War. In Korea, helicopters could rapidly transport wounded soldiers to MASH units with prefabricated surgical wards and supporting facilities roughly six to nine miles behind the front lines. Because there were only limited numbers of helicopters available, most casualties were still evacuated by foot or vehicle, and helicopter evacuations were saved for only the most seriously wounded. For much of the war, 25 CIBG evacuated its soldiers to a Norwegian MASH unit until 1953 when a Canadian one was established. Medical care certainly improved with the Korean War. During the Second World War, for every 1,000 soldiers wounded, 66 died; in Korea, that number was reduced to almost half that.

✦ ✦ ✦

A hockey match on the Imjin River in South Korea between teams from the 1st Princess Patricia's Canadian Light Infantry and the Royal 22nd Regiment (Van Doos), March 11, 1952.

By the summer of 1952, the Canadians in Korea experienced a fairly predict-able pattern of life: weeks spent at the front along the Jamestown Line conducting frequent patrols with the odd skirmish against aggressive Chinese forces, a small but steady drain of casualties sapping front-line strength, and a period in reserve where the men rested and trained before returning to the front to engage once again in patrols and the odd skirmish. While no major actions occurred during this period, the artillery, mortar, and machine-gun fire of the enemy was all too real to the men being shot at, and in August alone 18 Canadians were killed.

By this point, the Canadians were primarily on the defensive. While patrolling and ambushes were still conducted, no major offensive operations were allowed, which meant the Chinese dominated the ground "outside the wire"[16] while choosing the time and place for battle. In many ways, the Canadians and other U.N. forces were now forced into fighting at a disadvantage because of political decisions from above.

The Chinese certainly took advantage of this. One of those times was October 23 against the RCR, which was now defending the infamous Saddle. After a sustained curtain of artillery and machine-gun fire was dropped on the Canadians, bugles and whistles rang out across the valley signalling a

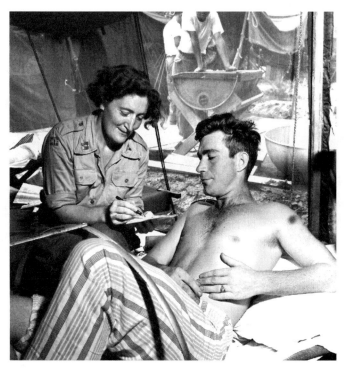

Captain Petra Drabloe (left) from a Norwegian Mobile Army Surgical Hospital tends to Lance Corporal M.R. Stevens from North Bay, Ontario, in South Korea, date unknown.

Chinese attack. Like the Van Doos before them, the RCR found itself in a brutal hand-to-hand scrap defending Little Gibraltar. For 48 hours, they beat back a numerically superior enemy that had infiltrated the Canadian trenches. When grenades and light machine guns failed, it fell to bayonets and clubs to do the awful work. Lieutenant Russell Gardner was shot three times before falling onto his own wire and playing dead to avoid capture by the Chinese storming past him. Lieutenant John Clark, born in England but living in Quebec, emptied every weapon at his disposal, including a Sten, a Bren, and all his grenades, before leading the remnants of his platoon to safety while carrying a wounded comrade. He was awarded the Military Cross. By early morning of the next day, the RCR recaptured its lost positions, with 18 killed and 35 wounded.

Skirmishing continued throughout the winter and into the spring of 1953. By this point, 25 CIBG was on its third battalion rotation and its third brigade commander. Rockingham had been rotated out in April 1952, and replaced by Brigadier-General M.P. Bogert, who had served in Sicily and Italy during the Second World War. He, in turn, was rotated out a year later for Brigadier-General Jean Victor Allard, who had commanded the Van Doos in Italy during the previous war. Five days after Allard took command of the brigade, peace talks once again resumed at Panmunjom.

This time, though, the strategic situation had shifted in favour of the U.N. forces. Soviet leader Joseph Stalin, North Korea's main benefactor, had died. The Chinese economy was suffering heavily under the weight of continued fighting, and the Americans had just elected Dwight D. Eisenhower as president. Eisenhower was the former Supreme Commander of the Allied Forces in Western Europe and came to office with a very clear message that America was not backing down. Thus, the talks that began in late April appeared as if they were on their way to some sort of tangible conclusion. Regardless, the Chinese were still attempting to improve their current position along the front before an armistice was reached.

In early May, 25 CIBG was positioned at the centre of the 1st Commonwealth Division's front along the Jamestown Line when the Chinese attacked. The assault was aimed at Hill 123, held by the RCR. Despite intelligence suggesting an attack was coming, Allard was in Seoul on May 2 having dinner with General Maxwell Taylor, the new commander of the Eighth Army. He was forced to cut his meal short and return to the front when news of Chinese activity reached him. Then the storm hit. An RCR patrol ran smack into the first wave of Chinese attackers and quickly fell back. The sound of bugles and whistles signalled the main Chinese assault, and soon the RCR, and the Van Doos sent to support them, were overrun.

The enemy was in among the Canadian positions, dropping grenades into trenches and engaging Canadian soldiers in close-combat fighting for every slit trench and bunker. Like so many battles before, Canadian mortar and artillery fire was eventually called down right on top of the battle, inflicting heavy damage on the exposed attackers. As morning came and the Canadians prepared to recapture their lost positions, the Chinese inexplicably withdrew. This was a short, brutal battle that after only 12 hours ended up being the costliest single engagement for the Canadians, but also their last major engagement. Twenty-six died, 27 were wounded, and seven were taken prisoner. Less than two months later, an armistice agreement was signed.

Twenty-two thousand Canadians served in the army in Korea, 312 were killed, 1,202 were wounded, and 32 were taken prisoner. By the spring of 1954, only one battalion of Canadians (the Black Watch) remained to help oversee the armistice. A year later, only 500 Canadians remained in country. The last Canadian combat soldier to leave did so in June 1957. The war ended in a stalemate, the two sides almost exactly where they had been when North Korea had originally invaded. While 1950 and 1951 saw both sides launch large-scale offensives that achieved significant gains, by the end of 1951, politicians and generals had decided the U.N. forces would fight a defensive war, and a stalemate was the natural result. Nonetheless, U.N. forces had prevented a northern takeover of the south, with 370,000 South Korean, American, Commonwealth, and Allied soldiers paying the ultimate price to achieve it.

The Korean War certainly escaped the public imagination and for a long time became Canada's forgotten war, much to the frustration of its veterans. Canada's participation in the conflict did spark a renewed interest in defence matters among Canadian politicians. If the end of the Second World War witnessed a decline in defence spending, the Korean War triggered the exact opposite. For the Canadian government under Louis St. Laurent, the Korean War convinced it that Communism was, indeed, an ideology of aggression and enhanced the possibility of a war against the Soviet Union in Europe. Thus, Canada had to be ready to share the burden of European defence with its NATO allies. In May 1951, Brooke Claxton, minister of defence, announced that Canada would send a brigade group overseas, one that would end up being stationed around the town of Soest, as part of the British Army of the Rhine. To ensure adequate reinforcements for the brigade, after 1953 known as the 1st Canadian Infantry Brigade (1 CIB), Guy Simonds was able to expand the size of the regular force. It would now consist of 15 infantry battalions drawn from six regular infantry regiments: the original three (the PPCLI, the RCR, and the Van Doos), and three new regiments (the Queen's Own Rifles, the Black Watch, and the Canadian Guards). Defence spending by this point was 10 times higher than in 1947.

By 1957, 1 CIB provided one-sixth of the British Army's strength along the Rhine River and was, in the view of the British Army of the Rhine commander, one of the finest fighting formations in Europe, if not in the world.[17] The brigade was extremely well trained, and though it could not boast having the best equipment possible (much of it was still British-made), it enjoyed high morale, and was committed to Europe for the long haul. This brigade marked what Canadian military historian Jack Granatstein has called "the golden age of Canadian military professionalism" where efficiency, funding, and professionalism created a potent trifecta of military excellence.[18]

While the army certainly benefited from dramatic increases in defence spending, the air force was the greatest benefactor. In early February 1951, Claxton announced a significant expansion of the RCAF to 40 (later 41) regular and reserve squadrons with 3,000 aircraft; a personnel establishment increase to just over 26,000, plus 6,500 civilian members; a new radar system; an expansion of the RCAF's training infrastructure; and increased investments in Canada's aircraft industry. Claxton called for the creation of the "Big Air Force," and Canada, briefly, found itself as one of the world's top five airpowers. Part of the RCAF expansion also included the commitment to an air division in Europe, further bolstering Canada's NATO presence overseas. Operational in 1955, the RCAF's 1 Air Division consisted of 12 squadrons and was placed under the command of the American-led 4th Allied Tactical Air Force stationed at four airfields in eastern France and West Germany.

The navy also profited from this unusually generous period of defence spending. While the Korean War certainly stretched the navy's resources, it did spur the government to agree to a fairly sizable expansion that included 14 new destroyers, seven of which were the up-gunned and technologically improved Restigouche class. By 1955, the RCN could boast over six naval aviation squadrons as well as more than four dozen ships, including one carrier (*Magnificent*) and one cruiser (*Quebec*), with another 16 vessels still under construction. In 1957, HMCS *Magnificent* was decommissioned and replaced by the brand-new *Bonaventure* ("*Bonnie*"), a modern aircraft carrier that carried Banshee jet fighter aircraft, Tracker anti-submarine aircraft, and Sikorsky helicopters for anti-submarine operations. Like her sister services, the navy was now modern and flexible and the largest it had ever been in Canadian peacetime history.

By the time the *Bonnie* had been launched, Canada's military was already being deployed in a form that would come to dominate the public imagination for much of the 20th century — U.N. peacekeeping. Two factors really drove Canada's participation in this: concern over the spread of

Communism into war-torn regions and the fear of a "hot war," as in Korea, escalating into armed conflict between the two nuclear superpowers. Of course, as the Canadian public began to embrace this "supposedly non-combative" form of military participation, Canadian politicians accepted it even more and thus so much of the second half of the 20th century would be dominated by images of blue-helmeted Canadian soldiers on every continent of the globe, though the myth that emerged around peacekeeping would obscure the far more complicated truth behind this era in global Canadian military activity.

Majestic-class aircraft carrier HMCS *Bonaventure*, 1963.

9

THE ERA OF PEACEKEEPING

It is a commonly embraced myth that Canadian peacekeeping was born on the sands of the Sinai Desert during the Suez crisis of 1956–57. But like so many myths, it simply does not stand up to reality. The template for U.N. interpositional peacekeeping was established nearly a decade before. In 1948, the United Nations asked for military observers to patrol the demarcation line between India and Pakistan in Kashmir. While there was very little enthusiasm for such a task, eventually eight Canadian officers were sent. In fact, a Canadian, Brigadier-General Harry H. Angle, was given command of this small peacekeeping force. Angle had commanded the British Columbia Dragoons during the Second World War, and after the war maintained his officer rank in the reserves while fruit farming in Kelowna, British Columbia. In early 1950, he was made chief military observer of the U.N. Military Observer Group in India-Pakistan but tragically died in July in a plane crash — Canada's first soldier to die on peacekeeping duties.

In 1953, the United Nations asked for peacekeepers to bolster the fledgling U.N. Truce Supervision Organization struggling to maintain a crumbling peace between Israel and its Arab neighbours. Early the next year, four regular-force Canadian officers were sent, one of whom, former I Canadian Corps commander Major-General E.L.M. Burns, was named the organization's chief of staff. Tragically, one of Burns's fellow officers, Lieutenant-Colonel George Flint from Outremont, Quebec, was killed by a sniper while attempting to stop active shooting between Israeli and Arab police forces.

A cadre of 150 Canadian military officers and diplomats was sent in 1954 to the newly established country of Vietnam, which had seen years of brutal fighting between the French and Vietminh. Canada's contribution was part of a three-nation International Control Commission initiated by the U.N. Security Council to attempt to bring a stable peace to the region formerly known as French Indochina. Canada, alongside Poland and India, made some headway with the new countries of Laos and Cambodia, but the commission splintered and then fell apart when it came to Vietnam, and that nation once again collapsed into decades of war as a result.

The Suez Crisis

The Suez crisis began two years after Canada took part in the International Control Commission. By the early 1950s, Egypt had undergone dramatic change when a revolution toppled its monarch, King Farouk, and established a new government, eventually headed by the charismatic nationalist Colonel Gamal Abdel Nasser. In 1956, Nasser nationalized the Suez Canal, partly as a punitive measure toward the British, who refused to sell him weapons, but mostly to pay for a massive hydroelectric project known as the Aswan Dam. The canal was co-owned by the British and the French, who relied on it to get their oil from the Middle East.

Prime Minister Anthony Eden of Britain, who had been a deputy to former prime minister Winston Churchill, saw Nasser as a new Hitler and authorized secret negotiations with the French and Israelis to attack the Egyptians. On October 29, 1956, this alliance launched its attack, with the British sending in soldiers to "protect" the canal. Nobody was deceived by this. It was clear the British had orchestrated an assault to take back the important waterway. The Americans, Soviets, Canadians, and most of the United Nations denounced the action. By November, however, the Egyptian military was soundly beaten, the Israelis were deep into the Sinai Desert, and French and British forces were on the east bank of the Suez Canal.

It was in early November, as the U.N. General Assembly prepared to pass a resolution requesting the withdrawal of Anglo-French-Israeli forces, that Lester B. Pearson, the Canadian secretary of state for external affairs, proposed a U.N. military force to step in between the warring sides and enforce peace in the region. Of course, as with any U.N. endeavour, this one was chock full of diplomatic layers. Domestically, this U.N. peacekeeping force was roundly criticized by John Diefenbaker, the Conservative Party Opposition Leader, who felt it was a betrayal of Great Britain. Internationally, Canadian diplomats attempted to soothe an irate United States, which blamed the British for causing a serious international incident. It was in Canada's diplomatic interests to ensure their two closest allies, Great Britain and the United States, were on good terms, and Canadian diplomats believed they were uniquely positioned to bring about an accord between the former and current superpower.[1]

At the same time, Canada was also very concerned about the potential for any conflict to escalate. The Korean War had taught Canadian politicians to fear the potential nuclear conclusion of any escalating conflict. At the same time, NATO security concerns made it imperative that the Soviet Union be prevented from sending troops to help a beleaguered Egypt, which could give the Soviet Union a foothold in the Middle East.

Pearson's proposal was thus accepted, and the United Nations Emergency Force (UNEF) was dispatched in December. While at first the Canadian government offered the Queen's Own Rifles to be the core of this peacekeeping force, Nasser rejected this. To Nasser, Canada was not some benign neutral country but one seen very much as part of the British sphere. The Canadian flag had the Union Jack on it, Canadian soldiers spoke English and wore British-patterned uniforms, and even the regiment's name was a direct link to the British monarchy. Although no Canadian soldiers were initially allowed to be part of UNEF, the commander of the force was a Canadian, Major-General E.L.M. Burns, who was in Jerusalem commanding the U.N. Truce Supervision Organization. Burns was able to walk a fine diplomatic line during his year in command, earning the respect of the Israelis but also establishing himself as relatively trustworthy to the Egyptians.[2]

Thus, despite UNEF being a Canadian initiative and led by a Canadian officer, the initial contingent, nearly 3,200 strong, was made up of countries either associated with Egypt or from non-aligned nations. Half of the force

Major-General E.L.M. Burns (centre) meeting with Dag Hammarskjöld (far left), secretary-general of the United Nations, and personnel of the United Nations Emergency Force (UNEF), 1956.

was from India and Yugoslavia, while other soldiers included Colombians, Swedes, Norwegians, Danes, and Finns. Once UNEF was settled into its facilities at Abu Suweir and El Ballah, it was quickly realized that the force was desperately short of supplies. After some diplomatic haggling, the Egyptians were convinced to permit 300 Canadian troops to work in logistic and administrative roles, which became vital to fixing UNEF's supply shortage. In late November, RCAF C-119s began flying supply runs from Italy to the airport at Abu Suweir. In January, Canada's aircraft carrier, HMCS *Magnificent*, arrived in Port Said, bringing with it 154 vehicles, 78 trailers, four Otter aircraft, over 200 boxes of ammunition, and crates of much-needed other supplies.

By late March 1957, Nasser relented on his anti-Canadian position, and the Canadian contingent expanded in size, so that by the next year, when UNEF moved its base close to Gaza City, the Canadian contribution made up one-sixth of the entire UNEF force. Eventually, 1,200 Canadians arrived to serve with UNEF as a signal and transport squadron, infantry in a training capacity, an air transport unit, and a reconnaissance squadron. The reconnaissance squadron was responsible for patrolling a 35-mile section of

Canadian scout car in the Sinai Desert as part of UNEF, August 11, 1964.

the Israeli-Egyptian border, with regular patrols to stop border infiltrations, investigate truce violations, and generally make the U.N. presence known in the region. While most patrols were routine and without serious incident, there was always a sense that violence could erupt. In late November 1959, a patrol was ambushed by Egyptian soldiers, killing one Canadian. The Egyptians pleaded a case of mistaken identity, but it was clear an ambush had been purposefully organized.[3] Mines were also scattered throughout the region and posed a threat to Canadians. In one instance, a Canadian soldier was wounded by an exploding mine and taken care of by friendly Bedouins until help arrived.

In the end, UNEF achieved its immediate objectives. It stopped the fighting while also preventing any escalation toward a Soviet-American conflict, though interestingly both the Soviets and Americans were on the same side in their denunciation of the Anglo-French-Israeli attack. The British and French were allowed to withdraw, effectively saving face, and the Suez Canal was opened to international shipping. For his efforts, Pearson won the 1957 Nobel Peace Prize. In the long term, UNEF was simply a Band-Aid on a bullet wound. It did not contribute to any lasting peace in the region, and in 1967 when Egypt was about to launch an attack against Israel, the Egyptians simply ordered the U.N. force to withdraw completely, which it did.

The Suez crisis was significant in other ways. Because of Pearson's Nobel Peace Prize, many Canadians began to embrace peacekeeping as a uniquely Canadian foreign policy. This idea was further stoked by politicians, and many in the public started to think of Canadians as "natural" peacekeepers who had a particular national temperament suited to such a task. Public support for this form of international participation thus began to grow, and Canada participated in nearly every U.N. peacekeeping mission for the next four and a half decades.[4]

Other less obvious consequences came because of UNEF. Egyptian concern over the fact that Canadian soldiers looked very much like British soldiers pushed many within the Canadian military to seek a more distinctive Canadian appearance for its soldiers. Finally, Egypt's reluctance to accept Canadian soldiers spurred Pearson's interest in finding a distinctive national flag for the country, one that did not have a Union Jack on it.[5]

The Congo

The perceived success of UNEF played a role in Canada's decision to send peacekeepers into the Congo in 1960. In the aftermath of the Congo's independence in June of that year, the former Belgian colony collapsed into chaos. Political, tribal, and ethnic violence erupted throughout the country while two areas seceded with the backing and support of the Belgian military still present in the region. Despite being rivals in the Congo, President Joseph Kasavubu and Prime Minister Patrice Lumumba rallied together in July 1960 to request U.N. support. While the U.N. plan was to send a force made up primarily of soldiers drawn from African nations, the Canadian public and news media called upon Prime Minister John Diefenbaker's Progressive Conservative government to provide a significant contribution, even though no such contribution was initially requested by the United Nations.

Diefenbaker was reluctant to commit Canadian soldiers, and rightfully so. He understood the potentially disastrous optics of white soldiers enforcing peace in the Congo, especially white soldiers from a NATO country allied to Belgium, which had brutally and violently exploited the region for decades.[6] However, there were very real fears that chaos in the Congo would be exploited by Communist agents and the country could become the front line for the Cold War in Africa. Diefenbaker was certainly faced with a dilemma: participate in a U.N. action and potentially be perceived as an agent of neo-colonialism or do nothing and incur the wrath of the Canadian public while possibly leaving the Congo to Communist influences.

While mired in this dilemma, Diefenbaker was eventually asked by the United Nations to send Canadian troops. Similar to UNEF, the initial U.N. contingent being deployed for the United Nations Operation in the Congo lacked several support services, including logistics, signals, aircraft, and specialized personnel. The United Nations' secretary-general, Dag Hammarskjöld,[7] thus turned to Diefenbaker and requested a Canadian signals contingent made up with as many bilingual personnel as possible. This was the perfect solution, since it allowed Diefenbaker to appease the Canadian public and help bring stability to the Congo without making white Canadian soldiers the spearhead of the operation.

In early August, despite vocal Soviet objections, the Canadian government authorized the dispatch of nearly 200 soldiers, a number of them drawn from the French-speaking Van Doos, along with the necessary vehicles and equipment. The United Nations Operation in the Congo became one of the largest U.N. peacekeeping missions in history with upward of 20,000 peacekeepers, though the Canadian contingent never exceeded 500 personnel.

Even before the signals contingent arrived in the Congo, a dozen Canadian officers seconded from UNEF and the U.N. Truce Supervision Organization were already working at U.N. headquarters on the staff of U.N. commander General Carl von Horn from Sweden. As well, RCAF North Stars were carrying out supply lifts, bringing desperately needed food into the region. By the end of August, most of the Canadian contingent was in theatre and several detachments of signallers were stationed throughout the country, ensuring communication between various U.N. positions.

Despite the Canadians clearly playing a supporting role, they were not immune to danger. In mid-August, several Canadian peacekeepers were physically assaulted by a group of Congolese soldiers at N'Djili Airport outside Léopoldville (today's Kinshasa). One of the continual problems was the fact that white Canadian soldiers were often mistaken for white Belgian soldiers and until identity could be confirmed were often treated harshly by the Congolese military. This was the reasoning behind another attack in late August when two Canadian peacekeepers were beaten so badly by a

Canadian peacekeepers arrive in the Congo.

Congolese crowd that they were hospitalized. Notwithstanding the inherent risks, sporadic violence, and a continually fraught political situation, the Canadian presence remained, and the first rotations were carried out successfully after six months.

In 1963, with the Canadian presence entering its third year, Brigadier-General Jacques Dextraze, the same man who had commanded the Van Doos in Korea, was appointed chief of staff of the U.N. forces under the command of Thomas Aguiyi-Ironsi, the difficult and often inebriated Nigerian general. While in this position, Dextraze planned and executed a series of small-scale raids to rescue civilians caught up in internecine violence. For this he was named a Commander of the Order of the British Empire. Dextraze also oversaw the Canadian withdrawal from the Congo, which was completed in July 1964.

Over 1,800 Canadian soldiers served in the Congo, and once again the immediate objectives of the peacekeeping mission were achieved. The country's territorial integrity had been preserved and peacekeepers established law

THE ERA OF PEACEKEEPING

and order, though at times just barely maintaining it. The mission had also effectively brought desperately needed relief supplies to the civilian population. Yet the nation continued to deal with localized uprisings throughout the tenure of the operation, and within two years of the U.N. withdrawal, Joseph Mobutu seized power in a coup and ran a brutal and corrupt dictatorship for the next three decades.

The Arrow, Bomarc, and Cuban Missiles

By the time the United Nations Operation in the Congo was wrapped up, the golden age of Canadian defence spending came to an end. The postwar boom that had made Canada one of the wealthiest nations on the planet was over by the late 1950s, and defence spending began to decline as a result. This did not necessarily mean Canada's military commitments lessened, only that the Department of National Defence was forced to find ways to cut expenses. In 1959, John Diefenbaker's government rightly cancelled the far-too-costly and poorly managed Avro Arrow jet interceptor fighter program.[8] Cost was certainly one, if not *the*, main reason for the cancellation, whose story has been polluted with Canadian nationalist rhetoric ever since. Another reason, touted by Diefenbaker's administration, was that the growing threat from the Soviet Union was not its bombers but its intercontinental ballistic missiles, the Soviets having first successfully tested theirs in 1957. Diefenbaker's government thus opted for the much cheaper Bomarc B surface-to-air missiles to counter the intercontinental ballistic missiles danger.

The purchase of U.S. Bomarc Bs highlighted growing Canadian-American defence co-operation during this period. The same year that the Soviets tested their intercontinental ballistic missiles, the joint protection of the skies over North America was formalized with the creation of the North American Air Defense Command, or NORAD, now known as the North American Aerospace Defense Command. Canada also co-operated with the United States in developing a series of radar station lines to warn against a Soviet attack. While the Pinetree and Mid-Canada Lines proved largely ineffective, it was the Distant Early Warning Line running across Canada's far northern Arctic region that proved the most capable.

THE ERA OF PEACEKEEPING

and order, though at times just barely maintaining it. The mission had also effectively brought desperately needed relief supplies to the civilian population. Yet the nation continued to deal with localized uprisings throughout the tenure of the operation, and within two years of the U.N. withdrawal, Joseph Mobutu seized power in a coup and ran a brutal and corrupt dictatorship for the next three decades.

The Arrow, Bomarc, and Cuban Missiles

By the time the United Nations Operation in the Congo was wrapped up, the golden age of Canadian defence spending came to an end. The postwar boom that had made Canada one of the wealthiest nations on the planet was over by the late 1950s, and defence spending began to decline as a result. This did not necessarily mean Canada's military commitments lessened, only that the Department of National Defence was forced to find ways to cut expenses. In 1959, John Diefenbaker's government rightly cancelled the far-too-costly and poorly managed Avro Arrow jet interceptor fighter program.[8] Cost was certainly one, if not *the*, main reason for the cancellation, whose story has been polluted with Canadian nationalist rhetoric ever since. Another reason, touted by Diefenbaker's administration, was that the growing threat from the Soviet Union was not its bombers but its intercontinental ballistic missiles, the Soviets having first successfully tested theirs in 1957. Diefenbaker's government thus opted for the much cheaper Bomarc B surface-to-air missiles to counter the intercontinental ballistic missiles danger.

The purchase of U.S. Bomarc Bs highlighted growing Canadian-American defence co-operation during this period. The same year that the Soviets tested their intercontinental ballistic missiles, the joint protection of the skies over North America was formalized with the creation of the North American Air Defense Command, or NORAD, now known as the North American Aerospace Defense Command. Canada also co-operated with the United States in developing a series of radar station lines to warn against a Soviet attack. While the Pinetree and Mid-Canada Lines proved largely ineffective, it was the Distant Early Warning Line running across Canada's far northern Arctic region that proved the most capable.

One of the major debates over continental defence revolved around Canada's use of nuclear weapons. While Diefenbaker was an early advocate for nuclear weapons, he had changed his tune by the end of the 1950s. Even though the Bomarc B missiles were supposed to be armed with nuclear warheads, Diefenbaker wanted them without. The CF-101 Voodoos that were the much cheaper replacements for the cancelled Arrow were also supposed to be armed with nuclear missiles, but Diefenbaker's government refused to allow that, as well. However, international events proved to challenge Diefenbaker's anti-nuclear stance when in October 1962 it was discovered that the Soviets were building missile platforms in Cuba. A tense standoff ensued, and NORAD went to defence readiness condition (DEFCON) 3, a heightened state of alert in anticipation of mobilization. The U.S. Navy surrounded the island, with Royal Canadian Navy (RCN) vessels relieving U.S. Navy ships so they could participate in the blockade, and awaited the Soviet navy on its way to deliver the missiles. As the world fretted over a potential superpower clash, Nikita Khrushchev, the Soviet Union's premier, blinked and ordered his navy to return home. The world breathed a sigh of relief.

The Cuban Missile Crisis convinced many Canadians that Canada needed a nuclear arsenal. The issue of nuclear armament even split Diefenbaker's own Cabinet, with his minister of national defence, Douglas Harkness, resigning in protest. Diefenbaker's opponent, Liberal leader Lester B. Pearson, announced that his party would support full nuclear armament if elected. While not the only political issue at stake, it certainly drew a very clear line in the sand, and in the 1963 federal election, Pearson won a minority government with overwhelming voting support from Canada's military personnel.[9] With that victory, the Liberals made good on their nuclear promise: the Bomarcs got their warheads and the Voodoos got their missiles. In Europe, as part of the NATO contingent, Canadian CF-104 Starfighters received their nuclear armament, and the Canadian forces adopted the Honest John surface-to-surface nuclear missile system.

One of the benefits of nuclear weapons was that they were cheaper than conventional forces. Despite this, budget cuts continued. Under both Diefenbaker and Pearson, the Canadian Army's reserve force saw its funding and size continually reduced, and Canada's NATO contingent in Europe felt the sting of budget cutbacks in its lack of armoured personnel carriers.

Cyprus

Peacekeeping continued, though. Small groups of Canadian peacekeepers were deployed to Lebanon and were also part of a U.N. security force in Dutch West New Guinea as it transferred to Indonesian authority. It was in Cyprus, however, that Canada committed to its longest peacekeeping operation.

By 1963, Cyprus, which had only just received its independence from Britain three years earlier, was descending into chaos as Greek and Turkish Cypriots clashed over the political future of the island. Intercommunal violence was spreading, so much so that it threatened to pull NATO members Greece and Turkey into war with each other. In March 1964, with the British already on the island, the U.N. Security Council authorized the deployment of U.N. forces. Within a few months, more than 6,000 U.N. personnel were deployed as part of the United Nations Forces in Cyprus. In Canada, Prime Minister Pearson recognized that the Mediterranean was a key strategic

Canadian peacekeepers in Cyprus, date unknown.

region for NATO — its southern flank effectively — and certainly understood the importance of maintaining NATO cohesion during the Cold War. The Americans, too, were concerned about a NATO rupture in the face of the crisis and put pressure on Pearson to act. He thus agreed to send a battalion-sized contingent, whose vehicles were transported to Cyprus on HMCS *Bonaventure*, and from 1964 onward rotations of Canadian soldiers spent six months patrolling the Green Line, which separated Turkish and Greek Cypriots in the capital of Nicosia.

While service during the first decade was rather monotonous, that all changed rapidly in July 1974 when a coup overthrew the Cypriot president and established a pro-Greek administration. In response, Turkey deployed 40,000 troops to the island, ostensibly to protect the Turkish minority. Violence erupted and Canadian peacekeepers were caught in the middle, sometimes being fired on by both sides at the same time. In one instance, Canadians even returned fire against Greek forces attacking a Turkish patrol under U.N. protection.[10] Seventeen Canadians were wounded during this period and two were killed. In reaction to this fighting, Canadian reinforcements were dispatched to Cyprus along with armoured personnel carriers and anti-tank weapons. After this short but intense period, the U.N. mission returned to its more familiar routine of impasse and continued that way for nearly two decades. The bulk of the Canadian commitment was eventually withdrawn in 1993 as Canada shifted its U.N. commitments to the Balkans, though a Canadian officer continued to be sent to Cyprus every year to support mission headquarters.

The Liberal Party, the Military, and Peacekeeping

While Canadian soldiers served in Cyprus, substantial changes were occurring in Canada's military under a succession of Liberal governments. In 1964, Pearson's Liberal government published the very important *White Paper on Defence*, which stressed Canada's commitment to North American defence, the critical importance of participation in U.N. peacekeeping operations, and finally a call for a more unified structure of the Canadian military. The principal author of this paper was Paul Hellyer, minister of national defence from 1963 to 1967, who, with Pearson's blessing, implemented the very controversial program of unification.

Hellyer inherited a defence establishment based on three separate, independent services, all with distinct access to the defence minister. The minister hoped to reduce defence costs by integrating the three separate services into one unified administrative organization with a single Chief of the Defence Staff overseeing powerful branches, or commands as they were called. The objective was improved efficiency and better co-operation. There was resistance, of course. Unification threatened long-standing loyalties to the individual services and would remove a large degree of autonomy from the service chiefs. Several senior military personnel resigned in protest. Regardless, in February 1968, the Canadian Forces Reorganization Act became law and the Canadian Armed Forces (CAF) was officially born. Gone was the "Royal" from Canada's navy and air force and in its place was Maritime Command, Air Defence Command, and Air Transport Command, while the army was now Mobile Command.

By this time, the Canadian social landscape was dramatically different from a decade earlier. The counterculture movement was in full swing, America's unpopular war in Vietnam was a major focus on both sides of the 49th parallel, anti-nuclear and pro-peace organizations proliferated, and there was a growing concern over the emerging Quebec separatist movement. All of this characterized a Canadian society shifting in values and concerns. This also meant a Canadian public that cared less and less about its military, reflected in its elected officials, as well. Continual cutbacks saw the size of the CAF reduced by 10,000 personnel, while Canada's air contribution to NATO was cut to six squadrons.

When Liberal prime minister Pierre Elliott Trudeau came to power in 1968, reductions continued. Trudeau was generally skeptical of Pearson's internationalism, and his administration completely reshuffled Canada's defence priorities. Peacekeeping and NATO, traditionally at the top of Canadian defence priorities, were now pinned at the bottom, which meant Canadian defence spending was harmonized in line with that. Canada's NATO contribution in Europe was gutted, its size decreased by half, the Honest Johns junked, and the contingent eventually lost its Centurion tanks. The regular force lost five regiments, the reserve strength was cut from 23,000 to 19,000, and the *Bonnie* (HMCS *Bonaventure*), fresh off a multi-million-dollar refit, was scrapped.

Trudeau was certainly willing to use the military, though. In October 1970, terrorists from the Front de libération du Québec (FLQ) kidnapped

James Cross, the British trade commissioner, and Pierre Laporte, the Quebec labour minister. The FLQ had already conducted a campaign of bombings and robberies that had left eight people dead, but it was the October kidnappings that triggered federal involvement. On October 15, Robert Bourassa, Quebec's premier, at the strong urging of Trudeau, requested aid to the civil power from the federal government.[11] The next day, Trudeau shocked the nation by invoking the War Measures Act to deal with the crisis. Never had a Canadian leader used this act during peacetime. Within days, thousands of Canadian soldiers were deployed throughout Quebec, most of them in Montreal, guarding key sites and patrolling the streets while police rounded up hundreds of suspects. Trudeau's heavy-handed approach to the crisis is still hotly debated, yet the military deployment was successful in rapidly bringing order to the situation without any civilian casualties (one soldier died when he accidentally tripped with his loaded weapon). Cross was eventually freed, though, sadly, Laporte was murdered by his kidnappers.

Despite a 1971 White Paper placing peacekeeping at the bottom of Canada's defence priorities, Trudeau continued sending Canadians overseas to wear the blue helmet. When Egypt and Syria attacked Israel in early October 1973 — UNEF had been humiliatingly expelled by Egypt in 1967 — tension once again threatened to boil over into a Cold War collision of superpowers. The United Nations was quick to intervene to impose a ceasefire between the warring nations. Just over 1,000 Canadians made up the largest contribution to UNEF II, which arrived in Egypt in late October 1973. In June 1974, Austrian, Peruvian, Polish, and Canadian (albeit small) contingents arrived in Syria as part of the United Nations Disengagement Observer Force to maintain the ceasefire between Syria and Israel. Two hundred and fifty CAF personnel were also dispatched to Vietnam as part of the International Commission of Control and Supervision. Canada played a role in this peace observation mission from January to July 1973 during which one Canadian died in a helicopter crash (likely shot down) and two others were held captive for 17 days by the Vietcong. As well, when fighting again erupted in Cyprus in July 1974, it was Pierre Trudeau who sent in reinforcements to bolster the Canadian presence. Trudeau was thus a bit of a paradox when it came to the military. He was not interested in the CAF or generally in defence issues affecting it, but he was certainly willing to use it nearly as much as his predecessors.

It is worth pointing out that by the 1970s there were some critics of Canada's continued role in U.N. peacekeeping operations. The decade-long stalemate on Cyprus and the ignominious departure of U.N. forces from UNEF I highlighted some of the limits of peacekeeping, yet these critics were few, and peacekeeping continued to resonate with many Canadians who saw internationalism as a core Canadian value.

Trudeau oversaw some serious cultural changes within the military itself. The first was a major push to increase francophone representation within the CAF. This was part of a broader process by which both Pearson and Trudeau sought to increase francophone representation throughout Canadian society. Pearson commissioned the 1963 Royal Commission on Bilingualism and Biculturalism, the famous B and B Commission, and Trudeau's government passed the 1969 Official Languages Act, making French and English both the official languages of Canada. Trudeau was particularly concerned with the rising tide of Quebec separatism that seemed to be growing exponentially during the 1960s. Increasing French-language representation in government and within the military were weapons helping to prevent growing support for that movement.

While there had always been some francophone presence in the military (French regiments such as the Van Doos or the Collège militaire royal in Saint-Jean), the CAF was a predominantly anglophone organization. There were far fewer French-speaking recruits, French-speaking soldiers stayed in the military for much shorter periods, and it was more difficult for unilingual French speakers to be promoted, especially to senior ranks. The push for bilingualism in the military was championed by Chief of the Defence Staff Jean Victor Allard and Léo Cadieux, Canada's first French-speaking defence minister, who had successfully lobbied for the creation of several French-language units in the last year of Pearson's government. Under Trudeau, a 28 percent quota was set for francophones in the military, and by 1983, that was nearly achieved. However, it was not without controversy. Many anglophones were left embittered during this period because they saw French speakers get promoted faster and more often. By 1997, senior officers were required to be functional in both languages to gain promotion. The implementation of bilingualism in the military certainly had its hiccups, but it worked.

The other major cultural change within the CAF was the process of "civilianization." In 1972, a new National Defence Headquarters integrated the headquarters of the CAF with the Department of National Defence, creating an organization in which military and civilian personnel worked alongside one another to both advise on defence matters while running the armed forces. While this move was intended to create a more efficient and streamlined system of military management, it also served to erode military morale.[12] The military was starting to be organized and run like any other bureaucratic department within the Canadian government. Civilian bureaucrats and military managers began to outrank command officers, while civilian business models were imposed upon military decision-making. There was growing concern among Canada's military leadership that civilianization was, in fact, destroying the military ethos of the CAF and replacing it with a civilian business/management culture. As the 20th century rolled on, CAF personnel, officers in particular, were expected to behave more like managers of a corporate team than as leaders on a battlefield.

Trudeau's first two administrations let the military erode. However, shortly after winning the 1974 election, in his third administration, he approved a series of defence budget increases. The problem was that serious inflation meant that even with these budgetary increases the purchasing power of the military declined. Yet global events would make defence spending a greater priority than it had ever been under Trudeau.

In 1979, the Soviets invaded Afghanistan, triggering an intensification of the Cold War. The next year, the United States elected ardent Cold War warrior Ronald Reagan as president. Reagan reignited the arms race, and suddenly pressure was put on America's NATO allies to pull their own weight. Trudeau's relationship with Reagan was difficult, made more so by the Canadian prime minister's world-tour peace initiative. After his stop in Washington, D.C., one senior member of Reagan's team even called Trudeau a "leftist high on pot."[13] Reluctantly, however, Trudeau agreed to a U.S. request to conduct cruise missile testing on Canadian territory.

The CAF benefited from this growing global tension with a wide range of purchases, though much of the equipment would not be ready until the mid to late 1980s. Nonetheless, 128 German-made Leopard tanks were bought for the NATO combat group, and a much-overdue commitment to the construction of new frigates and planes for the navy was made. The largest contract, however, went to the purchase of 137 new fighter jets — the CF-18 Hornet — for Air Defence Command.

Brian Mulroney, the Military, and Peacekeeping

The Progressive Conservatives led by Brian Mulroney promised to do even better both with Canada's relationship with Washington and when it came to Canada's military. Yet when they won the 1984 election, they failed to follow through on almost all of their promises. A significant federal deficit left by the Liberals meant Mulroney focused his administration on balancing the budget, and any increases to defence spending were minimal. However, in June 1987, Mulroney's new defence minister, Perrin Beatty, issued a White Paper on Canadian defence. It admitted that the CAF's equipment was either already obsolete or at risk of becoming so and that Canada's military needed an increase in resources combined with a decrease in commitments. This proved too good to be true. As Canadian military leaders were extolling the promises of Beatty's White Paper, the Soviet Union began to liberalize and then, almost unbelievably so, collapse. In November 1989, the Berlin Wall fell, the next year the two Germanys were reunited, and the year after that the Warsaw Pact was dissolved. By the end of 1991, the Soviet Union officially ceased to exist.

Now that the Cold War was over, the Soviet bogeyman was gone, and the 1990s, many optimistically believed, would usher in an unprecedented age of peace and global co-operation. This came on the heels of the 1988 Nobel Peace Prize awarded to the United Nations for its decades of peacekeeping. Many Canadians took pride in this since Canada had contributed roughly 10 percent of all peacekeeping forces beginning in 1948. Peacekeeping had become enshrined as a mythic building block of the nation. Now, many naively thought, peacekeeping could be used to shape a world order without fear of a superpower conflict. Yet for the Canadian military, the 1990s would be one of its most challenging decades since the end of the Korean War.

Canadians at the beginning of the 1990s had some very real domestic concerns. The Quebec separatist movement seemed to be heading full steam toward the completion of its goal, while Canada was entering its worst recession since the Great Depression. Even though much of the old Soviet Bloc was collapsing into chaos, it was difficult to convince Canadians that they should be invested in European stability when major problems existed at home. As well, with a massive deficit and no looming prospects of a Third World War, it was difficult to justify the $12 billion per year spent on Canada's 83,000 men and women in the CAF. This meant that despite supporters of defence spending within Brian Mulroney's administration, cuts were coming. The regular force was reduced to 76,000 and Canada's NATO commitment in Europe was officially wrapped up in July 1993. It wasn't all bad news, though. With money saved on salaries, the Department of National Defence could afford some new equipment: a small number of new corvettes, 228 armoured vehicles, communications hardware, and new helicopters, including 50 brand-new top-of-the-line EH-101 anti-submarine helicopters.

The Canadian military was kept as busy as ever. In March 1990, armed Kanien'keha:ka (Mohawk) from Kanehsatà:ke, 30 miles west of Montreal, erected barricades to protest the municipality of Oka's decision to approve a golf course expansion on unceded, ancestral land. In July, Quebec police attacked the barricades and shooting erupted, leaving one officer dead and the barricades remaining in place. In early August, the army was called in to do what the police could not. With the media spotlight on the standoff, Canadian soldiers surrounded the Kanien'keha:ka. Without further escalation, the Kanien'keha:ka decided to end the standoff after 78 days. In a final skirmish, as the Kanien'keha:ka walked out from behind the barricades, a young woman was bayoneted in the stomach by a soldier.

While many among the non-Indigenous Canadian public celebrated the army's role in ending the standoff, others were critical of the use of the police and the army in a local land dispute. The so-called "Oka Crisis," today referred to as the Kanehsatà:ke Resistance, brought to the surface pressing issues regarding the frustration and anger of many Indigenous peoples. As well, the image of the Canadian military being used to put down an Indigenous resistance over land reflected a long, violent history of struggle by Indigenous peoples over rights and claims to their historical territories.

In August 1990, not long after Canadian soldiers were deployed to Kanehsatà:ke, Iraq invaded the small, oil-rich country of Kuwait. In response to this aggression, President George H.W. Bush put together a coalition to liberate Kuwait, and Canada answered the call, despite vocal criticism from Jean Chrétien, the Liberal Opposition Leader. Canada thus entered its first war since Korea, but its contribution was small. The country's main effort was three ships and a CF-18 Hornet fighter squadron. By September, HMCS *Protecteur*, *Athabaskan*, and *Terra Nova* arrived in the Persian Gulf. The two destroyers, *Athabaskan* and *Terra Nova*, helped enforce the coalition

An M113 armoured personnel carrier in Oka, Quebec, during the Kanehsatà:ke Resistance, August 20, 1990.

blockade, while *Protecteur*, a supply vessel, assisted in refuelling the coalition fleet at sea and also conducted interdiction operations in support of the blockade. Canadian pilots conducted dozens of bombing runs against enemy targets. Military operations to liberate Kuwait began in earnest in mid-January 1991, and by the end of February, Iraqi forces had completely collapsed. Fifty-one hundred CAF personnel served in the Persian Gulf. Canada's army played no part in the actual ground war, and while training, logistics, reinforcements, and travel time all contributed to this, historian Jack Granatstein caustically writes: "Realistically, after years of cutbacks, the army could do little — and even that, not very well."[14]

More dramatic cuts came when the Progressive Conservatives were crushed in the 1993 federal election by Jean Chrétien and the Liberals. The regular force was further reduced, the EH-101 helicopter contracts were cancelled, bases throughout the country were abandoned, and Royal Roads Military College on Vancouver Island, the Collège militaire royal in Saint-Jean, and the National Defence College in Kingston were closed. Between 1993 and 1998, the defence budget was slashed by 23 percent. By the time Chrétien won his third election in 2000, the size of the regular force was down to 61,000 men and women.

The transition from Progressive Conservatives to Liberals may have resulted in cutbacks, but it meant little for the tempo of peacekeeping operations. Canadians continued to patrol the Israeli-Egyptian border, were part of the 1988 U.N. Iran-Iraq Military Observer Group, participated in anti-mine operations in Afghanistan, played a role in the U.N. mission in Nicaragua, and 300 soldiers were part of the U.N. Iraq-Kuwait Observer Mission. In fact, for an army that was continually reduced in size, its commitments were nearly untenable.

If there was one thing the governments of Brian Mulroney and Jean Chrétien had in common, it was that neither seemed willing to say no to the United Nations. Canadian soldiers were part of missions to Angola, Western Sahara, Cambodia, El Salvador, East Timor, Namibia, Haiti, Sierra Leone, the Central African Republic, Rwanda, Somalia, and the former Yugoslavia. By this time, peacekeeping images had been deployed on monuments, currency, stamps, and books. Songs had been written about Canadian peacekeepers, while *Heritage Minutes* and beer commercials celebrated them. Yet what made the operations of the 1990s different from previous decades was that these were not the interpositionary peacekeeping missions that had so resonated with the Canadian public in the past. In fact, the image of blue-helmeted Canadian soldiers placing themselves between two warring sides may have been what the Canadian public thought Canadian soldiers were still doing, but in many ways this had become anachronistic. Canadian soldiers were conducting armed interventions into conflict zones fully prepared to utilize force if attacked. This was the case in the former Yugoslavia.

Former Yugoslavia

When President Josip Broz Tito died in 1980, Yugoslavia began to slowly fall apart until by 1991 the country had splintered into violently competing nationalist groups conducting ethnic cleansing, murder, and rape against one another. In 1992, Canadian soldiers went in as part of a U.N. Protection Force to attempt to enforce a ceasefire. When Sarajevo in Bosnia-Herzegovina came under attack by Serbian forces, Canadian soldiers moved to protect the airport and humanitarian convoys coming into the besieged city. They watched helplessly as Serbian artillery and sniper fire killed Sarajevo citizens indiscriminately.

It was during this time that Canadian soldiers found themselves in Canada's largest battle since the Korean War, this time against Croatian forces. In September 1993, the 2nd Princess Patricia's Canadian Light Infantry (2 PPCLI), which contained nearly 40 percent reservists, was in the Medak region of Croatia, struggling to keep apart Croatian and Serbian forces. Supported by a small number of soldiers from the French Army, the battle group moved into a no man's land between the two sides to enforce a recently agreed upon ceasefire. On September 15, the battle group suddenly came under attack from Croatian forces and for 15 hours a vicious firefight ensued. When it ended, the Canadians had suffered no casualties, while Croatian casualties were estimated at 27. Despite the Canadians getting the better of their Croatian attackers, the Croatians still refused to withdraw while they conducted a brutal campaign of ethnic cleansing against Serbian villages. In a moment of genius, 2 PPCLI's commanding officer, Lieutenant-Colonel Jim Calvin, held a press conference at a Croatian-manned barricade, bringing to light Croatian activities. With the world watching, Croatian forces finally withdrew. When the Canadians moved into the area, all they found were empty villages, scorched homes, and bodies. To this day, the Croatians deny the Battle of the Medak Pocket ever took place.

The chaos in Yugoslavia only seemed to intensify. Serbian forces continued shelling Sarajevo and began to advance and occupy parts of eastern Bosnia and Herzegovina. In response to this Serbian aggression, NATO stepped in and started conducting air strikes against Serbian forces. Then, in late 1995, NATO increased its ground presence in the region and Canada contributed just over 1,000 soldiers to the NATO Implementation Force. At the same time, the Canadian navy contributed ships to a NATO blockade and Canadian pilots helped enforce a no-fly zone over the region. It seemed as if the commitment to the former Yugoslavia was draining more and more of Canada's resources. In 1999, when the Albanian majority region of Kosovo sought to split from Serbia, war erupted once again and NATO intervened on behalf of the Kosovars. Canadian pilots returned to the skies over the former Yugoslavia, this time conducting bombing runs against Serbian forces (during which Canadian pilots carried out 10 percent of

NATO's strike missions) while a Canadian ground force, 1,300 strong, took part in a NATO-led mission to enforce a ceasefire.

Somalia

While Canadians faced challenges within the collapsing Yugoslavia, events in Africa damaged the reputation of the Canadian military. In December 1992, a Canadian contingent was sent to Somalia as part of a U.S.-led Unified Task Force, an armed humanitarian intervention to impose peace as famine spread across the state torn apart by warring factions.[15] The contingent consisted of an armoured squadron — the Royal Canadian Dragoons — and the Canadian Airborne Regiment (CAR).

The CAR was a problem regiment by the time it arrived in Somalia. What began in 1968 as an elite formation had by the early 1990s become a dumping ground for troublesome soldiers.[16] Regardless, for the first couple of months, the CAR carried out its job effectively. Living in dusty, fly-infested conditions, subsisting on ration packs and bottled water, the men patrolled constantly and brought a semblance of stability to the area, forcing local gangs

A member of the Canadian Airborne Regiment behind a group of bound and blindfolded Somali civilians, date unknown.

to retreat into the countryside. However, the regiment dealt with increasing hostility from local inhabitants, sporadic firefights, and rising cases of theft of its supplies. On March 16, 1993, soldiers from 2 Commando CAR caught 16-year-old Shidane Arone sneaking into the base. Arone was bound, detained, tortured, and ultimately murdered.

This was just the beginning. Over the next several years, a series of hazing videos were leaked to the media showing drunk CAR soldiers, some with swastikas tattooed on their bodies, uttering racist remarks and conducting disturbing hazing rituals on new recruits. The murder of Arone, coupled with these videos, shattered the Canadian public's image of Canadian soldiers as the pre-eminent peacekeepers. In March 1995, almost exactly two years after the murder of Arone, the CAR was disbanded. The 1997 findings of an inquiry commission was further damning for the Canadian Armed Forces, exposing a litany of offences committed in Somalia and highlighting serious failures in leadership by several senior Canadian officers.

Rwanda

After years of friction between the feuding majority Hutu and minority Tutsi people in the former Belgian colony of Rwanda, a full-scale civil war broke out in the country in 1990. A Uganda-backed rebel group, mostly Tutsi with some moderate Hutu, was fighting the Hutu-dominated Rwandan government. In February 1993, Rwanda and Uganda asked the United Nations to set up the U.N. Observer Mission Uganda-Rwanda to monitor the border between the two countries, which it did in July 1993, appointing Roméo Dallaire, a Canadian general, as chief military observer. A few months later, in October, the United Nations replaced the observation mission with the U.N. Assistance Mission for Rwanda, with Dallaire in command of an eventual 2,548-strong contingent.

The U.N. Assistance Mission for Rwanda was intended to enforce the recently agreed upon peace accords and help bring order to the country, which was facing a steadily increasing refugee problem, widespread famine, and a worsening civil war. Despite the arrival of U.N. forces, violence continued to escalate, and in January 1994, Dallaire sent word to Canada's Major-General Maurice Baril, military adviser to the U.N. secretary-general, that he had intelligence indicating that government-trained civilian militias were carrying out the registration of Tutsi minorities and were, in fact, planning an all-out attack against the Tutsi civilian population. Dallaire informed Baril of his intention to use the U.N. mission's forces to pre-empt such attacks but was denied permission to do so.

On April 6, 1994, a plane carrying Juvénal Habyarimana, Rwanda's president and a Hutu, was shot down. Believing this to be the work of the Tutsi rebels, Hutu militias began to brutally attack and murder Tutsi and some moderate Hutu civilians. The genocide had begun. Despite Dallaire's pleas to authorize U.N. intervention, the United Nations denied him permission. At the time, there was little international political will to support armed intervention, including none by the Canadian government. Incredibly, the United Nations even authorized a reduction in strength for the U.N. Assistance Mission for Rwanda, and by end of April, Dallaire's contingent was down to 270 troops.

As U.N. soldiers withdrew from their operating bases, Hutu militias moved in to slaughter the Tutsi and moderate Hutu who had been relying on them for protection. Dallaire and his soldiers did what they could to save them, but his paltry force could do little to stop the tide of wanton mass murder. The United Nations finally intervened with the authorization of a second U.N. Assistance Mission for Rwanda, which began arriving in July 1994, including 350 Canadians, at which point the massacres had largely stopped due to the rebels' seizure of Kigali, the Rwandan capital. It's been estimated that by then 800,000 Rwandans had died, most of them Tutsi.

Haiti

Much as in Rwanda, a complicated political situation faced Canadians in 1995 when they took part in peacekeeping operations in Haiti. In 1991, the democratically elected president, Jean-Bertrand Aristide, was overthrown in a military coup. Amid growing human-rights abuses under the new military junta, as well as international demands for Aristide's return to power, the United Nations authorized the U.N. Mission in Haiti in September 1993. Yet instability within the country and the obstinance of the military junta prevented this mission from implementing its mandate from the beginning.

In October, ratcheting up its pressure on the Haitian military regime, the United Nations authorized the reimposition of an oil-and-arms embargo on Haiti that was first applied in June 1993. The CAF's Maritime Command participated in this operation, carrying out nearly 1,400 armed boardings and diverting 119 ships from delivering goods to Haiti.

In July 1994, with reports coming back to the United Nations indicating an alarming increase in violence and human-rights infractions within Haiti, the U.N. Security Council passed Resolution 940, authorizing a Multinational Force to enter the country and restore Aristide to power (Operation Uphold Democracy), which it did unopposed in September 1994. The military government was overthrown, Aristide was restored to the presidency, and the U.N. Mission in Haiti finally commenced its work.

Canada's initial contribution was 500 CAF personnel, though that was later expanded to 750 in March 1996 as part of the evolving U.N. Support Mission, with Canada continuing to play a role in what evolved into the U.N. Transition Mission in Haiti. By this point, Canada had both military and police personnel working in the country. In 1997, the United Nations deemed Haiti stabilized and most of the U.N. force was withdrawn.

However, in February 2004, Aristide suspiciously stepped down as Haiti's leader and the new interim president, Boniface Alexandre, requested U.N. help in the face of domestic instability. A U.N.-authorized, U.S.-led multinational force, including Canadian personnel, arrived in the region in late February as part of Operation Secure Tomorrow. In June, this force passed peacekeeping responsibility over to the U.N. Stabilisation Mission in Haiti, to which Canada contributed 500 military personnel as well as 100 police officers to assist with the delivery of humanitarian aid and the continuing development of the Haitian National Police.

In 2010, when a devastating earthquake struck Haiti, the CAF sent a joint task force made up of air, land, and naval components to support the country. Canadian peacekeepers remained in the region, primarily police personnel, and in September 2023, there were still two Canadian police officers serving in Haiti.

Requiem for Canadian Peacekeeping

By the mid-1990s, Canadian participation in U.N. peacekeeping missions reached an all-time high with 3,336 personnel deployed, ranking Canada as the third-largest contributor to world peacekeeping operations. Yet the remainder of the decade saw a reduction in commitments. The combination of defence cuts, the aftermath of the murder of Shidane Arone in Somalia, the public response to the horrific violence in Rwanda, and a shift toward greater Canadian participation in NATO all contributed to this decline. Under Jean Chrétien's Liberal government, Canada's involvement in U.N. peacekeeping was reduced to less than 300 active peacekeepers, a trend that continued into the 21st century under Chrétien's successor, Paul Martin, who by the time he left office in February 2006 saw Canada ranked 33rd in the list of contributing nations. The final nails in the coffin for Canadian peacekeeping were hammered home under the Conservative government of Stephen Harper; by the end of his first year in government, Canada ranked 49th.

The end of the 20th century did not just see a decline in Canadian participation in U.N. peacekeeping missions but also a troubling deterioration in morale among the CAF.[17] A series of scandals came to light, including the expropriation of funds, further evidence of hazing rituals, and gender-based abuse, all of which contributed to a very difficult decade for the CAF. The bottom line was that successive Canadian governments continued to commit the military to missions while repeatedly slashing budgets. The CAF was asked to punch way above its weight time and time again. Despite most CAF personnel performing their duties admirably, it was no surprise that a breaking point came, and the 1990s seemed to be just that. However, it was not that there were no success stories. While the former Yugoslavia was chaotic in the long term, the Balkans were stabilized. As well, the CAF acted admirably supporting civilian populations at home during massive flooding in Quebec and Manitoba and the terrible ice storm of 1998.

Under General Maurice Baril, who became Chief of the Defence Staff in 1997, small steps were made toward recuperation. Although he was unable to get any dramatic budget increases, Baril secured pay raises for the troops; implemented new officer education programs; improved CAF medical care, particularly for soldiers suffering from post-traumatic stress disorder (PTSD); and made new equipment purchases, including up-gunned Leopard tanks.

Perhaps more important than new equipment, Baril was able to convince the government to limit its commitment to U.N. missions. This was important, since Canada's defence spending, as a percentage of overall government expenditures, was the lowest among NATO nations besides Luxembourg.

The end of the 20th century brought down the last vestiges of the peacekeeping myth. Canadians had eagerly embraced the image of blue-helmeted Canadian soldiers breaking up fights, and over the course of the last half of the 20th century, this myth had become part of the vast, complicated mosaic that made up the building blocks of Canadian identity. It was felt that peacekeeping was uniquely Canadian and that somehow Canadians were naturals at it. Some of this had to do with our constant goal of defining ourselves in opposition to Americans. Americans went to war, Canadians enforced peace, or so many believed. But the peacekeeping myth was just that — a myth.

Peacekeeping was far more multifarious and nuanced than the altruistic and humanitarian rhetoric surrounding it. It was for most of the Cold War a very real extension of Cold War policy designed to prevent the spread of Communism and maintain NATO cohesion.[18] As well, the celebrated idea that it was "not war" flew in the face of the 130 Canadian peacekeepers who died while serving. The Congo, Cyprus, Croatia, and Somalia missions sharply contrasted with the public's perception of peacekeeping. The results of these interventions were mixed. In some cases, such as Yugoslavia, the U.N. and NATO missions were ultimately successful; in others, such as the Congo and Rwanda, they were not; and in places, such as Cyprus, the mission continues. The peacekeeping myth was perpetuated by successive governments from all political spectrums, maintained by the media and even in our education systems, and thus accepted all too eagerly by the Canadian public. The 1990s damaged the foundations of that myth and then it officially collapsed after September 11, 2001.

The Push for Further Diversification in Canada's Military

During the later stages of Canada's involvement in peacekeeping, a major cultural change occurred within the CAF with the full integration of women into the armed forces. Despite the important contributions of women in the armed services in the Second World War, by 1945, the Canadian government and public were already transitioning back into a pre-war state of mind when it came to gender in Canadian society, and that meant mass demobilization of women. When the Korean War broke out, nursing sisters were once again recruited, as were smaller numbers of women in more traditionally accepted military occupations. The emerging Cold War meant a larger peacetime force, and by 1955, there were 5,000 women serving in the CAF. Ten years later, this number was inexplicably reduced as a cap was placed on enlistment at 1,500 personnel, 1.5 percent of the total CAF.

It was not until 1970 that things began to permanently change. That year a published report from the Royal Commission on the Status of Women made a number of recommendations, including the removal of any recruitment caps. A wider range of military occupations became available, though by 1971 women made up only 1.8 percent of the personnel in the CAF. Two years later, the CAF set a goal of 8,000 women by 1983. To do this effectively, more and more opportunities had to be made available. By 1975, women made up 3.6 percent of the regular force and 13.4 percent of the reserves, and some even went on to serve in the Canadian peacekeeping contribution to UNEF II.

While more opportunities were being opened up, there was still resistance within the CAF to women entering combat roles, serving in remote locations, or performing at sea. Many within the military strongly believed that women in combat would increase the risk to Canadian soldiers. At the same time, the hyper-masculine culture of the Canadian military — some might even say a toxic masculine culture — meant that many women challenging gender norms within the organization faced discrimination, harassment, and even violence.[19]

The 1978 Canadian Human Rights Act, the 1982 Charter of Rights and Freedoms, and the 1985 *Equality for All* report (published by the Parliamentary Committee on Equality Rights) increased pressure on the military to integrate women further into the armed services, but the military continued to drag its feet. This was highlighted by two administrative orders issued in 1986 by the Chief of the Defence Staff: Canadian Forces Administrative Order (CFAO) 49-14 and CFAO 49-15. The former opened all trades to women *as long as* it ensured operational effectiveness. The latter stated that some trades would remain all male while others would maintain a minimum male requirement. That same year also saw the release of the findings from the Service Women in Non-Traditional Environments and Roles (SWINTER) trials. These SWINTER trials included a wide range of interviews, assessments, and studies for air, sea, and land components, evaluating more thoroughly whether the integration of women into certain roles would hurt operational effectiveness. The findings of these trials concluded that women were, indeed, capable of serving in all roles and implied that they should be given the opportunities to do so. However, the survey and interview data from these same trials also found that there was serious resistance to gender integration from male service personnel. Further to that, the CAF rejected the findings as inconclusive regarding the effectiveness of women in combat.[20]

By 1989, women represented just under 10 percent of all CAF personnel, yet things were about to change dramatically. That year the last of 14 hearings wrapped up in the milestone case of *Brown v. the Canadian Armed Forces*, a merger of five complaints made against the CAF to the Canadian Human Rights Tribunal. In its findings, the tribunal ordered the CAF to fully integrate women by 1999. Adhering to these findings, the CAF officially removed all barriers for women, except on submarines, which were opened to women in 2001. Yet women continued coming up against informal barriers to their full integration, highlighted by a series of *Maclean's* articles in 1998 identifying a culture of harassment within the CAF and accusing senior officers of ignoring or covering up a number of sexual assaults on female personnel.[21]

The LGBTQ2S+ community also struggled to gain acceptance within the CAF. The period from the 1940s to the 1990s has often been referred to as the LGBT purge.[22] For much of this period, gays and lesbians in the government and the military were deemed security threats, and a purge of confirmed and suspected homosexuals occurred within both the Department of National Defence and the CAF. Even after the 1969 decriminalization of homosexuality, the military continued to conduct investigations into the sexuality of its members — until 1973, homosexuality was still classified as a mental disorder. These investigations were carried out by Special Investigation Units under the auspices of Regulation CFAO 19-20, which banned homosexuals from serving.

As more women entered the military in the 1970s and 1980s, greater emphasis was placed on identifying and expelling lesbian servicewomen in what became known as the "Witch Hunts."[23] By the end of that decade, however, while gays and lesbians were still barred from serving in the military, the CAF announced it would no longer conduct investigations into the sexuality of its members. In 1990, former CAF member Michelle Douglas, who once served in a Special Investigation Unit, filed a discrimination suit against the CAF for being wrongly dismissed because she was a lesbian. Two years later, this resulted in the CAF removing all restrictions on LGBT recruitment though the military.

Yet the deeply embedded warrior ethos, rooted in heteronormative masculinity, continued to impose a barrier in creating a diverse and inclusive environment for members of the LGBTQ2S+ community. Change imposed upon any institution with deeply entrenched cultural and social norms inevitably results in pushback, and harassment and sexual misconduct

Colonel Bertrand, commander of the 2nd Division Headquarters, raises the LGBTQ+ pride flag at Canadian Forces Base Montreal, May 17, 2023.

remained a continuing problem within the military while diversity and inclusivity persisted as an ongoing challenge. Despite very real issues, by the time Canada went to war in Afghanistan in 2001, its military was the most diverse it had ever been.

10

A TUMULTUOUS 21ST CENTURY: FROM PEACEKEEPERS TO PEACE ENFORCERS

Afghanistan

Afghanistan has had a long history of resistance to outsiders. Alexander the Great invaded through the Khyber Pass in 330 BCE, leaving behind several cities named after him, including Kandahar. Genghis Khan and his Mongol forces ravaged Afghanistan in 1219, and his successor, Ögedei, secured large tracts of it for the Mongol Empire. In the 19th century, the British fought two wars in Afghanistan to ensure the region's position within its sphere of influence. In 1919, the British became embroiled in a third war in Afghanistan, and the peace settlement ultimately led to the nation becoming fully independent.

The largest of the 21 ethnic groups in Afghanistan, primarily speaking four languages, are the Pashtuns, making up about 40 percent of the total population. Yet the Pashtuns, like the other ethnic groups, are further divided into clans, many of them hostile to one another and with a long chronicle of blood feuds.

In the late 1970s, Afghanistan's central government collapsed. This precipitated a violent Soviet invasion that lasted 10 years. After the Soviet withdrawal in 1989, violence continued as warlords, clan leaders, and ethnic groups vied for control. During this chaotic period, a Pakistani-backed religious militia known as the Taliban came to prominence, calling for Afghanistan to be governed under strict Islamic law. By the late 1990s, the Taliban had gained significant support, and by the end of the century, had secured control of nearly all the country except for a small portion in the north.

One of the Taliban's supporters and allies was wealthy Saudi Osama bin Laden, who had financially supported the Taliban during their rise to power. When the Taliban won control of Afghanistan, it became a haven for Bin Laden and Al-Qaeda, his terrorist organization. Al-Qaeda sought to establish a global caliphate and carry out a holy war against the enemies of Islam. It was particularly focused on the West, specifically the United States, which after 1990 had troops stationed in Saudi Arabia, a decided affront to Bin Laden.

It took American authorities 24 hours to identify that Bin Laden and Al-Qaeda were behind the terrorist attacks of September 11, 2001, and were operating out of Afghanistan. With the backing of the United Nations and NATO, the latter invoking Article 5 for the first time in the organization's existence — that an attack against one of its members was an attack against all — the United States demanded the Taliban hand over Bin Laden and disband Al-Qaeda's training camps. When the Taliban's leader, Mullah Omar, refused, a joint American-British offensive was launched. In co-operation with an alliance of northern Afghan tribes, the last holdouts to the Taliban regime, an offensive smashed both the Taliban and Al-Qaeda. By November 2001, the capital of Kabul fell, and by December, any serious resistance was scattered into the more remote regions of the country while the leadership fled over the mountainous border into Pakistan.

In Canada, the 9/11 attacks resulted in an almost complete shutdown of the U.S.-Canada border. Suddenly, Canada's economic vulnerability, via its heavy reliance on trade with the United States, was exposed. The economic consequences of the border shutdown made 9/11 and any future terrorist attacks a very real threat to Canada's economic and national security. North–south trade had to remain open. At the same time, the government of Prime Minister Jean Chrétien felt that it needed to show the Americans that Canada was a committed partner in the global fight against terrorism. With Article 5 lending legitimacy to military participation, on October 7, Chrétien announced that Canada would deploy its military in support of the American-led coalition into Afghanistan.

The first appearance of the Canadian Armed Forces (CAF) was HMCS *Halifax*, which deployed in early November. Further naval assets were sent to the Arabian Sea, the Persian Gulf, and the Indian Ocean, conducting boarding and inspection missions while also providing logistics support for the coalition. At peak operation, the Canadian naval contribution included 1,500 personnel and six warships, and by the end of the war, 18 of Canada's 20 surface vessels and 4,000 sailors were deployed to the region.

Canadian pilots and ground crew were also involved, with Canadian planes transporting supplies, conducting maritime surveillance, shuttling troops, and evacuating casualties. In December 2008, the air contribution solidified into Joint Task Force Afghanistan Air Wing based out of Kandahar Airfield.

Canada's largest contribution to Afghanistan was on the ground, which began with Operation Apollo, the name given to Canada's military contribution to Operation Enduring Freedom, the U.S. global war on terror. In

Halifax-class frigate HMCS *Halifax* en route to Haiti, January 2010.

Afghanistan, this meant helping the United States eliminate the last of Al-Qaeda's holdouts in the country's southern provinces. In December 2001, Canada's special operations force, Joint Task Force 2 (JTF-2), arrived. Largely unknown at the time, Canada's elite force quickly proved its status working alongside the American special operations force hunting Taliban and Al-Qaeda members. Together, they successfully conducted several reconnaissance, snatch-and-grab, and direct-action missions.

In January 2002, a battle group comprising the 3rd Battalion Princess Patricia's Canadian Light Infantry (3 PPCLI BG), which included an armoured vehicle reconnaissance squadron from Lord Strathcona's Horse and combat service support elements, arrived in Afghanistan as part of Operation Apollo. Delivered on American planes, 3 PPCLI BG immediately set to work taking part in a number of difficult missions.

The Canadian battle group worked closely with its American counterparts during this period, often carrying out missions alongside each other. The 3 PPCLI BG conducted operations in the Tora Bora cave complex in eastern Nangarhar Province, as well as in Kandahar and Zabul Provinces. Although the Canadians suffered personnel shortages and equipment deficiencies, the

Flight Engineer Corporal Steve J. Laing mans a Dillon 7.62 mm M134 minigun mounted on the side of a CH-146 Griffon helicopter, 2009.

American military developed an immense respect for the fighting power of the Canadians.[1] Tragically, in April 2002, Canada suffered its first casualties when an American plane mistakenly dropped a bomb on Canadian soldiers conducting a live-fire training exercise near Kandahar Airfield, killing four and wounding eight others. A small number of Canadian aircraft and ships also participated in Operation Apollo, transporting soldiers, providing logistics, conducting reconnaissance, and helping to prevent the escape of any Al-Qaeda or Taliban fighters from the region.

When Apollo wrapped up in October 2003, the second phase of Canada's ground war began with Operation Athena Phase 1, which was the Canadian contribution to the International Security Assistance Force (ISAF) in Kabul. ISAF had been established by the U.N. Security Council in 2001 and had been operating in and around Kabul since December of that year. By 2003, ISAF was NATO-led and sought to support the interim Afghan government by providing security and stability to the city and its outlying regions while also training the Afghan National Security Forces, all of which spoke to the complexities of the mission in Afghanistan. It was not going to be enough to simply defeat the enemy on the battlefield. State-building objectives had to be achieved to ensure that Afghanistan, broken after decades of war, could be rebuilt.

The summer of 2003 saw the 3rd Battalion Royal Canadian Regiment, an infantry battle group, arrive in Kabul. In August, just as it began active operations, Major-General Andrew Leslie from Ottawa, whose paternal grandfather was General Andrew McNaughton, was appointed deputy commander of ISAF. The following year, a Canadian became leader of ISAF: Rick Hillier, future Chief of the Defence Staff and at the time a lieutenant-general, was appointed commander for a six-month rotation starting in February 2004. At that point, ISAF included 6,500 soldiers from 35 different countries.

The first phase of Athena lasted until late 2005, and during that time, Canadian soldiers operating out of Camp Julien conducted constant foot patrols throughout Kabul as well as reconnaissance and surveillance missions in outlying areas. They disrupted potential attacks, took part in raids, and uncovered numerous illegal weapons caches. Two months after 3rd Battalion Royal Canadian Regiment went operational, Sergeant Robert Alan Short and Corporal Robbie Christopher Beerenfenger were killed when their vehicle hit a roadside bomb. Early the next year, Corporal Jamie Murphy was killed

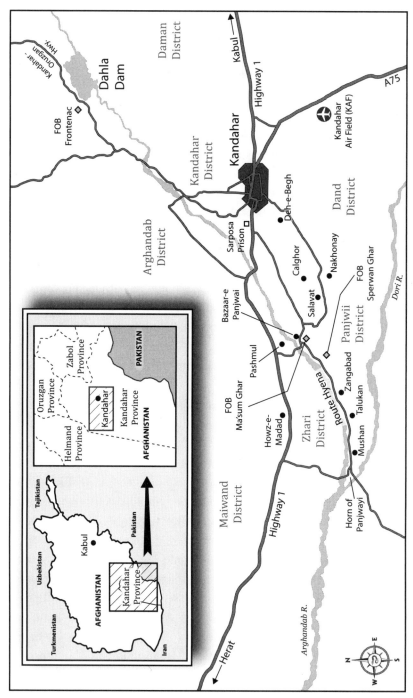

Map of Kandahar Province in Afghanistan.

by a suicide bomber who also wounded three other Canadians. Despite the ever-present threat of danger, ISAF was effective in bringing security and stability to the region. This was highlighted by the October 2003 visit of Prime Minister Chrétien three months after Canada officially opened its embassy in Kabul. Chrétien's visit included a meeting with Hamid Karzai, Afghanistan interim president, and marked the first time in history a Canadian prime minister had visited Kabul. The most significant achievement during this period, however, was the successful holding of Afghanistan's first-ever democratic election in October 2004, an event that could not have been held had security not been brought to the region.

When Chrétien's successor, Paul Martin, won the June 2004 election, he faced pressure to increase Canada's role in Afghanistan. Of particular concern were the frayed relations between Ottawa and Washington over the former's refusal to commit Canada to the American ballistic missile defence program.[2] Thus, to raise Canada's standing with the Americans while also helping to meet stated security objectives of the Afghanistan government, the Canadian role in Afghanistan was expanded dramatically. This came in the form of a Strategic Advisory Team to Kabul, which arrived in mid-2005. As part of Canada's "whole-of-government" approach, this was a multi-agency team made up of military personnel and civilians sent to support and advise the government of Afghanistan in accordance with the Afghanistan National Development Strategy.[3]

The expansion of Canada's role also meant taking over one of the most dangerous provinces in the country. By 2005, ISAF began extending its operational jurisdiction over most of Afghanistan, and Canadian soldiers were redeployed to the extremely volatile Kandahar Province. The redeployment to that province, known as Operation Athena Phase II, marked the third and most deadly phase of Canada's ground war in Afghanistan.

This phase began in earnest in March 2006 when Task Force Orion went into action — a battle group comprised of 1,900 soldiers and consisting of headquarters, infantry drawn from the 1st Princess Patricia's Canadian Light Infantry (1 PPCLI), artillery (to be used in battle for the first time since the Korean War), combat engineers, and armoured reconnaissance vehicles. A powerful, versatile force, it started conducting a wide range of aggressive counter-insurgency operations to root out insurgents from several Taliban-controlled villages. Contact with the enemy was frequent and firefights a

Prime Minister Stephen Harper is greeted by General Rick Hillier in Afghanistan, March 2006.

regular occurrence. During those first six months — the standard length of a rotation in theatre — 1 PPCLI BG, utilizing light armoured vehicles, travelled extensively to every corner of the province, asserted ISAF's presence, encountered the enemy more than 100 times, and engaged in 50 serious firefights.

Private Robert Costall was killed during one of these engagements when his platoon, as part of a quick reaction force, was sent in to support Afghan National Army troops that had come under attack by insurgents near a forward operating base roughly 68 miles northwest of Kandahar. In the early morning darkness of March 28, Costall and his platoon were flown in by American helicopters and deposited right in the middle of a fierce firefight. Sadly, during the battle, Costall was killed by friendly fire and three other Canadians were wounded, though the enemy attackers were repulsed with an estimated 30 insurgents killed.

Along with this battle group, Canada also took responsibility for the Kandahar Provincial Reconstruction Team (KPRT). The KPRT, at its peak numbering 330 people, combined the resources and expertise of the CAF with civilian agencies such as the Department of Foreign Affairs and International Trade, the Canadian International Development Agency, the

Canadian soldiers rest during a patrol in Badula Qulp, Helmand Province, Afghanistan, during Operation Helmand Spider, February 7, 2010.

Royal Canadian Mounted Police, and the Correctional Service of Canada. The mandate for the KPRT was to foster security through the mentoring and training of the Afghan army and police and to promote infrastructure development within the province while also strengthening local governance specifically in the areas of justice and corrections. The KPRT's responsibilities were thus wide-ranging.

The team's CAF component provided security for its civilian personnel and for its projects. The Department of Foreign Affairs and International Trade engaged with local government leaders while the Canadian International Development Agency was responsible for investment in infrastructure such as the Dahla Dam, irrigation projects, refurbishment of schools, and even providing polio vaccinations to children. Correctional Service of Canada personnel provided mentoring at Kandahar's Sarposa Prison while Royal Canadian Mounted Police personnel provided mentoring and advice for Afghan police. Although there were some fairly serious organizational challenges in the first two years, the KPRT was an integral contributor to the overall mission in Kandahar Province. It was not enough to simply defeat the enemy on the battlefield. The nation had to be rebuilt in a stable and secure way, and the work of the KPRT would be crucial if NATO was to achieve this long-term objective.[4]

However, security challenges persisted. When spring came, re-inforcements for the insurgency started to trickle in through the porous Afghanistan-Pakistan border, and growing numbers of enemy found support from disaffected clans and narcotics gangs throughout the province. By that summer, it was clear the Canadians were facing a buildup of insurgents around the Green Belt, a fertile area of farmland and villages running through the Zharey and Panjwayi Districts fed by the Arghandab River. Particularly concerning were efforts by the Taliban to create a stronghold in Pashmul, a collection of villages on the west bank of the Arghandab that contained a mosque where the Taliban had first organized back in the 1990s. The Panjwayi District was the spiritual heartland of the Taliban, and Pashmul was its centre. This was not just a symbolically important place but also strategically important, since from here the enemy could dominate the Green Belt and threaten the all-important Highway One. Numerous Canadian efforts were made to eliminate the enemy presence there.

On May 17, 200 Canadian and Afghan soldiers were conducting a sweep through this region when they came under attack from Taliban hidden in nearby houses. Ambushed, the Canadian-Afghan force effectively fought its way out but not before its commander, Captain Nichola Goddard, was killed by shrapnel from a rocket-propelled grenade as she monitored the battle from the turret in her light armoured vehicle. Goddard was the first Canadian female soldier to be killed in combat — 10 percent of all Canadians deployed to Afghanistan were women — and was posthumously awarded the Meritorious Service Medal.[5]

On August 3, Canadian forces were once again met with fierce opposition during a sweep in Pashmul when Sergeant Patrick Tower, a veteran of the Medak Pocket in Croatia, sprinted across 164 yards of bullet-swept ground to take command of a platoon whose commander had been killed in the fighting. Tower was able to successfully lead the remaining Canadian troops out of the firefight while inflicting significant damage on the enemy. For his actions, Tower received the Star of Military Valour. The Star of Military Valour and the Meritorious Service Medal were uniquely Canadian decorations created in the early 1990s. The Star of Military Valour is second only to the Victoria Cross, and Tower was the first-ever recipient of it.

A Canadian M777 howitzer firing, 2007.

Despite aggressive Canadian patrolling, the enemy was growing confident in its ability to hold Pashmul. There was, of course, a propaganda element to this. The longer the insurgents remained in the region the more effective they were at showing local Afghans that the new NATO-backed Afghanistan government was unable to secure its own country. As Jack Granatstein wrote, "The Task Force would put its finger in the dike, but there was too much water, too many holes ..."[6] It was clear that a major offensive was needed to root out the growing insurgency, which set the stage for Operation Medusa.

A major operation, Medusa was designed to eliminate the Taliban's hold on Pashmul. It was overseen by Brigadier-General David Fraser, a Canadian who commanded a coalition force that included Americans, Dutch, Afghans, Danes, and Canadians, numbering roughly 1,400 soldiers. The core of it was the men and women of 1 Royal Canadian Regiment (RCR), newly arrived in theatre as part of Roto 2 — the second rotation of Canadian soldiers in and out of Afghanistan — along with a company of the PPCLI. While not as many troops as Fraser wanted, this shortage of infantry was made up for by significant firepower in the form of artillery and tactical air support, including rockets, cannons, and precision-guided munitions. The hope was that the overwhelming firepower would destroy the morale of most of the 1,200

Members of 2 Platoon, Bravo Company, 1 RCR, prepare to storm a compound during Operation Medusa, September 4, 2006.

insurgents estimated to be in the area, thus leaving a much smaller number of hard-core fighters to be dealt with by the attacking infantry.

Medusa got off to a terrible start. C Company of 1 RCR BG settled in on a high feature on the opposite bank of the Arghandab River from Pashmul to direct air and artillery fire onto enemy positions. However, despite intense NATO firepower, no enemy activity was detected and Fraser controversially ordered the company to cross the river much earlier than originally planned. When C Company made it to the other side of the mostly dry riverbed on the morning of September 3, it walked right into a trap. The enemy had been lying in wait behind irrigation ditches and the high clay walls of the village compounds. The Canadians thus found themselves in a killing zone against well-entrenched insurgents who had centred their defensive position on a white schoolhouse, the same place where Sergeant Tower had won his Star of Military Valour back in August. Two Canadians were killed in this ambush and a number wounded before the company commander ordered the withdrawal back across the river. During this retreat, a light armoured vehicle was abandoned after it had crashed, and two more Canadians were killed before the company finally made it back across. Tragically, more Canadians from C Company died the next day when an American attack helicopter mistook them for insurgents and opened fire. Less than 72 hours into Operation Medusa, the Canadians had suffered four dead and 40 wounded.

With C Company so beat up, Fraser readjusted his attack plan. The remnants of C Company were incorporated into a makeshift battle group, Task Force Grizzly, that focused on the southern battle line while the main thrust into Pashmul now came from the north, spearheaded by 1 RCR's B Company with support from a company of the PPCLI. At the same time, Task Force 31, made up of American special operations forces, pushed toward the objective from the southeast. By September 5, this three-pronged assault began squeezing the enemy on all sides, and Taliban bodies began to pile up. By September 12, Pashmul was occupied, and by September 15, the Taliban were fleeing west and Medusa was over. Five hundred and twelve enemy dead were counted, though some commanders estimated that between 1,000 and 1,500 enemy were actually killed.[7]

As with much of the fighting in Afghanistan, the period of conventional battle devolved into a longer and more deadly period of unconventional warfare. In the aftermath of Medusa's success, ISAF sought to construct a new road, known as Route Summit, to connect Pashmul to Highway One and thus better integrate Pashmul into Kandahar's urban economy. The Canadian battle group now focused on protecting this construction effort while insurgents attacked frequently. Improvised explosive devices (IEDs), hit-and-run attacks, and ambushes led to 10 more Canadian deaths over the next month alone. The Taliban also launched a program of intimidation and terror against the local population. Threats, arson, and assassination were all tools they directed against anyone thought to be co-operating with ISAF forces. In some parts of Zharey and Panjwayi Districts, the Taliban even established their own local parallel government.[8] The problem in combatting all this was that the Canadian battle group simply did not have enough soldiers to both protect the road and conduct large-scale sweeps westward where surviving insurgents were gathering.

Medusa was a great tactical success, but it was clear that it did not eliminate the Taliban threat in the province. Enemy reinforcements and supplies began trickling in from Pakistan mere weeks after the conclusion of Medusa. The enemy was regrouping in an area known as the Horn of Panjwayi where the Arghandab and Dowrey Rivers meet to the southwest of Pashmul. A new series of operations now had to be conducted to establish an ISAF presence in the villages making up this growing insurgent base. One such operation was Falcon Summit, launched in December 2006, in which the Canadians, along with a smattering of NATO forces and Afghan National Army allies, attacked a Taliban stronghold near the village of Howz-e Madad supported by NATO airpower and artillery, as well as firepower from Canadian Leopard tanks.

The operation was a success, but the problems came afterward when the Canadians passed the region over to the Afghan National Police to provide a more permanent security presence. The Afghan police struggled to do this effectively. It lacked the proper training, carried inadequate equipment, and suffered from widespread corruption, which often alienated the local population whose co-operation was so crucial in countering the insurgency. Time and again, the Canadians cleared an area, passed it on to the national police, and had to return in force later as the insurgents filtered back in. With reinforcement and supplies fed continuously into the region from Pakistan, and with the civilian population neutral or even hostile to ISAF's presence, operations in the Horn came to a frustrating deadlock and Canadian casualties in this region continued. On September 18, a suicide bomber on a bicycle detonated near a large group of Canadian soldiers, killing four and wounding 21.

A Canadian soldier fires an M72 rocket launcher at insurgents.

Meanwhile, with their hopes set on retaking Kandahar, the Taliban shifted their focus to the north of the city and sought to gain control of Arghandab District. By the end of October 2007, they had established such a strong presence there that once again Kandahar was under threat. The Canadian battle group acted quickly. This time it was the 3rd battalion of the Royal 22nd Regiment (the Van Doos of Roto 4), which along with Afghan National Army forces and superior firepower drove the enemy out. Unlike during Medusa, the Taliban refused to stand and fight and melted away in the face of the overwhelming attack of the Van Doos. Yet while conventional fighting once again ended in a Canadian victory, the insurgency went on. IEDs, ambushes, targeted assassinations of sympathetic village leaders, and attacks on Afghan police stations continued throughout the district. To counter this, the Canadians established a new forward operating base, called FOB Frontenac, in early 2008 to guard the northern approaches to Kandahar while protecting the all-important Dahla Dam. Despite this presence, the Taliban continued to act boldly.

In June, the Taliban attacked Sarposa Prison on the western outskirts of Kandahar and successfully released hundreds of prisoners, many of whom were captured Taliban fighters. Two days later, they launched an attack into Arghandab District, and despite the rapid response by the Canadian battle group and its Afghan allies, the enemy melted away before being drawn into a conventional battle. In the summer months that followed, seven more Canadian soldiers were killed. Attacks like these were propaganda victories for the Taliban, who showed they had the offensive capacity to strike at targets throughout the province and undermine ISAF's ultimate objective to provide security in the region.

By this point, it was clear that the strategy in Kandahar was not working. Local tactical successes were frequent but of a short-term nature, and any sustained long-term success was difficult due to the limited number of NATO troops in the region and the fact that the Afghan National Security Forces, a combination of Afghan police and military, were simply not ready to take on the responsibility of ensuring permanent security. While media reports filtering back to Canada emphasized the successes — defeating insurgents in battle, constructing schoolhouses, fighting the opium trade, et cetera — the reality on the ground was much different. In August 2008, a mechanized assault by Canadian and Afghan forces cleared Taliban insurgents out of

Correctional Service Canada representative Paula Milino speaks with an administrator at Sarposa Prison in Kandahar City, November 17, 2008.

a region in the Zharey District west of Kandahar. Despite an unmitigated tactical victory, no Afghan governance was established in the area and the Taliban remnants were back in place within hours.[9] So far, 78 Canadian soldiers and one Canadian diplomat, Glyn Berry, had died, and it seemed as if the fighting in Kandahar was turning into a deadly and frustrating game of never-ending "whack-a-mole."

Fresh off his 2006 election victory, Conservative prime minister Stephen Harper made support of the Afghan mission a hallmark of his administration. For Harper, Canada's Afghanistan commitment placed Canada in an international leadership role while at the same time buttressed its perception of reliability within Washington. Under Harper, the size of the Canadian contingent was increased to 2,800, defence spending rose, new equipment was purchased, recruiting for the CAF was expanded, and Harper committed $1 billion in aid to Afghanistan's reconstruction. With public support for the war still fairly strong, Harper sought to extend the mission beyond its end date of February 2009. To do this, he convened a committee in late 2007 called the Independent Panel on Canada's Future Role in Afghanistan, led by John Manley, the former Liberal Party minister of foreign affairs and deputy prime minister.

When it was released in January 2008, the conclusion of the Manley Report surprised the Canadian public but also provided the impetus for a mission extension. Instead of confirming the widespread belief that the mission was going well, Manley's report identified that southern Afghanistan had, in fact, become more destabilized over the past year. The best way to combat this, the report argued, was to increase the NATO presence in the volatile regions of the country. Manley's report stated that the CAF mission in Kandahar should continue only if another 1,000 NATO troops were sent to reinforce it. The report also identified a desperate need for attack helicopters and unmanned aerial vehicles for surveillance. The Harper government agreed to follow its recommendations and proposed an extension to the Kandahar mission, which was put in front of Parliament to vote on. The Liberals, desperate to avoid an election with the war as the central issue, agreed to an extension but also negotiated a firm withdrawal date set for 2011.[10]

The Americans had also come to the conclusion that more troops were needed, and in early 2009, President Barack Obama committed 20,000 more to the country, which meant the Canadians would be receiving their much-needed ground reinforcements. However, the Canadian presence was also bolstered by the arrival of air support when in December 2008 Joint Task Force Afghanistan Air Wing was formed at Kandahar Airfield. This task force included Hercules transport aircraft, along with the helicopters and unmanned aerial vehicles identified in Manley's report: Chinook heavy-lift helicopters, Griffon escort helicopters, and six medium-lift helicopters contracted from the private company SkyLink Aviation. In addition, Tactical Heron unmanned aerial vehicles arrived, borrowed from the Americans. The Canadian air wing was a vital addition to the Kandahar mission and gave the Canadian battle group far greater operational flexibility and reconnaissance capabilities.[11]

With reinforcements arriving and the battle group having the support of its own air wing, Canadian operations could now focus specifically on Kandahar City and its immediate surrounding areas. At this stage, Canadian strategy shifted to what was deemed the "village approach" whereby the Canadian battle group and its Afghan army allies would focus their counter-insurgency efforts on a specific village. Counter-insurgency (COIN) doctrine called first for the establishment of security in that specific village followed by its maintenance for a lengthy period with the responsibility of security being slowly transitioned to local Afghan forces. At the same time, ISAF forces, often as part of a provincial reconstruction team, would identify and overcome local economic, administrative, and infrastructure problems to undermine any local support for the insurgency — winning the "hearts and minds" of the local population.

The entire COIN process was often summed up with the phrase "clear-hold-build," which meant that Canadian soldiers were often engaged in a wide spectrum of activities at the same time: conducting offensive operations to engage and destroy enemy forces, establishing security for the civilian population and government officials and administrators, and providing humanitarian aid and assisting in economic development. The successful application of COIN doctrine required extensive resources, and once NATO reinforcements arrived in the province, the Canadians could better focus theirs on specific villages instead of being spread out too thinly to effectively carry out the "clear-hold-build" concept.[12]

In June 2009, this approach was tested on the village of Deh-e-Begh, just south of Kandahar City in the Dand District. It contained about 900 people and was thought to be relatively sympathetic to the current Afghan

A Canadian soldier greets an Afghan woman during the celebration of Eid al-Adha organized by the Kandahar Provincial Reconstruction Team.

government. Afghan National Security Forces led by Canadian soldiers established regular security patrols while construction projects improving road infrastructure and irrigation canals were completed. The work in Deh-e-Begh was considered a success, even though the Taliban continually attempted to disrupt efforts, including an attempted assassination of the district governor and attacks against ISAF forces. On September 6, 2009, an IED killed two Canadians from the 5 Combat Engineer Regiment, and in late December, an IED destroyed a Canadian armoured vehicle, killing four soldiers and Michelle Lang, a Canadian journalist.

Despite these casualties, the work in Dand provided a template for COIN operations elsewhere, and focus shifted to the Panjwayi District, which had continued to take a deadly toll on Canadian soldiers (in September of that year, IEDs in the area killed two Canadians and injured 15). To apply the village approach, the Canadian battle group targeted a tri-village complex nine miles southwest of Deh-e-Begh based around the main village of Nakhonay, which had been under Taliban influence since 2007. This was a crucial part of their network to funnel fighters into Kandahar proper. In November 2009, 1 PPCLI and Afghan National Army troops launched Operation Hydra to clear the enemy out of this area. While successful, the insurgents who survived fled to other parts of the Panjwayi where the coalition forces had yet to impose a serious presence and continued to threaten stability operations, particularly from the Horn of Panjwayi.

After Operation Hydra was launched, President Obama announced in December 2009 that a further 30,000 American soldiers would be sent to Afghanistan. This surge meant that by 2010, coalition forces, including 100,000 U.S. soldiers, had the manpower to effectively impose ISAF stability throughout southern Afghanistan, with particular focus on the strategically important Kandahar Province and its problematic districts of Arghandab, Zharey, and Panjwayi. Operation Hamkari followed in 2010, a large-scale offensive that emphasized the "clear-hold-build" concept of COIN doctrine. Over the summer and fall of that year, the American-led operation with the largest deployment of Afghan National Security Forces to date resecured Kandahar City, removed the Taliban presence from Arghandab District, and shifted to the Zharey District where they dismantled the enemy presence there before completing military operations in the Horn of Panjwayi where a series of insurgent strongholds were destroyed.[13]

Canadian troops were particularly active in the last phase of Hamkari in Panjwayi where the 1st Battalion Van Doos BG (of Roto 10) occupied positions in western Panjwayi to prevent insurgents fleeing from the U.S.-led push into the district. Toward the end of 2010, a Canadian infantry-armour assault on the village of Zangabad, colloquially known as "Zangaboom" because of the abundance of IEDs in the region, cleared out the remaining Taliban troops in that cluster of villages, which had been a stronghold for the enemy for years. In accordance with COIN doctrine, CAF personnel remained in the region in the months that followed, co-operating with village elders and supporting building operations seeking to improve the living conditions of the locals.

Of particular importance was the construction of Route Hyena, designed to improve local farmers' access to markets while also better linking the western end of the Horn of Panjwayi to forward operating base Sperwan Ghar, a dominating piece of high ground in the eastern end of the Horn. Like Route Summit before it, insurgents sought to disrupt the construction of this road with IEDs, ambushes, and intimidation of the locals. The construction work required heavy security, and Canadian, American, and Afghan lives were lost while the road was built.

Canadian counter-insurgency operations continued on a regular basis throughout the Kandahar region right up to the end of Canada's combat mission in the country. On July 7, 2011, Task Force Kandahar was handed over to the U.S. 4th Infantry Division, concluding Canada's nine years of combat. From this point onward, Canada entered the fourth phase of its time in Afghanistan as part of Operation Attention.

Operation Attention was the NATO training mission of Afghan National Security Forces in Kabul, Mazar-e-Sharif, and Herat. While initially the Conservative-Liberal agreement regarding the 2011 deadline had meant a complete Canadian withdrawal from the country, pressure from the United States to maintain some sort of visible support for the war effort led to Prime Minister Harper agreeing to the training mission. The CAF presence in Afghanistan was thus reduced to 950, along with 45 police officers.

This final phase was a non-combat one focused on improving the quality of the Afghan National Security Forces, including police, army, and air force components; providing guidance to Afghan leaders; delivering humanitarian aid; and helping to build infrastructure. It was a mission designed so that

Afghanistan could govern itself effectively while providing for its own security. Canada was the second-largest contributor to the mission. This phase wrapped up in 2014, and by March of that year, the last of Canada's soldiers left the country. Between 2001 and 2014, 40,000 Canadians served in theatre, nearly 2,000 were wounded, 109 decorations for military valour were awarded, approximately 9,000 CAF men and women received treatment for PTSD, and 158 Canadian soldiers made the ultimate sacrifice in the longest war in Canadian history.

Ten years after the departure of Canadian troops, the complicated legacy of Canada's role in Afghanistan was still being assessed. There were some successes: The Taliban were removed — temporarily, of course. A new Afghan government was established, supported, and mentored by Canadian personnel. National-level government mechanisms and infrastructure were put in place that helped prevent an Afghan civil war breaking out in the years following the ousting of the Taliban. As well, a national development strategy was accepted by the Afghan government in Kabul, and the international community was convinced to help finance it. Finally, not only did the CAF help stabilize Kabul and its surrounding regions but it then maintained operations in the volatile Kandahar Province against an increasingly sophisticated insurgency and effectively handed over that province to the Americans.

The mission also resulted in some longer-term successes: Al-Qaeda was no longer able to use the country as its operating base, and its global mission of insurgency and terrorism was seriously disrupted. The fighting in Afghanistan engendered a cultural change within the CAF whereby the demoralizing legacy of the Somalia affair was put to bed and the risk-aversion policies practised in the deployments of the 1990s were slowly abandoned. This led to the CAF becoming one of the most reliable military partners in Afghanistan, improved morale within the Canadian military, enhanced standing within NATO, and most importantly, better relations with the United States, which had been tumultuous under the Chrétien and Martin governments. As well, in Canada, the CAF underwent a dramatic shift in its perception by the Canadian public, finally shedding the decades-long, blue-helmeted peacekeeper myth.

At the same time, the events that unfolded in Afghanistan after the last American troops left in July 2021 have forced many to take a hard, sober look at that aspect of the mission.[14] The Taliban steamrolled the Afghan National Army in the days following the American withdrawal, reinstated themselves in power, and are now utilizing much of the governance infrastructure that was built up by ISAF. For instance, there are police services where there were none prior to the 21st century. But the police, the military, and the government all suffer from widespread corruption and the country continues to be a major narcotics producer. Recently, a jihadist movement called the Islamic State — Khorasan Province has ramped up its murderous activities in Afghanistan against the Taliban, including suicide bombings and assassinations.

Libya

While the war in Afghanistan was certainly Canada's major military commitment in the first quarter of the 21st century, men and women of the CAF continued in operations elsewhere. In early 2011, popular protests ripped across Libya, challenging the despotic rule of Colonel Muammar Ghadhafi, who responded with widespread attacks on the civilian population. The country

Captain Barrie Ransome, a CP-140 pilot with Sicily Air Wing, flies the first intelligence, surveillance, and reconnaissance mission over Libya before conducting the first overland SCAR-C mission executed by the CP-140 crews.

then ruptured into civil war. In response, the United Nations called for an international arms embargo, and by March, passed a resolution strengthening the embargo while also imposing a no-fly zone over the country.

Stephen Harper's government was quick to commit Canadian forces, and Operation Mobile was the name given to Canada's participation in the Libyan conflict, which saw air and naval assets deployed in support of this mission. At first, the Canadian air force was utilized in a non-combat role evacuating civilians. However, by March, this changed to a U.S.-led mission to enforce the no-fly zone over the country. The air force's contribution, flying out of bases in Italy, consisted of a contingent of seven CF-18 Hornets that flew an average of six sorties a day, comprising just over 10 percent of all coalition combat missions over Libyan airspace. This included attacks against Libyan regime targets such as vehicles, ammunition dumps, bunker complexes, and infrastructure. In early October, Major James "Buca" Kettles flew his 50th combat mission, the first Canadian air force pilot to do so since the Korean War. Canada's Polaris and Hercules planes offered important logistic support through air-to-air refuelling while two CC-140 Auroras flew reconnaissance missions, including the first ever all-Canadian strike coordination and reconnaissance–coordinator (SCAR-C) mission, which directed strike aircrafts to suitable targets — a brand new capability for the Canadian air force.[15]

HMCS *Charlottetown* arrived in mid-March and joined a carrier-based task group enforcing the blockade along Libya's coastline. *Charlottetown* was replaced by HMCS *Vancouver* in mid-August, which continued the work. When the Libyan mission transitioned from a U.S.-led one to a NATO-led one in late March, it was a Canadian who was placed in charge: Lieutenant-General Charles Bouchard, who was born in Chicoutimi, Quebec. Bouchard commanded the mission until it wrapped up at the end of October, by which time Ghadhafi's forces had been thoroughly beaten and Ghadhafi himself had been captured by opposition forces and executed.

Recent Developments for the Canadian Armed Forces

Since the end of the war in Afghanistan, CAF personnel have remained busy elsewhere, as well. Over 900 CAF personnel from all three branches were part of the initial contribution to NATO's Operation Reassurance in Central and Eastern Europe, boosting NATO presence in the region in response to Russia's aggression in Crimea in 2014. In July 2023, Prime Minister Justin Trudeau announced an increase in the size of Canada's forces in Latvia as part of Operation Reassurance to include 2,200 CAF personnel, doubling the commitment, and 15 Leopard 2 battle tanks by 2026. Two hundred CAF personnel were also in Ukraine training Ukrainian security forces prior to Russia's 2022 invasion of the remainder of the country.

As of 2024, Canadians are in the Middle East helping to build the military capabilities of Iraq, Jordan, and Lebanon to assist these countries in engaging and defeating the Islamic State of Iraq and Syria (ISIS), also known as the Islamic State of Iraq and the Levant (ISIL). ISIS/ISIL is a Salafist jihadist group that emerged in the early 2000s during the Iraqi insurgency that resulted from the collapse of Saddam Hussein's regime and the failure of the U.S. military to secure the country. In the chaos that followed the U.S.-led invasion of Iraq, ISIS/ISIL flourished, and by 2014, it had established control of parts of northwestern Iraq and eastern Syria. Canadian pilots began flying combat missions in November 2014 against ISIS targets and supply missions supporting coalition troops fighting it. Within two years, coalition forces nearly eliminated the extremist organization's presence in the Middle East. In March of 2023 the mission was extended for the third time, set to expire in March 2025. Operation Impact continues as a "whole-of-government" approach to training and state-building to achieve stability and security against the threat of ISIS.

At home the Canadian Armed Forces were used regularly to enforce fishing regulations in Canadian waters, respond to natural disasters, and carry out search-and-rescue missions from the air. Frequent exercises and patrols have been conducted in Canada's North to enforce the country's sovereignty in the Arctic. In the spring of 2020, when the Covid-19 pandemic struck, 1,600 CAF personnel were deployed as part of Operation Laser. The deployed soldiers provided much-needed assistance to long-term-care facilities in Quebec and Ontario that were on the brink of total collapse. CAF personnel continued to support medical infrastructure across the country and help with vaccine distribution.

Despite this great work, institutional challenges have plagued the CAF. In 2015, an external review into military sexual violence, known as the Deschamps Report, was released. Its findings confirmed that the military consisted of a sexually hostile culture toward women and LGBTQ2S+ personnel. A Statistics Canada survey conducted the following year found that one in four women in the regular force and one in three in the reserves had experienced sexual assault during their service.[16]

In response to the Deschamps Report, Chief of the Defence Staff Jonathan Vance launched Operation Honour, a CAF mission to address and prevent sexual harassment and discrimination within the ranks. Two years later, as part of the Department of Defence's official defence policy "Strong, Secure, and Engaged," Vance announced recruitment target increases for women from 14.9 percent in 2016 to 25 percent by 2026, Indigenous peoples from 2.6 percent in 2016 to 3.5 percent by 2026, and visible minorities from 6.7 percent to 11.8 percent. However, these objectives encountered serious systemic obstacles highlighted by a series of sexual misconduct accusations and investigations. In 2019, a $900 million settlement was reached in a class-action lawsuit against the CAF on behalf of current and former members who experienced sexual misconduct.

Two years later, Lieutenant-Colonel Eleanor Taylor, the first Canadian woman to lead an infantry company in combat and recipient of the Meritorious Service Medal for her service in Afghanistan, publicly resigned in response to sexual misconduct allegations that had come to light regarding senior officers in the CAF. Taylor accused the CAF of failing to adequately address harassment within the organization. Shockingly, Vance was one of these senior officers. In the summer of 2021, he was the subject of an investigation by military police into sexual misconduct, and in March 2022, he pled guilty to obstruction of justice.

Along with institutional challenges, securing adequate defence spending continued to pose a problem for the CAF. The sudden 2008 recession meant the Harper government was focused on stimulus packages for the Canadian economy, and defence spending was put on the back burner. Things did not change much when Harper won the 2011 election. This was the year that the service branches were once again allowed to refer to themselves using their royal designations, though informally most people had already been using them for years. It also marked a shift in Harper's support for the military. Despite the prime minister's continued vocal backing, defence priorities continued to wane. Defence spending fell by 16 percent in the ensuing years and funds allocated for procurement projects were stripped from the Department of National Defence to help Harper's administration balance the budget. By 2014, spending was less than 1 percent of Canada's gross domestic product, the lowest it had been since the demobilization days post–Second World War and half of NATO's recommended spending target of 2 percent.[17]

Things did not get better for the CAF with the election of Justin Trudeau and the Liberals in 2015. Despite lofty public promises, defence spending remained a low priority, which was in stark contrast to a broad platform of Liberal spending that ran up billions of dollars in new debt. Canada was, of course, not the only NATO nation to be below the 2 percent spending target, and this issue became a focus for newly elected President Donald Trump, who after winning the 2016 U.S. presidential election made it clear that America expected its NATO allies to open up their wallets. Regardless of presidential pressure, defence spending remained a low priority under the Liberals, rising only slightly so that by 2019 defence spending was 1.28 percent of Canada's gross domestic product (the average among the NATO powers is 1.55 percent; the United States spends approximately 3.4 percent).[18]

In 2017, however, the Liberals offered a ray of hope in their defence White Paper. Despite widespread pessimism, the White Paper surprised many, since it turned out to be a well-thought-out document that provided a solid vision for Canadian defence going forward. It called for significant increases in spending with particular emphasis on the purchase of new frigates and fighter aircraft, the expansion of the CAF by 5,000 personnel, and greater investment in cybersecurity and warfare.

On paper, all of this looked good for the CAF and even garnered public approval from James Mattis, the U.S defence secretary.[19] The problem, however, was that most of the spending was scheduled to be done after the next election, meaning the Liberals were able to portray themselves as supporters of the military without having to take much action to prove it. Frankly, the ambitious vision laid out in the 2017 White Paper was on shaky ground.

While many were already pessimistic about the government's long-term commitment to the plan, Covid-19 further destabilized it, and in September 2023 the Liberal government announced it would be cutting $1 billion in defence spending. Whatever political party is in power in Canada in the future, it is hoped that it will recognize how important and valuable a strong, capable military is in such an uncertain world.

IN SUMMARY

When examining the history of the Canadian Armed Forces (CAF), it is clear that Canada's military has overcome incredible challenges. It has often discovered, much to our own detriment as a nation, that one of the greatest of these challenges has been to prove its relevance time and again to the Canadian public and to Canadian politicians. This began as early as the first days of nationhood when a paltry organization served to reinforce Canada's control over its own territory and support Great Britain's imperial hegemony. At that time, the greatest test for the Canadian military was securing enough funding for the fledgling and poorly run force. While some certainly sought reforms, it was an organization that was so deeply intertwined with political patronage that many fought tooth and nail to resist any attempts to change it.

Canada's participation in the Second Boer War finally led to some of the most-needed reforms, while the years leading up to the First World War saw both the Permanent Force and Non-Permanent Active Militia undergo significant improvements. Those same years also witnessed Canada get its own navy, though it truly was a "tinpot" one. The debate over the navy highlighted how issues of defence were heavily partisan but also fed into tensions between French and English Canada and differing views on Canada's role in the wider British imperial world.

The First World War shook Canada to its core. The country's army ballooned in size. Hundreds of thousands of Canadians served in the conflict,
most in the Canadian Expeditionary Force, but many others in Britain's Royal
Navy and Royal Flying Corps. The war left an indelible imprint on Canadian
society. Places such as Ypres, Vimy Ridge, Passchendaele, and Amiens,
among others, adorn cenotaphs across the country, while names such as
Arthur Currie, Billy Bishop, Francis Pegahmagabow, and so many more have
become imprinted on the Canadian historical psyche. The Canadian Corps
fought and won numerous battles and by 1918 was one of the finest fighting
formations on the Western Front. Dozens of regiments claimed numerous
battle honours, and in the postwar period, regimental spirit thrived in the
wake of such victories. The veteran community was further consolidated by
the numerous Royal Canadian Legions that popped up in towns and cities
across the country. A national military identity was developing.

The war did not just leave an imprint on those who served. The duplici-
tous tactics of Prime Minister Robert Borden that gave his Union government victory in the 1917 general election and a large number of Canadian
women the right to vote, resulted in the implementation of conscription, an
issue that nearly tore the country apart. Further chaos ensued when Canada
entered a brutal postwar recession leading to numerous violent eruptions of
discontent across the nation while countless families still mourned the loss
of loved ones.

As Canadians sought to rebuild their lives after the trauma of war, its
military atrophied. Despite the excitement over the military's newest branch,
the Royal Canadian Air Force, defence budgets were continually slashed,
both the Permanent Force and Non-Permanent Active Militia returned to
their pre-war levels, and the Royal Canadian Navy fought a desperate struggle for survival. On the political stage, Canada's First World War exploits
gave Prime Minister King the leverage to push for a new role within the
British Commonwealth. However, when it came to actual defence spending,
general uninterest coupled with the Great Depression meant little was going to happen. When war did come in 1939, Canada was, as in 1914, totally
unprepared for the commitments it was about to make.

The sad state of Canada's military in 1939 made its achievements in the
Second World War all that more amazing. On land, at sea, and in air, hundreds of thousands of Canadian men and women donned uniforms to serve

their country. Canada provided training infrastructure for tens of thousands of pilots, helped secure the North Atlantic Run of convoys, liberated vast swathes of Europe, and aided in the controversial destruction of German cities, all the while providing vast quantities of war *matériel* to Great Britain. By the end of the war, Canada's military was a force to be reckoned with. The Second World War was a catalyst for Canada to re-emerge onto the international stage as a leading middle power, as well as a wealthy, vibrant country moving deeper into the American sphere of influence while fostering a welfare state system that came to define it for decades afterward.

The Cold War tensions of the postwar world made Canadian defence issues more relevant than ever before during peacetime. The formation of NATO, Canada's participation in the Korean War, and the creation of NORAD all shone a spotlight on real Canadian fears about the spread of Communism and the prospect of nuclear conflict. Thus, the Canadian state supported unprecedented levels of peacetime defence spending. With such a powerful military it was no surprise that Canada was willing to use it in an active international role. From the late 1940s onward, Canadian military personnel were deployed all around the world, primarily under the banner of the United Nations. From this emerged the powerful peacekeeping myth: an "ideal" foreign policy whereby Canadian military personnel were seen by the Canadian public and the international community as trying to stop war — a poignant counter to the growing perception of an increasingly belligerent America. But as history has proven, peacekeeping was far more complicated than most Canadians understood.

By the end of the 1960s, the global antiwar movement coupled with dramatic changes to Canada's social landscape led to a decline in support for Canada's defence establishment. Budget cuts followed. This did not, however, mean that the tempo of operations diminished for Canadian military personnel — far from it. Successive Canadian governments continually reduced the capacity for the Canadian Armed Forces to operate while eagerly deploying them both domestically and internationally.

At the same time, the CAF underwent organizational changes, "civilianized" in such a way as to operate more like any other bureaucratic branch of the Canadian government, "bilingualized" to better incorporate French-speaking Canadians and perhaps temper the growing support for the Quebec separatist movement, and reluctantly, culturally modernized in response to growing pressure to create more opportunities for women and minorities. Some of these changes worked very well, others took much longer to become fully realized.

Despite a brief period of defence optimism in the 1980s, the collapse of the Soviet Union was a major nail in the growing decline of the importance of the Canadian defence establishment. When a series of military scandals came to light in the 1990s, public support for the CAF hit an all-time low. The peacekeeping myth had been shattered, NATO seemed irrelevant, and for some of the more naive, it even seemed like defence issues were becoming obsolete. Then Al-Qaeda carried out a shocking attack on American soil on September 11, 2001, and ruptured the very nature of the international order. All of a sudden, Canada was at war. Defence mattered again. The dark decade of the 1990s was long behind as Canadian soldiers, sailors, and aircrew were now called upon to fight. The Canadian government and public were forced to wake up fast to the chaotic realities of the 21st century and the need for the Canadian Armed Forces.

The CAF will continue to play an important role for Canada both domestically and internationally. What is less clear is the kind of support it will receive from the government that uses it. This is, of course, problematic because it is very difficult to predict what future deployments are going to look like. Will they continue to be state-building in the Middle East? Reassurance operations in Eastern Europe? Co-operation exercises with our allies around the world? Rescuing Canadians from war-torn regions? Will future operations be strictly humanitarian in nature, or will these future missions require Canadians to engage in combat? Most likely, they will be a combination of all of these.

What kind of domestic situations will our military face? Global warming, terrorism, disease, and Arctic sovereignty will continue to create challenges for Canada going forward. As well, what challenges will the CAF face as it continues to evolve culturally, socially, and institutionally? How damaging will the recent spate of high-profile sexual misconduct cases be to its organizational morale and long-term growth?

There is no question that for the CAF to gain the support it needs from the public and thus the politicians it will have to take serious and effective steps to address very real institutional issues that could potentially embarrass any government throwing support behind our armed forces. At the same time, the geopolitical realities of a conventional war in Europe and rising tensions in Asia cannot be ignored.

Because of this, it is important for the CAF to ensure that all the great work it does on a constant basis is not overlooked by the public. As uncomfortable as some Canadians are when it comes to recognizing our nation's military achievements, this is exactly what needs to happen. For those uncomfortable with even that sentence, let me be clear: "military achievements" does not solely mean a battle being fought and won. It refers to the extensive and positive work our military does constantly at home and around the world. Often this work does not make it into the news and remains little known to the average Canadian. Perhaps, if this trend were reversed, greater pressure could be brought to bear on our politicians to better support our military.

If there is anything history teaches us, it is that any fool brave enough to predict the future often remains a fool. We can certainly make some educated guesses but too many times history has shown that the best-educated guesses often end up in the annals of science fiction. At the end of the day, our military must be ready for a wide variety of challenges. The efforts of Russia to destabilize Eastern Europe could pull more of our forces there, while the continued power projections by China might shift our forces more to the Pacific. Failed states in any corner of the world might become our focus, while a wide range of issues might suddenly arise, as Covid-19 did, requiring the rapid assistance of the CAF. The threat of terrorism at home and abroad, the growing importance of cyberwarfare, and the potential danger to drinking water and food resources are all part and parcel of the myriad of challenges our nation and thus our military might face.

Without having a crystal ball, the only option is to ensure the CAF remains a highly trained force with strong morale and equipped with the most modern equipment to allow it to be flexible and adaptable. To do this, though, the financial resources must be provided and the military must show the Canadian public it deserves them, which is one of the greatest current challenges for the CAF. Canadian military leaders are constantly forced to do more with less, "punching above their weight," as many are apt to say, while now dealing with a string of public-relations disasters.

But how long can any organization or institution continue to be effective with the "doing more with less" model? At some point either the resources for the CAF must be increased or our government needs to reduce the military's commitments. The trend seems to indicate that neither of these will happen. Defence is not an expense; it is an asset. In an unpredictable world, such as the one we face, it is a dangerous game to continue to keep defence matters low on the priority list.

ACKNOWLEDGEMENTS

I was so lucky to have some incredible people read and comment on my work over the course of its creation. I cannot express my gratitude enough to the following people for their help in bringing this book to life: Alex Fitzgerald-Black and the Juno Beach Centre; Max Hamon; Lieutenant Commander James Brun, *Ready, Aye, Ready*; Jeff Keshen; Keith Maxwell; Kevin Spooner; Sean Maloney; Sean Carleton; Mike Bechthold; Maya Eichler; Tim Cook; Major Barrie K. Ransome; Lieutenant Colonel Alan Lockerby; James Calhoun and the Seaforth Highlanders of Canada Museum, *Cuidich'n righ*; Johnny and the team at the Directorate of Material Policy and Procedures in the Department of National Defence; Shannyn Johnson and the team at the Canadian War Museum; Gaëlle Rivard Piché; the University of British Columbia's Department of History; and Langara College's Department of History, Latin, and Political Science. And, finally, I'd like to thank Kathryn Lane, Michael Carroll, Elena Radic, and the whole team at Dundurn for their great work.

Of course, nothing I have accomplished would be possible without the incredible, unending, and unconditional support of my family: *Familia mea, meum fundamentum* — my family, my foundation.

Appendix 1

CAST OF CHARACTERS

Edwin Alderson (1859–1927): British general; commander Canadian Corps, 1915–16.

Harold Alexander (1891–1969): British Army field marshal; commander I Corps, 1940–42; commander 15th Army Group, 1943–45; governor general of Canada, 1946–52.

Jean Victor Allard (1913–96): Canadian general; commander Royal 22nd Regiment (Van Doos), 1943–45; commander 25th Canadian Infantry Brigade, Korea, 1953–54; Chief of the Defence Staff, 1966–69.

Maurice Baril (1943–): Canadian general; military adviser to the United Nations secretary-general, 1992–97; Chief of the Defence Staff, 1997–2001.

Perrin Beatty (1950–): Canadian politician; minister of national defence, 1986–89.

R.B. Bennett (1870–1947): Conservative Party prime minister of Canada, 1930–35.

Big Bear (circa 1825–88): Plains Cree Chief and leader during North-West Resistance.

M.P. Bogert (1908–99): Canadian general; General Officer Commanding (GOC) 2nd Canadian Infantry Brigade, 1944–45; GOC 25th Canadian Infantry Brigade in Korea, 1952–53.

Frederick Borden (1847–1917): Canadian Liberal Party minister of militia and defence, 1896–1911.

Robert Borden (1854–1937): Conservative Party prime minister of Canada, 1911–20.

Charles Bouchard (1956–): Canadian general; commander of NATO's Operation Unified Protector in Libya, 2011.

E.L.M. Burns (1897–1985): Canadian general and diplomat; GOC 5th Canadian Armoured Division, January–March 1944; GOC I Canadian Corps, March–November 1944; chief of staff of United Nations Truce Supervision Organization, 1954–56; commander of United Nations Emergency Force (UNEF), 1956–59.

George H.W. Bush (1924–2018): U.S. president, 1989–93.

George W. Bush (1946–): U.S. president, 2001–9.

Julian Byng (1862–1935): British Army general and GOC Canadian Corps, 1916–17; GOC British Third Army, 1917–18; governor general of Canada, 1921–26.

Jim Calvin: Canadian Army officer; commander 2 PPCLI Battle Group during Battle of the Medak Pocket, 1993.

A.J.H. Cassels (1907–96): British general; commander 1st British Commonwealth Division, Korea, 1951–52.

Jean Chrétien (1934–): Liberal Party prime minister of Canada, 1993–2003.

Winston Churchill (1874–1965): British Conservative Party prime minister, 1940–45, 1951–55.

Mark W. Clark (1896–1984): U.S. major general; commander U.S. Fifth Army, 1943–44; commander 15th Army Group, 1944–45.

Brooke Claxton (1898–1960): Canadian politician and veteran of the First World War; minister of national defence, 1946–54.

Douglas Cochrane, Earl of Dundonald (1852–1935): GOC Militia of Canada, 1902–4.

Harry Crerar (1888–1965): Canadian Chief of the General Staff (CGS), 1940–41; general commanding First Canadian Army, 1944–45.

Piet Cronjé (1836–1911): South African general in Second Boer War, defeated by British at Battle of Paardeberg, 1900.

Arthur Currie (1875–1933): Canadian general commanding Canadian Corps, 1917–19; CGS, 1919–20; principal and vice-chancellor of McGill University, 1920–33.

CAST OF CHARACTERS

Roméo Dallaire (1946–): Canadian general, diplomat, activist, and politician; commander of the United Nations Assistance Mission for Rwanda (UNAMIR), 1993–94; Liberal Party senator since 2005.

Jacques Dextraze (1919–93): Canadian general; commander 2nd Battalion, Royal 22nd Regiment (Van Doos), 1950–52; chief of staff Opération des Nations Unies au Congo, 1963–64; Canadian Chief of the Defence Staff, 1972–77.

John Diefenbaker (1895–1979): Progressive Conservative Party prime minister of Canada, 1957–63.

Gabriel Dumont (1837–1906): Métis activist and Louis Riel's military commander during North-West Resistance in 1885.

Anthony Eden (1897–1977): British Conservative Party prime minister, 1955–57.

Dwight D. Eisenhower (1890–1969): Supreme Allied Commander of Allied Expeditionary Force, 1943–45; U.S. president, 1953–61.

Joseph Flavelle (1858–1939): Canadian businessman and chairman of the Imperial Munitions Board in First World War.

Ferdinand Foch (1851–1929): French field marshal; chief of staff French Army, 1917–18; Supreme Allied Commander, 1918–20.

Charles Foulkes (1903–69): British-Canadian general; commander I Canadian Corps, 1944–45; CGS, 1945–51.

David Fraser: Canadian general; commander of NATO forces during Operation Medusa (September 2006).

Douglas Haig (1861–1928): British field marshal commanding British Expeditionary Force, 1915–19.

Stephen Harper (1959–): Conservative Party prime minister of Canada, 2006–15.

Arthur "Bomber" Harris (1892–1984): Royal Air Force (RAF) air chief marshal; commander RAF Bomber Command, 1942–45.

Rick Hillier (1955–): Canadian general; commander Multinational Division (South-West, Bosnia), 2000–1; Canadian Chief of Land Staff, 2003–5; Canadian Chief of the Defence Staff, 2005–8.

Adolf Hitler (1889–1945): Dictator of Germany, 1933–45.

Bert Hoffmeister (1907–99): Canadian general; commander Seaforth Highlanders, 1942–43; commander 2nd Canadian Infantry Brigade, 1943–44; commander 5th Canadian Armoured Division, 1944–45; commander Canadian Pacific Force, 1945.

Walter Hose (1875–1965): Royal Canadian Navy (RCN) rear-admiral considered father of Canada's Naval Service; captain of HMCS *Rainbow* in First World War.

Sam Hughes (1853–1921): Canadian politician and soldier who served in the Second Boer War (1899–1902); Canadian minister of militia and defence, 1911–16.

Edward Hutton (1848–1923): GOC Canadian Militia, 1898–1900; commander 1st Mounted Infantry Brigade, 1900, Second Boer War.

Albert Kesselring (1885–1960): German field marshal; commander Army Group C, 1943–44; high commander West, 1945.

William Lyon Mackenzie King (1874–1950): Liberal Party prime minister of Canada, 1921–26, 1926–30, 1935–48.

Wilfrid Laurier (1841–1919): Liberal Party prime minister of Canada, 1896–1911.

John K. Lawson (1886–1941): Canadian general; commander West Brigade Hong Kong, 1941.

Oliver Leese (1894–1978): British general; commander XXX Corps, 1942–43; commander British Eighth Army, 1943–44; commander Allied Land Forces, Southeast Asia, 1944–45.

Douglas MacArthur (1880–1964): Supreme Commander Allied Forces Southwest Pacific, 1942–45; Supreme Commander Allied Powers, 1945–51; commander U.N. Command, 1950–51.

John A. Macdonald (1815–91): Conservative Party prime minister of Canada, 1867–73, 1878–91.

Alexander Mackenzie (1822–92): Liberal Party prime minister of Canada, 1873–78.

Christopher Maltby (1891–1980): British general; commander British troops Hong Kong, 1941; prisoner of war, 1941–45.

Paul Martin (1938–): Liberal Party prime minister of Canada, 2003–6.

Richard McCreery (1898–1967): British Army general; commander U.K. Eighth Army, 1944–45.

Andrew McNaughton (1887–1966): Canadian general; CGS, 1929–35; minister of defence, 1944–45.

George Meade (1815–72): U.S. general; commander Army of Potomac, 1863–65; arrested Fenians in 1870.

Malcolm Mercer (1859–1916): Canadian general; commander 1st Brigade, 1st Canadian Division, 1914–15; commander 3rd Canadian Division, 1916.

Frederick Middleton (1825–98): British Army general commanding Canadian forces during the North-West Resistance in 1885.

Walter Model (1891–1945): German field marshal; commander Ninth Army, 1942–43; commander Army Group B, 1944–45.

Bernard "Monty" Montgomery (1887–1976): British Army field marshal; commander British Eighth Army, 1942–44; commander 21st Army Group, 1944–45.

Louis Mountbatten (1900–79): British admiral of the fleet; chief of Combined Operations, 1942–43; Supreme Allied Commander, Southeast Asia, 1943–45.

Brian Mulroney (1939–2024): Progressive Conservative Party prime minister of Canada, 1984–93.

Leonard Murray (1896–1971): Canadian rear-admiral appointed commander-in-chief of Canadian Northwest Atlantic, 1943–45.

Benito Mussolini (1883–1945): Dictator of Italy, 1922–43.

Barack Obama (1961–): U.S. president, 2009–17.

John Osborn (1899–1941): Winnipeg Grenadiers sergeant-major, Hong Kong, 1941; first Canadian awarded Victoria Cross in Second World War.

William Otter (1843–1929): Canadian commanding officer who led attack at Battle of Cut Knife in May 1885 during the North-West Resistance; commanded first contingent of Canadians during the Second Boer War; CGS, 1908–10.

George S. Patton (1885–1945): U.S. general; commander U.S. II Corps, March–April 1943; commander U.S. Seventh Army, June 1943–44; commander U.S. Third Army, 1944–45.

Lester B. Pearson (1897–1972): Canadian politician, diplomat, and veteran of the First World War; secretary of state for external affairs, 1948–57; Liberal Party prime minister of Canada, 1963–68.

Poundmaker (circa 1842–86): Plains Cree Chief and leader during North-West Resistance.

J.L. Ralston (1881–1948): Canadian minister of national defence, 1926–30, 1940–44.

Ronald Reagan (1911–2004): U.S. president, 1981–89.

Matthew Ridgway (1895–1993): U.S. general; commander U.S. Eighth Army, 1950–51; Supreme Commander U.N. Forces, Korea, 1951–52; Supreme Allied Commander Europe, 1952–53; chief of staff U.S. Army, 1953–55.

Louis Riel (1844–85): Métis activist and leader of the Red River (1870) and North-West Resistance (1885).

John Hamilton "Ham" Roberts (1891–1962): Canadian general; commander 2nd Canadian Division, 1941–43; commander 2nd Division at Dieppe Raid, 1942.

John "Rocky" Rockingham (1911–87): Canadian general; GOC 9th Canadian Infantry Brigade, 1944–45; GOC 25th Canadian Infantry Brigade, 1950–52.

Erwin Rommel (1891–1944): German field marshal; commander Panzer Army Africa/Army Group Africa, 1941–43; commander Army Group B, 1943–44.

Franklin D. Roosevelt (1882–1945): U.S. president, 1933–45.

Guy Simonds (1903–74): Canadian general; GOC II Canadian Corps, 1944–45; CGS 1951–55.

Louis St. Laurent (1882–1973): Liberal Party prime minister of Canada, 1948–57.

Thomas Bland Strange (1831–1925): British general; commander of field force at Battle of Frenchman's Butte during North-West Resistance, 1885.

Justin Trudeau (1971–): Liberal Party prime minister of Canada, 2015 to present.

Pierre Elliott Trudeau (1919–2000): Liberal Party prime minister of Canada, 1968–79, 1980–84.

Harry Truman (1884–1972): U.S. president, 1945–53.

Donald Trump (1946–): U.S. president, 2017–21.

Richard Turner (1871–1961): Canadian general; commander 3rd Brigade, 1st Canadian Division, 1914–15; commander 2nd Canadian Division, 1915–16.

Jonathan Vance (1964–): Canadian general; Chief of the Defence Staff, 2015–21.

Chris Vokes (1904–85): Canadian general; commander 1st Canadian Infantry Division, 1943–44; commander 4th Canadian Armoured Division, 1944–45.

Wandering Spirit (circa 1845–85): Plains Cree Chief and leader during North-West Resistance.

David Watson (1869–1922): Canadian general; commander 4th Division, 1916–18.

Woodrow Wilson (1856–1924): U.S. president, 1913–21.

Garnet Wolseley (1833–1913): British general commanding Red River (1870) and Nile Expeditions (1884–85); commander-in-chief British Army, 1895–1901.

Appendix 2

TIMELINE

July 1, 1867: British North America Act creates Canada.

December 8, 1869: Métis-led Provisional Government of Red River formed.

March 4, 1870: Thomas Scott executed.

May 1870: Wolseley expedition sets out for Red River Settlement.

August 1870: Wolseley expedition arrives at Fort Garry.

July 5, 1884: Louis Riel returns to Canada.

March 26, 1885: Battle of Duck Lake.

May 2, 1885: Battle of Cut Knife Hill.

May 9–12, 1885: Battle of Batoche.

October 7, 1885: Canadian voyageurs arrive in Alexandria, Egypt, in preparation for Nile Expedition.

November 16, 1885: Louis Riel hanged in Regina.

October 11, 1899: Second Boer War breaks out.

February 18–27, 1900: Battle of Paardeberg.

November 7, 1900: Battle of Leliefontein.

May 31, 1902: Second Boer War ends.

August 4, 1914: Britain declares war on Germany.

April 22–May 25, 1915: Second Battle of Ypres.

July 1, 1916: Somme Offensive begins.

September 15–22, 1916: Battle of Flers-Courcelette.

April 9–12, 1917: Battle of Vimy Ridge.

July 31–November 10, 1917: Third Battle of Ypres (Passchendaele).

August 15–25, 1917: Battle of Hill 70 and Lens.

December 17, 1917: Robert Borden's Union Party wins federal election.

March 28–April 1, 1918: Anti-conscription Easter Riots in Quebec.

August 8, 1918: The Hundred Days Campaign begins with Battle of Amiens.

November 11, 1918: First World War ends.

June 28, 1922: National Defence Act passed, effectively creating Department of National Defence (DND).

December 11, 1931: Statute of Westminster passed.

September 10, 1939: Canada declares war on Germany.

August 30, 1941: Convoy SC 42 sails out of Sydney, Nova Scotia.

December 7, 1941: Japanese attack Pearl Harbor, Hawaii. United States declares war on Japan, December 8, 1941, then declares war on Germany, December 11, 1941.

December 7, 1941: Canada declares war on Japan.

December 8, 1941 (Japanese time): Japan attacks Hong Kong.

August 19, 1942: Dieppe Raid launched.

July 9, 1943: Operation Husky, Allied invasion of Sicily, begins.

July 24–28, 1943: Firebombing of Hamburg.

September 3, 1943: Allied invasion of mainland Italy begins.

December 20–28, 1943: Battle for Ortona, Italy.

June 6, 1944: D-Day.

October 2–November 8, 1944: Battles for the Scheldt Estuary in Belgium and the Netherlands.

February 26–March 3, 1945: Operation Blockbuster.

April 30, 1945: Adolf Hitler commits suicide.

May 7, 1945: Germany surrenders.

September 2, 1945: Japan surrenders.

October 24, 1945: United Nations (U.N.) created.

April 4, 1949: North Atlantic Treaty Organization (NATO) created.

June 25, 1950: North Korea invades South Korea, starting the Korean War.

December 4, 1950: Captain Brock's task force aids in evacuation of Chinnamp'o.

April 22–25, 1951: Battle of Kapyong.

November 22–25, 1951: Battle of Hill 355.

July 27, 1953: Korean War Armistice Agreement signed.

November 12, 1956: Canadian General E.L.M. Burns and command elements of U.N. Emergency Force (UNEF) arrive in Cairo in response to Suez crisis.

May 12, 1958: North American Air Defense Command (later North American Aerospace Defense Command) created.

July 1960–June 1964: Canadian peacekeepers deployed to Congo as part of U.N. Opération des Nations Unies au Congo (ONUC).

March 4, 1964: United Nations approves deployment of peacekeepers to Cyprus as part of U.N. Peacekeeping Force in Cyprus (UNFICYP).

October 16, 1970: Prime Minister Pierre Elliott Trudeau invokes War Measures Act in what eventually becomes known as the October Crisis.

June 1986: Canadian Forces Administrative Order (CFAO) 49-14 and CFAO 49-15 issued.

February 1989: Canadian Human Rights Tribunal issues findings in regard to *Brown v. the Canadian Armed Forces.*

July 11, 1990: The 78-day Kanehsatà:ke Resistance begins.

February 21, 1992: United Nations authorizes deployment of peacekeepers to former Yugoslavia as part of U.N. Protection Force (UNPROFOR).

December 3, 1992: United Nations authorizes deployment of peacekeepers to Somalia as part of U.N. Unified Task Force (UNITAF).

October 5, 1993: United Nations establishes U.N. Assistance Mission for Rwanda (UNAMIR).

April 6, 1994: Rwandan president Juvénal Habyarimana killed in plane crash, setting off Rwandan genocide.

March 5, 1995: Canadian Airborne Regiment officially disbanded.

September 11, 2001: Al-Qaeda carries out series of terrorist attacks on U.S. soil.

October 7, 2001: Prime Minister Jean Chrétien announces Canada will deploy its military in support of an American-led invasion of Afghanistan.

November 2, 2001: HMCS *Halifax* begins counterterrorism operations in the Arabian Sea as part of Operation Apollo.

December 2001: Canadian Special Forces (Joint Task Force 2) arrive in Afghanistan.

February 2006: Task Force Orion completes arrival in Kandahar Province.

September 2–17, 2006: Operation Medusa.

January 22, 2008: Manley Report released.

February 25, 2011: Operation Mobile, deployment of Canadian forces to Libya, begins.

March 12, 2014: Canadian mission in Afghanistan ends.

April 30, 2015: Deschamps Report released.

Appendix 3
MILITARY FORMATIONS

CANADA (ARMY)

Pre-Second Boer War
Permanent Force (PF)
Non-Permanent Militia (NPM)
Red River Expedition (Wolseley expedition)
9th Voltigeurs of Quebec
65th Carabiniers of Montreal
10th Royal Grenadiers
Queen's Own Rifles
Nile Expedition
Yukon Field Force

Second Boer War
2nd (Special Service) Battalion, Royal Canadian Regiment of Infantry (2 RCRI), later the 2nd Battalion, Royal Canadian Regiment (2 RCR)
Royal Canadian Field Artillery (RCFA)
Royal Canadian Dragoons (RCD)

1st and 2nd Canadian Mounted Rifles (1 CMR and 2 CMR)
Lord Strathcona's Horse

First World War
Canadian Expeditionary Force (CEF)/Canadian Corps
1st Division: 1st (2nd Battalion), 2nd (7th and 10th Battalions), and 3rd Brigades
2nd Division: Canadian Motor Machine Gun Brigade, 5th Brigade, 6th Brigade (27th Battalion)
3rd Division: 8th Brigade
4th Division
5th Division
Princess Patricia's Canadian Light Infantry (PPCLI)
Royal Canadian Regiment (RCR)
4th Canadian Mounted Rifles
Canadian Army Medical Corps
Canadian Cavalry Brigade
No. 2 Construction Battalion
Canadian Siberian Expeditionary Force

Second World War
I Canadian Corps
II Canadian Corps
First Canadian Army
1st Canadian Infantry Division (1 CID): 1st and 2nd Brigades
2nd Canadian Infantry Division (2 CID)
3rd Canadian Infantry Division (3 CID): 7th, 8th, and 9th Brigades
4th Canadian Armoured Division (4 CAD)
5th Canadian Armoured Division (5 CAD)
1st Canadian Infantry Brigade (1 CIB)
2nd Canadian Infantry Brigade (2 CIB)
11th Canadian Infantry Brigade (11 CIB)
2nd Canadian Armoured Brigade (2 CAB)
5th Canadian Armoured Brigade (5 CAB)
1st Canadian Army Tank Brigade (1st Canadian Armoured Brigade)
Royal 22nd Regiment (Van Doos)

C-Force (Winnipeg Grenadiers and Royal Rifles of Canada)

Calgary Tank Regiment (14th Armoured)

Fusiliers Mont-Royal (FMRs)

Queen's Own Rifles

Princess Patricia's Canadian Light Infantry (PPCLI)

Royal Canadian Regiment (RCR)

Royal Hamilton Light Infantry

Black Watch

4th Princess Louise Dragoon Guards (RCFA, 5 CAD)

British Columbia Dragoons (5 CAB, 5 CAD)

Perth Regiment (11 CIB, 5 CAD)

Hastings and Prince Edward Regiment

Loyal Edmonton Regiment

Three Rivers Regiment

Calgary Highlanders

48th Highlanders

Seaforth Highlanders

1st Canadian Parachute Battalion

Regina Rifle Regiment

1st Special Service Force

Post–Second World War

Canadian Army Special Force (CASF), renamed 25th Canadian Infantry
    Brigade Group (25 CIBG)

1st, 2nd, and 3rd Battalions, Princess Patricia's Canadian Light Infantry
    (1, 2, and 3 PPCLI)

1st, 2nd, and 3rd Battalions, Royal Canadian Regiment (1, 2, and 3 RCR)

Royal 22nd Regiment (Van Doos)

5 Combat Engineer Regiment

1st Canadian Infantry Brigade (1 CIB)

Black Watch

Canadian Guards

Lord Strathcona's Horse

British Columbia Dragoons

Royal Canadian Dragoons (RCD)

Queen's Own Rifles
Canadian Airborne Regiment (CAR) and 2 Commando CAR
Joint Task Force Afghanistan Air Wing (JTF-2)

CANADA (AIR FORCE)

Royal Air Force (Canadian) 242 Squadron
Royal Canadian Air Force 1, 110, 162, 405, 413, 417, 418, and 426 Squadrons
6 Bomber Group
Royal Canadian Air Force 331 Wing (402, 424, and 425 Squadrons)
Royal Canadian Air Force Women's Division
1 Air Division

CANADA (NAVY)

31st Canadian Minesweeping Flotilla
Women's Royal Canadian Naval Service (WRCNS or Wrens)

GERMANY (ARMY)

Second World War
Army Group B
Seventh Army
Tenth Army
Fourteenth Army
Fifteenth Army
Hermann Göring Division
12th SS Hitler Youth Division
21st Panzer Division
26th Panzer Division
29th Panzer Grenadier Division
90th Grenadier Division

Panzer Lehr Division
1st Parachute Division

UNITED KINGDOM AND ALLIES (ARMY)

First World War
British Expeditionary Force (BEF)
First Army
Second Army
Third Army
Fourth Army
Fifth Army
Eighth Army
28th Division
British Cavalry Corps
Royal Newfoundland Regiment
Australian Corps

Second World War
British Expeditionary Force (BEF)
15th Army Group
V British Corps
XXX British Corps
3rd British Division
8th Indian Division
6th Armoured Division
52nd Division
Polish II Corps
Royal Army Medical Corps

Post–Second World War
1st Commonwealth Division
27th British Commonwealth Infantry Brigade (27 BCIB)
28th British Commonwealth Infantry Brigade (28 BCIB)
29th British Infantry Brigade

British Army of the Rhine (BAOR)
Royal Australian Regiment (RAR)

UNITED KINGDOM (AIR FORCE)

Royal Air Force 249
Desert Air Force
Second Tactical Air Force (2TAF)

UNITED KINGDOM (NAVY)

Royal Navy
10th Destroyer Flotilla

UNITED STATES (ARMY)

Second World War
First Army
Fifth Army
Seventh Army
U.S. Medical Corps

Post-Second World War
Eighth Army
IX Corps (2nd Infantry Division)
4th Infantry Division
7th Infantry Regiment

UNITED STATES (AIR FORCE)

4th Allied Tactical Air Force

NOTES

Chapter 1: The Expanding Nation

1   Jennifer Reid, *Louis Riel and the Creation of Modern Canada: Mythic Discourse and the Postcolonial State* (Winnipeg: University of Manitoba Press, 2012), 9.

2   Much of this is discussed in chapters 6, 7, and 8 in M. Max Hamon's brilliant book, *The Audacity of His Enterprise: Louis Riel and the Métis Nation That Canada Never Was, 1840–1875* (Montreal: McGill-Queen's University Press, 2019).

3   Hamon, 176–80.

4   George Stanley argues this was, indeed, a major mistake in his book *Louis Riel* (Toronto: Ryerson Press, 1963), while Hamon attempts a more balanced look at Riel's decision to execute Scott on pages 198–99 of *The Audacity of His Enterprise*.

5   J.M. Bumsted, *The Red River Rebellion* (Winnipeg: Watson and Dwyer, 1996), 166.

6   A good description of the events of the expedition comes from the memoir of Captain G.L. Huyshe, one of Wolseley's staff officers: Captain G.L. Huyshe, *The Red River Expedition* (London and New York: Macmillan, 1871).

7   Hamon, 207.

8   Hamon, 144.

9   J.L. Granatstein, *Canada's Army: Waging War and Keeping the Peace*, 3rd ed. (Toronto: University of Toronto Press, 2021), 25.

10   This is a major focus of James Daschuk's groundbreaking work in *Clearing the Plains: Disease, Politics of Starvation, and the Loss of Indigenous Life* (Regina: University of Regina Press, 2019).

11   Daschuk, 19.

12   Daschuk, 20.

13   The military events of the North-West Resistance are well described in Bob Beal and Rod Macleod's *Prairie Fire: The 1885 North-West Rebellion* (Toronto: McClelland & Stewart, 1984).

14   Blair Stonechild and Bill Waiser, *Loyal Till Death: Indians and the North-West Rebellion* (Markham, ON: Fifth House Publishing, 1997), 96–99.

15   Daschuk, 152–53.

16   Stonechild and Waiser, 142.

17   Granatstein, *Canada's Army*, 30.

18   Much of this criticism came from the Canadian officers who served under him. Back in Ottawa, he was celebrated until a scandal involving stolen furs led to his resignation and return to England.

19   Reid, 29.

20   Daschuk, 159–60.

21   Granatstein, *Canada's Army*, 30.

Chapter 2: Fighting for the Empire

1   There is very little written on this event in Canadian military history. C.P. Stacey published one book and two articles on the subject in the 1950s (see Bibliography). More recently, Anthony P. Michel wrote a 2012 dissertation on the subject at Carleton University, which then became the basis for the article "To Represent the Country in Egypt: Aboriginality, Britishness, Anglophone Canadian Identities and the Nile Voyageur Contingent," *Histoire sociale* 39, no. 77 (Spring 2006): 45–77.

2   Jack Granatstein covers this extensively in Chapter 2 of *Canada's Army*.

3   Eirik Brazier, "Guardians of Empire? British Imperial Officers in Canada, 1874–1914," in *Fighting with the Empire: Canada, Britain, and Global Conflict, 1867–1947*, eds. Steve Marti and William Pratt (Vancouver: UBC Press, 2019).

4   Granatstein, *Canada's Army*, 35; Brereton Greenhous, *Guarding the Goldfields: The Story of the Yukon Field Force* (Toronto: Dundurn Press, 1996).

5   Geoff Keelan, *Duty to Dissent: Henri Bourassa and the First World War* (Vancouver: UBC Press, 2020).

6   Granatstein, *Canada's Army*, 36–37.

7   A more detailed exploration of Canadian military participation in the Second Boer War can be found in Carman Miller's *Painting the Map Red: Canada and the South African War, 1899–1902* (Montreal: McGill-Queen's University Press, 1993). Granatstein's *Canada's Army* provides a good summary on pages 37–45.

8   One of the best books on this subject is Elizabeth van Heyningen's *The Concentration Camps of the Anglo-Boer War: A Social History* (Johannesburg, South Africa: Jacana Media, 2013).

9   Keelan, *Duty to Dissent*, 26.

10 Carman Miller, "The Montreal Flag Riot of 1900," in *One Flag, One Queen, One Tongue: New Zealand, the British Empire, and the South African War, 1899–1902*, eds. John Crawford and Ian McGibbon (Auckland, NZ: Auckland University Press, 2003), 165–79.

11 Granatstein, *Canada's Army*, 46.

12 Granatstein, *Canada's Army*, 46.

13 Desmond Morton, *A Military History of Canada: From Champlain to Kosovo*, 4th ed. (Toronto: McClelland & Stewart, 1999), 124.

14 Siobhan J. McNaught, "The Rise of Proto-Nationalism: Sir Wilfrid Laurier and the Founding of the Naval Service of Canada, 1902–1910," in *A Nation's Navy: In Quest of Canadian Naval Identity*, ed. Michael L. Hadley (Montreal: McGill-Queen's University Press, 1996).

15 William Johnston, William G.P. Rawling, Richard H. Gimblett, and John MacFarlane, *The Seabound Coast: The Official History of the Royal Canadian Navy, 1867–1939*, Volume I (Toronto: Dundurn Press, 2011), 183–85.

Chapter 3: The First World War: 1914–1916

1   Geoff Keelan, "For King or Country? Quebec, the Empire, and the First World War," in *Fighting with the Empire: Canada, Britain, and Global Conflict, 1867–1947*, eds. Steve Marti and William Pratt (Vancouver: UBC Press, 2019).

2   Tim Cook, *At the Sharp End: Canadians Fighting the Great War, 1914–1916*, Volume One (Toronto: Viking Canada, 2007), 23.

3   This is covered very well in Tim Cook's *The Madman and the Butcher: The Sensational Wars of Sam Hughes and General Arthur Currie* (Toronto: Allen Lane Canada, 2010), 57–71.

4   Tim Cook, "He Was Determined to Go: Underage Soldiers in the Canadian Expeditionary Force," *Social History* 41, no. 81 (May 2008): 41–74.

5   There are numerous works providing important accounts of Canada's military participation in the First World War. G.W.L. Nicholson's official history is certainly one of them: *Canadian Expeditionary Force, 1914–1919* (Ottawa: Queen's Printer and Controller of Stationery, 1964). Tim Cook wrote an excellent two-volume series, *At the Sharp End: Canadians Fighting the Great War, 1914–1916* and *Shock Troops: Canadians Fighting the Great War, 1917–1918* (Toronto: Viking Canada, 2009).

6   Granatstein, *Canada's Army*, 61.

7   Cook, *At the Sharp End*, 154.

8   One of those casualties was Lieutenant Alexis Helmer. Inspired by Helmer's burial, his good friend Major John McCrae wrote a poem on May 3, 1915. It was published in the British magazine *Punch* and was entitled "In Flanders Fields."

9   Granatstein, *Canada's Army*, 80; Kandace Bogaert, "Patient Experience and the Treatment of Venereal Disease in Toronto's Military Base Hospital During the First World War," *Canadian Military History* 26, no. 2 (2017).

10   Granatstein, *Canada's Army*, 83.

11   Cook, *At the Sharp End*, 344.

12   Haig receives a well-balanced examination — and dare I say a slight rehabilitation — in Gary Sheffield's book *The Chief: Douglas Haig and the British Army* (London: Aurum Press, 2012).

13   One of the best books on Canadian tactics and technology on the Western Front is Bill Rawling's *Surviving Trench Warfare: Technology and the Canadian Corps, 1914–1918* (Toronto: University of Toronto Press, 1992).

14   Cook, *Madman and the Butcher*, 160–79.

15   Mark Osborne Humphries, *A Weary Road: Shell Shock in the Canadian Expeditionary Force, 1914–1918* (Toronto: University of Toronto Press, 2018).

16   Bohdan S. Kordan, "First World War Internment in Canada: Enemy Aliens and the Blurring of the Military/Civilian Distinction," *Canadian Military History* 29, no. 2 (2020).

17   Cook, *Shock Troops*, 40.

18   The social and cultural life of Canadian soldiers in the Great War is the subject of Tim Cook's masterful work *The Secret History of Soldiers: How Canadians Survived the Great War* (Toronto: Allen Lane Canada, 2018).

Chapter 4: The First World War: 1917–1918

1 Rawling, 98.
2 The battle and its place in Canadian mythology is the subject of Tim Cook's *Vimy: The Battle and the Legend* (Toronto: Allen Lane Canada, 2017).
3 Cook, *Vimy*, 152.
4 Cook, *Vimy*, 153–62
5 Keelan, "For King or Country," 125.
6 Martin F. Auger, "On the Brink of Civil War: The Canadian Government and the Suppression of the 1918 Quebec Easter Riots," *The Canadian Historical Review* 89, no. 4 (December 2008): 503–40.
7 Calvin W. Ruck, *Canada's Black Battalion: No. 2 Construction 1916–1920* (Halifax: The Society for the Protection and Preservation of Black Culture in Nova Scotia, 1986).
8 Dan Black, *Harry Livingstone's Forgotten Men: Canadians and the Chinese Labour Corps in the First World War* (Toronto: James Lorimer and Company, 2019).
9 Timothy C. Winegard, *For King and Kanata: Canadian Indians and the First World War* (Winnipeg: University of Manitoba Press, 2012).
10 Mark Osborne Humphries, "The Best Laid Plans: Sir Arthur Currie's First Operations as Corps Commander," in *Capturing Hill 70: Canada's Forgotten Battle of the First World War*, eds. Douglas E. Delaney and Serge Marc Durflinger (Vancouver: UBC Press, 2016), 78–101.
11 Nick Lloyd, *Passchendaele: A New History* (London: Viking, 2017), 253.
12 Granatstein, *Canada's Army*, 118.
13 Shane Schreiber, *Shock Army of the British Empire: The Canadian Corps in the Last 100 Days of the Great War* (Westport, CT: Praeger, 1997).
14 Linda J. Quiney has a great article on Canadian nurses in the war entitled "Gendering Patriotism: Canadian Volunteer Nurses as the Female 'Soldiers' of the Great War," in *A Sisterhood of Suffering and Service: Women and Girls of Canada and Newfoundland During the First World War*, eds. Sarah Glassford and Amy Shaw (Vancouver: UBC Press, 2012), 103–25.
15 Patrick Dennis's book looks at the contributions made by Canadian conscripts to the Hundred Days Campaign: *Reluctant Warriors: Canadian Conscripts and the Great War* (Vancouver: UBC Press, 2017).
16 David Borys, "Crossing the Canal: Combined Arms Operations at the Canal du Nord, September–October 1918," *Canadian Military History* 20, no. 4 (Autumn 2011).

17 Granatstein, *Canada's Army*, 157.

18 Cook, *Shock Troops*, 590.

19 Cook, *Shock Troops*, 590–96.

20 Benjamin Isitt, *From Victoria to Vladivostok: Canada's Siberian Expedition, 1917–1919* (Vancouver: UBC Press, 2010).

21 Dennis, *Reluctant Warriors*, 229.

Chapter 5: The Interwar Years

1 David Jay Bercuson, "The Winnipeg General Strike of 1919," in *Canada 1919: A Nation Shaped by War*, eds. Tim Cook and J.L. Granatstein (Vancouver: UBC Press, 2020), 148–61.

2 Brock Millman, *Polarity, Patriotism, and Dissent in Great War Canada* (Toronto: University of Toronto Press, 2020).

3 Lara Campbell, "'We Who Have Wallowed in the Mud of Flanders': First World War Veterans, Unemployment, and the Development of Welfare in Canada, 1929–1939," *Journal of the Canadian Historical Association* 11, no. 1 (2000): 125–49.

4 Campbell, "'We Who Have Wallowed in the Mud of Flanders,'" 141; also see Desmond Morton and Glenn Wright, *Winning the Second Battle: Canadian Veterans and the Return to Civilian Life, 1915–1930* (Toronto: University of Toronto Press, 1987).

5 Eric Brown and Tim Cook, "The 1936 Vimy Pilgrimage," *Canadian Military History* 20, no. 2 (Spring 2020): 38.

6 Cook, *Vimy*, 189.

7 Granatstein, *Canada's Army*, 165.

8 William McAndrew, "Canadian Defence Planning Between the Wars: The Royal Canadian Air Force Comes of Age," *Canadian Military History* 22, no. 1 (Winter 2013).

9 Sean M. Maloney, "Maple Leaf Over the Caribbean: Gunboat Diplomacy Canadian Style?," in *Canadian Gunboat Diplomacy: The Canadian Navy and Foreign Policy*, eds. Ann Griffiths, Richard Gimblett, and Peter Haydon (Halifax: Centre for Foreign Policy Studies, 2000).

10 Marc Milner, "Walter Hose to the Rescue: Navy, Part 13," *Legion*, January 1, 2006, legionmagazine.com/walter-hose-to-the-rescue.

11 Marc Milner covers the incredible work of Commodore Hose in saving the navy during the interwar period in Chapter 4 of his book *Canada's Navy: The First Century* (Toronto: University of Toronto Press, 2010).

12   This is well documented in Robert Teigrob's book *Four Days in Hitler's Germany: Mackenzie King's Mission to Avert a Second World War* (Toronto: University of Toronto Press, 2019).

Chapter 6: The Second World War: The Conflict at Sea and in Air

1   Granatstein, *Canada's Army*, 182.

2   F.J. Hatch, *Aerodrome of Democracy: Canada and the British Commonwealth Air Training Plan, 1939–1945* (Ottawa: Directorate of History and Heritage, 1983), 14.

3   Paul Dickson, "Crerar and the Decision to Garrison Hong Kong," *Canadian Military History* 3, no. 1 (1994): 102; Terry Copp, "The Decision to Reinforce Hong Kong: September 1941," *Canadian Military History* 20, no. 2 (2011): 5–6.

4   Granatstein, *Canada's Army*, 200–201.

5   David O'Keefe writes in *One Day in August: The Untold Story Behind Canada's Tragedy at Dieppe* (Toronto: Vintage Canada, 2014), 397: "Nothing could be clearer: this intelligence pipeline was central to the Dieppe Raid, and [Ian] Fleming was the final link in the chain designed to bring the pinched material home." Tim Cook writes in *The Necessary War: Canadians Fighting the Second World War, 1939–1945*, Volume 1 (Toronto: Penguin Canada, 2015), 255: "[Some historians have argued] that the entire Dieppe Raid was but a cover for the commando pinch. It was not."

6   Cook, *Necessary War*, 257.

7   Cook, *Necessary War*, 283.

8   Cook, *Necessary War*, 283.

9   Marc Milner, *North Atlantic Run: The Royal Canadian Navy and the Battle for the Convoys* (Toronto: University of Toronto Press, 1985).

10   Cook, *Necessary War*, 109.

11   Cook, *Necessary War*, 121.

12   Cook, *Necessary War*, 305.

13   Milner, *North Atlantic Run*, 103.

14   Cook, *Necessary War*, 181.

15   Cook, *Necessary War*, 304.

16   W.A.B. Douglas et al., *No Higher Purpose: The Official Operational History of the Royal Canadian Navy in the Second World War, 1939–1943*, Volume II, Part 1 (St. Catharines, ON: Vanwell Publishing, 2002), 339.

17 Isabel Campbell, "A Brave New World: 1945–1960," in *The Naval Service of Canada, 1910–2010* (Toronto: Dundurn Press, 2009). See also canada.ca /en/navy/services/history/naval-service-1910-2010.html.

18 W.A.B. Douglas et al., *A Blue Water Navy: The Official Operational History of the Royal Canadian Navy in the Second World War, 1943–1945,* Volume II, Part 2 (St. Catharines, ON: Vanwell Publishing, 2007), 185.

19 Cook, *Necessary War,* 45.

20 When referring to the Battle of Britain, Winston Churchill famously stated: "Never in the field of human conflict was so much owed by so many to so few." Canada's role in the Battle of Britain is well accounted for in Brereton Greenhous et al., *The Crucible of War 1939–1945: The Official History of the Royal Canadian Air Force,* Volume III (Toronto: University of Toronto Press, 1994), 166–99.

21 Brian Nolan, *Hero: The Buzz Beurling Story* (Toronto: Lester & Orpen Dennys, 1981).

22 Tim Cook, *Fight to the Finish: Canadians in the Second World War, 1944– 1945* (Toronto: Allen Lane, 2015), 168.

23 This included both air-to-air and air-to-ground targets.

24 Scot Robertson, "In the Shadow of Death by Moonlight," in *The Valour and the Horror Revisited,* eds. David Bercuson and S.F. Wise (Montreal: McGill-Queen's University Press, 1994), 153–79.

25 Cook, *Necessary War,* 317.

26 Robertson, 165.

27 Cook, *Fight to the Finish,* 100.

28 Cook, *Fight to the Finish,* 369.

29 Cook, *Fight to the Finish,* 372.

30 Cook, *Fight to the Finish,* 376.

31 Jeffrey A. Keshen, *Saints, Sinners, and Soldiers: Canada's Second World War* (Vancouver: UBC, 2004).

32 Keshen, 150–52.

33 Keshen, 175.

34 Tina Davidson, "'A Woman's Right to Charm and Beauty': Maintaining the Feminine Ideal in the Canadian Women's Army Corps," *Atlantis* 26, no. 1 (Fall/Winter 2001): 45–54.

35 Davidson, 45.

36 Keshen, 186.

37 R. Scott Sheffield, "'Of Pure European Descent and of the White Race': Recruitment Policy and Aboriginal Canadians, 1939–1945," *Canadian Military History* 5, no. 1 (Spring 1996): 8–15.

38 Keshen, 55.

39 J.L. Granatstein, "Staring into the Abyss," in *How Britain's Weakness Forced Canada into the Arms of the United States* (Toronto: University of Toronto Press, 1989), 21–40.

40 Granatstein, "Staring into the Abyss," 35.

41 J.L. Granatstein and Dean F. Oliver, "The Canadian Home Front in the First and Second World Wars," *Canadian Military History* 21, no. 4 (Autumn 2012).

42 One of the best edited volumes covering this topic is *Landscapes of Injustice: A New Perspective on the Internment and Dispossession of Japanese Canadians*, ed. Jordan Stanger-Ross (Montreal: McGill-Queen's University Press, 2020).

43 Arthur W. Gullachsen, *An Army of Never-Ending Strength: Reinforcing the Canadians in Northwest Europe, 1944–1945* (Vancouver: UBC Press, 2021).

44 Daniel Byers, *Zombie Army: The Canadian Army and Conscription in the Second World War* (Vancouver: UBC Press, 2016).

Chapter 7: The Second World War: The Conflict on Land

1   Cook, *Necessary War*, 352.

2   Cook, *Necessary War*, 371.

3   Robert Engen, *Strangers in Arms: Combat Motivation in the Canadian Army, 1943–1945* (Montreal: McGill-Queen's University Press, 2016).

4   Cook, *Necessary War*, 402.

5   Granatstein, *Canada's Army*, 241.

6   Montgomery had returned to Britain to prepare for D-Day.

7   Douglas E. Delaney, *The Soldiers' General: Bert Hoffmeister at War* (Vancouver: UBC Press, 2005), 143.

8   Cook, *Fight to the Finish*, 92.

9   Cook, *Fight to the Finish*, 285.

10 Cook, *Fight to the Finish*, 285.

11 Delaney, *Soldiers' General*, 168.

12 Engen, 110–15.

13 Granatstein, *Canada's Army*, 256.

14 Marc Milner, *Stopping the Panzers: The Untold Story of D-Day* (Lawrence, KS: University of Kansas Press, 2014).

15 Granatstein, *Canada's Army*, 260.

16 John English, *Monty and the Canadian Army* (Toronto: University of Toronto Press, 2021), 131.

17   Cook, *Fight to the Finish*, 215. John English writes: "From 'Epsom' up to the First US Army breakout on 25 July, German reactions saw between 520 and 725 panzers continuously deployed against the British sector, whereas during this same period the Americans rarely faced more than 190." *Monty and the Canadian Army*, 131.

18   *Bocage* refers to the agricultural fields of Normandy that were often enclosed by large hedgerows or groves of trees. Particularly prevalent in the American sector, these were ideal terrain for the camouflaging of enemy guns and posed a significant challenge to the U.S. ability to move quickly across the territory.

19   Terry Copp provides a masterful accounting of the battle in *Fields of Fire: The Canadians in Normandy* (Toronto: University of Toronto Press, 2003).

20   Gullachsen, 34.

21   David Borys, *Civilians at the Sharp End: First Canadian Army Civil Affairs in Northwest Europe* (Montreal: McGill-Queen's University Press, 2021).

22   Terry Copp, *Cinderella Army: The Canadians in Northwest Europe, 1944–1945* (Toronto: University of Toronto Press, 2006), 152.

23   Copp, *Cinderella Army*, 180.

24   English, 190.

25   Cook, *Fight to the Finish*, 392.

26   Borys, *Civilians at the Sharp End*, 177.

27   Borys, *Civilians at the Sharp End*, 198–99.

28   R. Scott Sheffield, *The Red Man's on the Warpath: The Image of the "Indian" and the Second World War* (Vancouver: UBC Press, 2004).

Chapter 8: International Challenges: The Cold War and Korea

1   In November 1940, the Permanent Active Militia became the Canadian Army while the Non-Permanent Active Militia became the Army Reserve.

2   Granatstein, *Canada's Army*, 317–18.

3   The term "United Nations" was used fairly extensively by both the British and the Americans in the latter years of the Second World War to describe the Allies. The intergovernmental organization that we recognize today was established in the aftermath of the Second World War. Fifty nations, including Canada, met in San Francisco in April 1945 to draft the U.N. charter, which was approved later in June the same year. The official start of the United Nations dates to October 24, 1945, when the organization began operating. It is headquartered in New York City and now includes 193 member states.

4   Norman Hillmer and J.L. Granatstein, *Empire to Umpire: Canada and the World to the 1990s* (Toronto: Irwin Publishing, 2000).

5   David Bercuson, *Blood on the Hills: The Canadian Army in the Korean War* (Toronto: University of Toronto Press, 2002), 32.

6   Bercuson, *Blood on the Hills*, 53.

7   Bercuson, *Blood on the Hills*, 58.

8   The Fairchild C-119 Flying Boxcar was an American military transport aircraft.

9   Michelle Fowler discusses the awarding of the Presidential Unit Citation in her article "'For Extraordinary Heroism and Outstanding Performance': Kap'yong, 2nd Battalion Princess Patricia's Light Infantry and the Controversy Surrounding the Presidential Citation," *Canadian Military History* 13, no. 4 (2004).

10   Department of National Defence, Directorate of History and Heritage, *Canada and the Korean War* (Montreal: Art Global, 2002), 35–36.

11   Van Fleet had been given command of the army when Matthew Ridgway was promoted to Supreme Commander U.N. Forces after General Douglas MacArthur was unceremoniously relieved of command by President Harry Truman back in April.

12   Granatstein, *Canada's Army*, 331.

13   Bercuson, *Blood on the Hills*, 152.

14   K. Meghan Fitzpatrick, "Prostitutes, Penicillin, and Prophylaxis: Fighting Venereal Disease in the Commonwealth Division During the Korean War, 1950–1953," *Social History of Medicine* 28, no. 3 (August 2015): 555–75.

15   Bercuson, *Blood on the Hills*, 177.

16   "Outside the wire" refers to anything beyond the outermost defences (often barbed wire) of a base or position.

17   Granatstein, *Canada's Army*, 335.

18   Granatstein, *Canada's Army*, 337.

Chapter 9: The Era of Peacekeeping

1   Hillmer and Granatstein, *Empire to Umpire*, 196.

2   Michael K. Carroll, *Pearson's Peacekeepers: Canada and the United Nations Emergency Force, 1956–1967* (Vancouver: UBC Press, 2009), 34.

3   Carroll, 145.

4   The development of this peacekeeping myth is the focus of Colin McCullough's book *Creating Canada's Peacekeeping Past* (Vancouver: UBC Press, 2016).

5   Granatstein, *Canada's Army*, 345.

6   Kevin A. Spooner, *Canada, the Congo Crisis, and UN Peacekeeping, 1960–1964* (Vancouver: UBC Press, 2009), 31–35.

7   En route to negotiate a ceasefire in the Congo, Hammarskjöld was killed on September 18, 1961, when his plane crashed near Ndola, Northern Rhodesia (now Zambia). The origins of the crash are still hotly debated.

8   Donald C. Story and Russell Isinger, "The Origins of the Cancellation of Canada's Avro CF-105 Arrow Fighter Program: A Failure of Strategy," *Journal of Strategic Studies* 30, no. 6 (2007): 1025–50.

9   Morton, *Military History of Canada*, 249.

10   Granatstein, *Canada's Army*, 350.

11   Granatstein, *Canada's Army*, 367.

12   Granatstein, *Canada's Army*, 374–75.

13   Patrick Gossage, *Close to the Charisma: My Years Between the Press and Pierre Elliott Trudeau* (Toronto: McClelland & Stewart, 1986), 260.

14   Granatstein, *Canada's Army*, 381.

15   Effectively, a rebel group called the United Somali Congress (USC) ousted the government of Siad Barre. However, in the aftermath of this coup, the USC fractured while other rebel groups such as the Somali Patriotic Movement and the Somali Democratic Alliance refused to recognize the USC's provisional government.

16   David J. Bercuson, *Significant Incident: Canada's Army, the Airborne, and the Murder in Somalia* (Toronto: McClelland & Stewart, 1996).

17   Granatstein, *Canada's Army*, 406.

18   Sean Maloney covers this extensively in a number of his pieces, including his book *Canada and UN Peacekeeping: Cold War by Other Means, 1945–1970* (St. Catharines, ON: Vanwell Publishing, 2002).

19   Andrea Lane, "Women in the Canadian Armed Forces," in *Canadian Defence Policy in Theory and Practice*, eds. Thomas Juneau, Philippe Lagassé, and Srdjan Vucetic (New York: Springer International, 2020), 355–57.

20   Charlotte Duval-Lantoine, *The Ones We Let Down: Toxic Leadership Culture and Gender Integration in the Canadian Forces* (Montreal: McGill-Queen's University Press, 2022), 30.

21   Major R.C. Mclean, "Equal but Unfair: The Failure of Gender Integration in the Canadian Armed Forces" (master's dissertation, Canadian Forces College, 2017), 51–55.

22   In 2021, Prime Minister Justin Trudeau officially apologized for the "LGBT Purge." See *Statement by the Minister of Defence on the LGBT*

Purge Fund Report, May 17, 2021, canada.ca/en/department-national
-defence/news/2021/05/statement-by-the-minister-of-national-defence
-on-the-lgbt-purge-report.html.

23   Carmen Poulin et al., "Discharged for Homosexuality from the Canadian
Military: Health Implications for Lesbians," in *Feminism and Psychology*
19, no. 4 (2009): 498.

Chapter 10: A Tumultuous 21st Century: From Peacekeepers to Peace Enforcers

1   Granatstein, *Canada's Army*, 414.

2   Justin Massie, "Why Canada Goes to War: Explaining Combat
Participation in US-Led Coalitions," *Canadian Journal of Political Science*
52, no. 3 (2019): 586.

3   Lieutenant-Colonel Michel-Henri St. Louis, "The Strategic Advisory
Team in Afghanistan: Part of the Canadian Comprehensive Approach to
Stability Operations," *Canadian Military Journal* 9, no. 3 (2009): 58–67.
Strategic Advisory Team-A was controversially cancelled in 2008.

4   Caroline Leprince offers an excellent look at the KPRT's work in her article
"The Canadian-led Kandahar Provincial Reconstruction Team: A Success
Story?," *International Journal* 68, no. 2 (2013): 359–77.

5   Granatstein, *Canada's Army*, 432.

6   Granatstein, *Canada's Army*, 435.

7   Major-General David Fraser, *Operation Medusa: The Furious Battle That
Saved Afghanistan from the Taliban* (Toronto: McClelland & Stewart, 2018).
Jack Granatstein tempers the bold claim by Fraser's title when he writes in
Canada's Army, 437: "That might overstate matters, but not by much."

8   T. Robert Fowler, *Combat Mission Kandahar: The Canadian Experience
in Afghanistan* (Toronto: Dundurn Press, 2016), 28.

9   Granatstein, *Canada's Army*, 445.

10   Granatstein, *Canada's Army*, 439–41.

11   Fowler, 53.

12   Sean M. Maloney, "Counter-Insurgency Versus 'COIN' in Bazaar-e
Panjwayi and Panjwayi District, 2008–2010," in *No Easy Task: Fighting
in Afghanistan*, eds. Bernd Horn and Emily Spencer (Toronto: Dundurn
Press, 2012), 232–55.

13   Carl Forsberg, *Counterinsurgency in Kandahar: Evaluating the 2010
Hamkari Campaign* (Washington, D.C.: Institute for the Study of War,
2010).

14 In 2014, Roland Paris published a policy brief for the Centre for International Policy Studies that provided a sober look at the results of Canada's work in Afghanistan in "The Truth About Canada's Mission in Afghanistan," *Policy Options* (March 2014), cips-cepi.ca/how-canada -failed-in-afghanistan. Sean Maloney gives his own, more nuanced assessment in his article "'Was It Worth It?' Canadian Intervention in Afghanistan and Perceptions of Success or Failure," *Canadian Military Journal* 14, no. 1 (Winter 2013): 19–31.

15 Karl P. Mueller ed., *Precision and Purpose: Airpower in the Libyan Civil War* (Santa Monica, CA: RAND Corporation, 2015).

16 Lane, 358; Marie Deschamps, *External Review into Sexual Misconduct and Sexual Harassment in the Canadian Armed Forces* (Ottawa: Department of National Defence, 2015), canada.ca/en/department-national -defence/corporate/reports-publications/sexual-misbehaviour/external -review-2015.html.

17 Adam Chapnick and Christopher John Kukucha, *The Harper Era in Canadian Foreign Policy: Parliament, Politics, and Canada's Global Posture* (Vancouver: UBC Press, 2016).

18 Andrew Richter, "The Liberal Government and Canadian Defence Policy: Three Critical Issues," *Journal of Military and Strategic Studies* 19, no. 1 (2019): 64–100.

19 Richter, 77.

SELECT BIBLIOGRAPHY

Auger, Martin F. "On the Brink of Civil War: The Canadian Government and the Suppression of the 1918 Quebec Easter Riots." *The Canadian Historical Review* 89, no. 4 (December 2008): 503–40.

Beal, Bob, and Rod Macleod. *Prairie Fire: The 1885 North-West Rebellion.* Toronto: McClelland & Stewart, 1984.

Bercuson, David. *Blood on the Hills: The Canadian Army in the Korean War.* Toronto: University of Toronto Press, 2002.

———. *Significant Incident: Canada's Army, the Airborne, and the Murder in Somalia.* Toronto: McClelland & Stewart, 1996.

———. "The Winnipeg General Strike of 1919." In *Canada 1919: A Nation Shaped by War,* edited by Tim Cook and J.L. Granatstein. Vancouver: UBC Press, 2020.

Black, Dan. *Harry Livingstone's Forgotten Men: Canadians and the Chinese Labour Corps in the First World War.* Toronto: James Lorimer and Company, 2019.

Bogaert, Kandace. "Patient Experience and the Treatment of Venereal Disease in Toronto's Military Base Hospital During the First World War." *Canadian Military History* 26, no. 2 (2017).

Borys, David. *Civilians at the Sharp End: First Canadian Army Civil Affairs in Northwest Europe.* Montreal: McGill-Queen's University Press, 2021.

———. "Crossing the Canal: Combined Arms Operations at the Canal du Nord, September–October 1918." *Canadian Military History* 20, no. 4 (Autumn 2011).

Brazier, Eirik. "Guardians of Empire? British Imperial Officers in Canada, 1874–1914." In *Fighting with the Empire: Canada, Britain, and Global Conflict, 1867–1947*, edited by Steve Marti and William Pratt. Vancouver: UBC Press, 2019.

Brown, Eric, and Tim Cook. "The 1936 Vimy Pilgrimage." *Canadian Military History* 20, no. 2 (Spring 2020).

Bumsted, J.M. *The Red River Rebellion*. Winnipeg: Watson and Dwyer, 1996.

———. *Trials and Tribulations: The Red River Settlement and the Emergence of Manitoba, 1811–1870*. Winnipeg: Great Plains Publications, 2003.

Byers, Daniel. *Zombie Army: The Canadian Army and Conscription in the Second World War*. Vancouver: UBC Press, 2016.

Campbell, Isabel. "A Brave New World: 1945–1960." In *The Naval Service of Canada 1910–2010*. Toronto: Dundurn Press, 2009. See also canada.ca/en /navy/services/history/naval-service-1910-2010.html.

Campbell, Lara. "'We Who Have Wallowed in the Mud of Flanders': First World War Veterans, Unemployment, and the Development of Welfare in Canada, 1929–1939." *Journal of the Canadian Historical Association* 11, no. 1 (2000): 125–49.

Carroll, Michael K. *Pearson's Peacekeepers: Canada and the United Nations Emergency Force, 1956–1967*. Vancouver: UBC Press, 2009.

Chapnick, Adam, and Christopher John Kukucha. *The Harper Era in Canadian Foreign Policy: Parliament, Politics, and Canada's Global Posture*. Vancouver: UBC Press, 2016.

Cook, Tim. *At the Sharp End: Canadians Fighting the Great War, 1914–1916*, Volume One. Toronto: Viking Canada, 2009.

———. *Fields of Fire: The Canadians in Normandy*. Toronto: University of Toronto Press, 2003.

———. "He Was Determined to Go: Underage Soldiers in the Canadian Expeditionary Force." *Social History* 41, no. 81 (May 2008).

———. *The Madman and the Butcher: The Sensational Wars of Sam Hughes and General Arthur Currie*. Toronto: Allen Lane Canada, 2010.

———. *The Necessary War: Canadians Fighting the Second World War, 1939–1945*, Volume 1. Toronto: Penguin Canada, 2015.

———. *The Secret History of Soldiers: How Canadians Survived the Great War*. Toronto: Allen Lane Canada, 2018.

———. *Shock Troops: Canadians Fighting the Great War, 1917–1918*, Volume Two. Toronto: Viking Canada, 2009.

———. *Vimy: The Battle and the Legend*. Toronto: Allen Lane Canada, 2017.

Copp, Terry. *Cinderella Army: The Canadians in Northwest Europe, 1944–1945*. Toronto: University of Toronto Press, 2006.

Daschuk, James. *Clearing the Plains: Disease, Politics of Starvation, and the Loss of Indigenous Life*. Regina: University of Regina Press, 2019.

Davidson, Tina. "'A Woman's Right to Charm and Beauty': Maintaining the Feminine Ideal in the Canadian Women's Army Corps." *Atlantis* 26, no. 1 (Fall/Winter 2001): 45–54.

Delaney, Douglas E. *The Soldiers' General: Bert Hoffmeister at War*. Vancouver: UBC Press, 2005.

Dennis, Patrick. *Reluctant Warriors: Canadian Conscripts and the Great War*. Vancouver: UBC Press, 2017.

Deschamps, Marie. *External Review into Sexual Misconduct and Sexual Harassment in the Canadian Armed Forces*. Ottawa: Department of National Defence, 2015. canada.ca/en/department-national-defence/corporate /reports-publications/sexual-misbehaviour/external-review -2015.html.

Dickson, Paul. "Crerar and the Decision to Garrison Hong Kong." *Canadian Military History* 3, no. 1 (1994).

Douglas, W.A.B. et al. *A Blue Water Navy: The Official Operational History of the Royal Canadian Navy in the Second World War, 1943–1945*, Volume II, Part 2. St. Catharines, ON: Vanwell Publishing, 2007.

——— et al. *No Higher Purpose: The Official Operational History of the Royal Canadian Navy in the Second World War, 1939–1943*, Volume II, Part 1. St. Catharines, ON: Vanwell Publishing, 2002.

Duval-Lantoine, Charlotte. *The Ones We Let Down: Toxic Leadership Culture and Gender Integration in the Canadian Forces*. Montreal: McGill-Queen's University Press, 2022.

Engen, Robert. *Strangers in Arms: Combat Motivation in the Canadian Army, 1943–1945*. Montreal: McGill-Queen's University Press, 2016.

English, John. *Monty and the Canadian Army*. Toronto: University of Toronto Press, 2021.

Fitzpatrick, K. Meghan. "Prostitutes, Penicillin, and Prophylaxis: Fighting Venereal Disease in the Commonwealth Division During the Korean War, 1950–1953." *Social History of Medicine* 28, no. 3 (August 2015): 555–75.

Flanagan, Thomas. *Louis 'David' Riel Prophet of the New World*. Toronto: University of Toronto Press, 1996.

Forsberg, Carl. *Counterinsurgency in Kandahar: Evaluating the 2010 Hamkari Campaign*. Washington, D.C.: Institute for the Study of War, 2010.

Fowler, Michelle. "'For Extraordinary Heroism and Outstanding Performance': Kap'yong, 2nd Battalion Princess Patricia's Light Infantry and the Controversy Surrounding the Presidential Citation." *Canadian Military History* 13, no. 4 (2004).

Fowler, T. Robert. *Combat Mission Kandahar: The Canadian Experience in Afghanistan*. Toronto: Dundurn Press, 2016.

Fraser, Major-General David. *Operation Medusa: The Furious Battle That Saved Afghanistan from the Taliban*. Toronto: McClelland & Stewart, 2018.

Granatstein, J.L. *Canada's Army: Waging War and Keeping the Peace*. 3rd ed. Toronto: University of Toronto Press, 2021.

Granatstein, J.L., and Dean F. Oliver. "The Canadian Home Front in the First and Second World Wars." *Canadian Military History* 21, no. 4 (Autumn 2012).

Greenhous, Brereton. *Guarding the Goldfields: The Story of the Yukon Field Force*. Toronto: Dundurn Press, 1996.

Greenhous, Brereton, et al. *The Crucible of War 1939–1945: The Official History of the Royal Canadian Air Force*, Volume III. Toronto: University of Toronto Press, 1994.

Gullachsen, Arthur W. *An Army of Never-Ending Strength: Reinforcing the Canadians in Northwest Europe, 1944–1945*. Vancouver: UBC Press, 2021.

Hamon, M. Max. *The Audacity of His Enterprise: Louis Riel and the Métis Nation That Canada Never Was, 1840–1875*. Montreal: McGill-Queen's University Press, 2019.

Hatch, F.J. *Aerodrome of Democracy: Canada and the British Commonwealth Air Training Plan, 1939–1945*. Ottawa: Directorate of History and Heritage, 1983.

Hillmer, Norman, and J.L. Granatstein. *Empire to Umpire: Canada and the World to the 1990s*. Toronto: Irwin Publishing, 2000.

Humphries, Mark Osborne. "The Best Laid Plans: Sir Arthur Currie's First Operations as Corps Commander." In *Capturing Hill 70: Canada's Forgotten Battle of the First World War*, edited by Douglas E. Delaney and Serge Marc Durflinger , 78–101. Vancouver: UBC Press, 2016.

———. *A Weary Road: Shell Shock in the Canadian Expeditionary Force, 1914–1918*. Toronto: University of Toronto Press, 2018.

Huyshe, Captain G.L. *The Red River Expedition*. London and New York: Macmillan, 1871.

Isitt, Benjamin. *From Victoria to Vladivostok: Canada's Siberian Expedition, 1917–1919*. Vancouver: University of British Columbia Press, 2010.

Johnston, William, et al. *The Seabound Coast: The Official History of the Royal Canadian Navy, 1867–1939*, Volume I. Toronto: Dundurn Press, 2011.

Keelan, Geoff. *Duty to Dissent: Henri Bourassa and the First World War.* Vancouver: UBC Press, 2020.

———. "For King or Country? Quebec, the Empire and the First World War." In *Fighting with the Empire: Canada, Britain, and Global Conflict, 1867–1947,* edited by Steve Marti and William Pratt. Vancouver: UBC Press, 2019.

Keshen, Jeffrey A. *Saints, Sinners, and Soldiers: Canada's Second World War.* Vancouver: UBC Press, 2004.

Kordan, Bohdan S. "First World War Internment in Canada: Enemy Aliens and the Blurring of the Military/Civilian Distinction." *Canadian Military History* 29, no. 2 (2020).

Lane, Andrea. "Women in the Canadian Armed Forces." In *Canadian Defence Policy in Theory and Practice,* edited by Thomas Juneau, Philippe Lagassé, and Srdjan Vucetic, 355–57. New York: Springer International, 2020.

Leprince, Caroline. "The Canadian-Led Kandahar Provincial Reconstruction Team: A Success Story?" *International Journal* 68, no. 2 (2013): 359–77.

Lloyd, Nick. *Passchendaele: A New History.* London: Viking, 2017.

MacLaren, Roy. *Canadians on the Nile, 1882–1898: Being the Adventures of the Voyageurs on the Khartoum Relief Expedition and Other Exploits.* Vancouver: UBC Press, 1978.

Maloney, Sean. *Canada and UN Peacekeeping: Cold War by Other Means, 1945–1970.* St. Catharines, ON: Vanwell Publishing, 2002.

———. "Counter-Insurgency Versus 'COIN' in Bazaar-e Panjwayi and Panjwayi District, 2008–2010." In *No Easy Task: Fighting in Afghanistan,* edited by Bernd Horn and Emily Spencer. Toronto: Dundurn Press, 2012.

———. "Maple Leaf Over the Caribbean: Gunboat Diplomacy Canadian Style?" In *Canadian Gunboat Diplomacy: The Canadian Navy and Foreign Policy,* edited by Ann Griffiths, Richard Gimblett, and Peter Haydon. Halifax: Centre for Foreign Policy Studies, 2000.

———. "'Was It Worth It?' Canadian Intervention in Afghanistan and Perceptions of Success or Failure." *Canadian Military Journal* 14, no. 1 (Winter 2013): 19–31.

Massie, Justin. "Why Canada Goes to War: Explaining Combat Participation in US-Led Coalitions." *Canadian Journal of Political Science* 52, no. 3 (2019).

McAndrew, William. "Canadian Defence Planning Between the Wars: The Royal Canadian Air Force Comes of Age." *Canadian Military History* 22, no. 1 (Winter 2013).

McCullough, Colin. *Creating Canada's Peacekeeping Past.* Vancouver: UBC Press, 2016.

Mclean, Major R.C. "Equal but Unfair: The Failure of Gender Integration in the Canadian Armed Forces." Master's dissertation, Canadian Forces College, 2017.

McNaught, Siobhan J. "The Rise of Proto-Nationalism: Sir Wilfrid Laurier and the Founding of the Naval Service of Canada, 1902–1910." In *A Nation's Navy: In Quest of Canadian Naval Identity*, edited by Michael L. Hadley. Montreal: McGill-Queen's University Press, 1996.

Michel, Anthony P. "To Represent the Country in Egypt: Aboriginality, Britishness, Anglophone Canadian Identities and the Nile Voyageur Contingent." *Histoire sociale* 39, no. 77 (Spring 2006).

Miller, Carman. "The Montreal Flag Riot of 1900." In *One Flag, One Queen, One Tongue: New Zealand, the British Empire, and the South African War, 1899–1902*, edited by John Crawford and Ian McGibbon, 165–79. Auckland, NZ: Auckland University Press, 2003.

——. *Painting the Map Red: Canada and the South African War, 1899–1902*. Montreal: McGill-Queen's University Press, 1993.

Millman, Brock. *Polarity, Patriotism, and Dissent in Great War Canada*. Toronto: University of Toronto Press, 2020.

Milner, Marc. *Canada's Navy: The First Century*. Toronto: University of Toronto Press, 2010.

——. *North Atlantic Run: The Royal Canadian Navy and the Battle for the Convoys*. Toronto: University of Toronto Press, 1985.

——. *Stopping the Panzers: The Untold Story of D-Day*. Lawrence, KS: University of Kansas Press, 2014.

Morton, Desmond. *A Military History of Canada: From Champlain to Kosovo*. 4th ed. Toronto: McClelland & Stewart, 1999.

Morton, Desmond, and Glenn Wright. *Winning the Second Battle: Canadian Veterans and the Return to Civilian Life, 1915–1930*. Toronto: University of Toronto Press, 1987.

Nicholson, G.W.L. *Canadian Expeditionary Force, 1914–1919*. Ottawa: Queen's Printer and Controller of Stationery, 1964.

Nolan, Brian. *Hero: The Buzz Beurling Story*. Toronto: Lester & Orpen Dennys, 1981.

O'Keefe, David. *One Day in August: The Untold Story Behind Canada's Tragedy at Dieppe*. Toronto: Vintage Press, 2013.

Paris, Roland. "The Truth About Canada's Mission in Afghanistan." *Policy Options*, March 2014, cips-cepi.ca/how-canada-failed-in-afghanistan.

Poulin, Carmen, Lynne Gouliquer, and Jennifer Moore. "Discharged for Homosexuality from the Canadian Military: Health Implications for Lesbians." *Feminism and Psychology* 19, no. 4 (2009).

Quiney, Linda J. "Gendering Patriotism: Canadian Volunteer Nurses as the Female 'Soldiers' of the Great War." In *A Sisterhood of Suffering and Service: Women and Girls of Canada and Newfoundland During the First World War*, edited by Sarah Glassford and Amy Shaw, 103–25. Vancouver: UBC Press, 2012.

Rawling, Bill. *Surviving Trench Warfare: Technology and the Canadian Corps, 1914–1918.* Toronto: University of Toronto Press, 1992.

Reid, Jennifer. *Louis Riel and the Creation of Modern Canada: Mythic Discourse and the Postcolonial State.* Winnipeg: University of Manitoba Press, 2012.

Richter, Andrew. "The Liberal Government and Canadian Defence Policy: Three Critical Issues." *Journal of Military and Strategic Studies* 19, no. 1 (2019): 64–100.

Robertson, Scot. "In the Shadow of Death by Moonlight." In *The Valour and the Horror Revisited*, edited by David Bercuson and S.F. Wise. Montreal: McGill-Queen's University Press, 1994.

Ruck, Calvin W. *Canada's Black Battalion: No. 2 Construction 1916–1920.* Halifax: The Society for the Protection and Preservation of Black Culture in Nova Scotia, 1986.

Schreiber, Shane. *Shock Army of the British Empire: The Canadian Corps in the Last 100 Days of the Great War.* Westport, CT: Praeger, 1997.

Sheffield, Gary. *The Chief: Douglas Haig and the British Army.* London: Aurum Press, 2012.

Sheffield, R. Scott. "'Of Pure European Descent and of the White Race': Recruitment Policy and Aboriginal Canadians, 1939–1945." *Canadian Military History* 5, no. 1 (Spring 1996): 8–15.

———. *The Red Man's on the Warpath: The Image of the "Indian" and the Second World War.* Vancouver: UBC Press, 2004.

Spooner, Kevin A. *Canada, the Congo Crisis, and UN Peacekeeping, 1960–1964.* Vancouver: UBC Press, 2009.

St. Louis, Lieutenant-Colonel Michel-Henri. "The Strategic Advisory Team in Afghanistan: Part of the Canadian Comprehensive Approach to Stability Operations." *Canadian Military Journal* 9, no. 3 (2009): 58–67.

Stacey, C.P. "Canada and the Nile Expedition of 1884–1885." *Canadian Historical Review* 33, no. 4 (December 1952).

———. *Records of the Nile Voyageurs, 1884–1884: The Canadian Voyageur Contingent in the Gordon Relief Expedition.* Toronto: Champlain Society, 2013.

Stacey, C.P., and E. Pye. "Canadian Voyageurs in the Sudan, 1884–1885." *Canadian Army Journal* 5 (1951).

Stanger-Ross, Jordan, ed. *Landscapes of Injustice: A New Perspective on the Internment and Dispossession of Japanese Canadians.* Montreal: McGill-Queen's University Press, 2020.

Stanley, George. *Louis Riel.* Toronto: Ryerson Press, 1963.

Stonechild, Blair, and Bill Waiser. *Loyal Till Death: Indians and the North-West Rebellion.* Markham, ON: Fifth House Publishing, 1997.

Story, Donald C., and Russell Isinger. "The Origins of the Cancellation of Canada's Avro CF-105 Arrow Fighter Program: A Failure of Strategy." *Journal of Strategic Studies* 30, no. 6 (2007): 1025–50.

Teigrob, Robert. *Four Days in Hitler's Germany: Mackenzie King's Mission to Avert a Second World War.* Toronto: University of Toronto Press, 2019.

Van Heyningen, Elizabeth. *The Concentration Camps of the Anglo-Boer War: A Social History.* Johannesburg, South Africa: Jacana Media, 2013.

Winegard, Timothy C. *For King and Kanata: Canadian Indians and the First World War.* Winnipeg: University of Manitoba Press, 2012.

IMAGE CREDITS

10   Courtesy of Missisquoi Historical Society, Stanbridge East, Quebec.

15   Courtesy of Provincial Archives of Saskatchewan, Regina.

18   Courtesy of Archives of Manitoba, Winnipeg.

20-21 From G.L. Huyshe, *The Red River Expedition*, 1871.

26   Courtesy of McCord Stewart Museum, Montreal.

29   Courtesy of Canadian Plains Research Centre Mapping Division, adapted from *Atlas of Saskatchewan*, 1999, courtesy of University of Regina Press.

31   Courtesy of McCord Stewart Museum, Montreal.

33   Unknown.

36   Photograph by James Peters. Courtesy of Provincial Archives of Saskatchewan, Regina.

37   Courtesy of McCord Stewart Museum, Montreal.

41   Unknown.

43   From the 1885 book *Gordon and the Mahdi: An Illustrated Narrative of the War in the Soudan*.

45   Photograph by Major James Matthews.

46   Unknown. Wikimedia, upload.wikimedia.org/wikipedia/commons /thumb/5/54/SouthAfrica1885.svg/2445px-SouthAfrica1885.svg.png.

47   Photograph by William James Topley.

48   Courtesy of Canadian War Museum, Ottawa.

50   From *The Great Boer War* by Arthur Conan Doyle, 1901.

51   Courtesy of National Army Museum, London, England.

54 (top & bottom) Courtesy of Canadian War Museum, Ottawa.

56   Unknown.

59   Unknown.

61 (top) Photograph by George Grantham Bain.

61 (bottom) Photograph by Major James Matthews.

66   Courtesy of Library and Archives Canada, Ottawa, 3622973.

68   Courtesy of Library and Archives Canada, Ottawa, 3394622.

70   Courtesy of Canadian War Museum, Ottawa.

71   Courtesy of Library and Archives Canada, Ottawa, 3195178.

76   Courtesy of Seaforth Highlanders of Canada Museum & Archives, Vancouver, item no. 1461.

77   Courtesy of Seaforth Highlanders of Canada Museum & Archives, Vancouver, item no 1285.

78   Courtesy of Library and Archives Canada, Ottawa, 3213524.

84   Courtesy of Seaforth Highlanders of Canada Museum & Archives, Vancouver, item no. 0684.

88   Courtesy of Library and Archives Canada, Ottawa, 3550154.

92   Courtesy of Library and Archives Canada, Ottawa, 3404878.

93   Courtesy of Library and Archives Canada, Ottawa, 3357570.

94   Courtesy of Seaforth Highlanders of Canada Museum & Archives, Vancouver, item no. 1351.

99   Courtesy of Library and Archives Canada, Ottawa, 3193206.

101   Courtesy of Library and Archives Canada, Ottawa, 3396798.

102   Courtesy of Library and Archives Canada, Ottawa, 3192219.

104   Courtesy of Seaforth Highlanders of Canada Museum & Archives, Vancouver, item no. 1612.

105   Courtesy of Library and Archives Canada, Ottawa, 3397846.

106   Courtesy of Nikkei National Museum & Cultural Centre, Burnaby, British Columbia.

107   Courtesy of Library and Archives Canada, Ottawa, 3397868.

108   Courtesy of Seaforth Highlanders of Canada Museum & Archives, Vancouver, item no. 2255.

111   Unknown. Historica, historica.fandom.com/wiki/Spring_Offensive?file=Spring_Offensive.jpeg.

114   Courtesy of Library and Archives Canada, Ottawa, 3622970.

115	Courtesy of Seaforth Highlanders of Canada Museum & Archives, Vancouver, item no. 3360.
116	George Metcalf Archival Collection, Canadian War Museum, Ottawa.
118	Courtesy of Seaforth Highlanders of Canada Museum & Archives, Vancouver, item no. 3392.
121	Library and Archives Canada, Ottawa, 3642873.
126	Courtesy of Library and Archives Canada, Ottawa, 3615116.
130	Courtesy of Library and Archives Canada, Ottawa, 4930589.
132	Courtesy of University of Calgary Digital Collections.
133	Courtesy of Library and Archives Canada, Ottawa, 3365730.
135	Courtesy of Library and Archives Canada, Ottawa, 3401124.
141	National Film Board of Canada/Department of National Defence/Library and Archives Canada, Ottawa, PA-136047.
143	Courtesy of Library and Archives Canada, Ottawa, 3228792.
144	Courtesy of Library and Archives Canada, Ottawa, 3617924.
148	Courtesy of Library and Archives Canada, Ottawa, 3195155.
150	Courtesy of Library and Archives Canada, Ottawa, 3194308.
151	Courtesy of Library and Archives Canada, Ottawa, 3203514.
152	Lieutenant Tanner, No. 5 Army Film and Photographic Unit.
153	Map by Dennis Richards, HMSO, London.
156	Unknown.
158	Unknown.
161	Courtesy of Library and Archives Canada, Ottawa, 3209599.
162	Unknown.
164	Courtesy of Library and Archives Canada, Ottawa, 3662049.
165	Courtesy of Library and Archives Canada, Ottawa, 3644108.
167	Courtesy of Library and Archives Canada, Ottawa, 4814396.
168	Photograph by Lyonde Studio.
172	Dowd J (Fg Off), Royal Air Force official photographer.
175	Courtesy of MONOVA: Museum & Archives of North Vancouver, inventory no. 12384.
176	Courtesy of Library and Archives Canada, Ottawa, 3193621.
178	Photograph by Captain Frank Boyd. Courtesy of Library and Archives Canada, Ottawa, 3381922.
183	Photograph by Tak Toyota. Courtesy of Library and Archives Canada, Ottawa, 3379268.
189	Courtesy of Juno Beach Centre, Courseulles-sur-Mer, France.
190	Courtesy of Seaforth Highlanders of Canada Museum & Archives,

Vancouver, item no. 030.

191   Photograph by Dale Dunlop.

192   Courtesy of Seaforth Highlanders of Canada Museum & Archives, Vancouver, item no, 032.

195   Photograph by Lieutenant Jack Smith. Courtesy of Library and Archives Canada, Ottawa, 3599873.

198   Courtesy of Library and Archives Canada, Ottawa, 4113916.

200   Photograph by United States Army Air Forces. Courtesy of National WW2 Museum, New Orleans, Louisiana.

202   Courtesy of United States Military Academy Department of History, West Point, New York.

208   Courtesy of United States Military Academy Department of History, West Point, New York.

210   Courtesy of United States National Archives and Records Administration, College Park, Maryland.

211   Photograph by Ken Bell. Courtesy of Library and Archives Canada, Ottawa, 3403235.

212   Photograph by Lieutenant H. Gordon Aikman. Courtesy of Library and Archives Canada, Ottawa, 3396123.

218   John Wyatt Greenlee of Surprised Eel Maps.

219   Courtesy of Canadian War Museum, Ottawa.

220   Photograph by Lieutenant Harold G. Aikman. commons.wikimedia.org/wiki/File:4th_Canadian_Armoured_Division_flamethrower_demonstration_across_canal_Balgerhoeke_Belgium_October_1944.jpg.

221   Photograph by Donald Grant. Courtesy of Library and Archives Canada, Ottawa, 3623235.

222   Photograph by Willem van de Poll. Courtesy of National Archives of the Netherlands, The Hague.

225   Courtesy of United States Military Academy Department of History, West Point, New York.

227   Courtesy of Canadian War Museum, Ottawa.

230   Courtesy of Library and Archives Canada, Ottawa, 3661954.

237   Courtesy of Naval History and Heritage Command, Washington, D.C., 80-G-642748.

238   John Wyatt Greenlee of Surprised Eel Maps.

242   Photograph by Bill Olson. Courtesy of Library and Archives Canada, Ottawa, 3397764.

244   Courtesy of Library and Archives Canada, Ottawa, 4482404.

250 Photograph by J.R. Marwick. Courtesy of Library and Archives Canada, Ottawa, 3237479.

251 Courtesy of Library and Archives Canada, Ottawa, 3397765.

252 Unknown.

256 U.S. Navy National Museum of Naval Aviation photo No. 1996.488.037.050.

260 Courtesy of Canadian War Museum, Ottawa.

261 Photograph by W.H. Cole. Courtesy of Library and Archives Canada, Ottawa, 4117928.

264 Courtesy of Library and Archives Canada, Ottawa, 4235671.

267 Courtesy of Library and Archives Canada, Ottawa, 4235917.

275 Courtesy of Library and Archives Canada, Ottawa, 5301259.

278 Courtesy of Library and Archives Canada, Ottawa, 3604003.

286 Photograph by Corporal Duchesne-Beaulieu. Courtesy of Department of National Defence.

291 Photograph by Kristopher Wilson. Courtesy of Department of National Defence, Ottawa.

292 Courtesy of Department of National Defence, Ottawa.

294 John Wyatt Greenlee of Surprised Eel Maps.

296 Photograph by Jason Ransom. Courtesy of Library and Archives Canada, Ottawa, 5543256.

297 Photograph by U.S. Air Force Technical Sergeant Efren Lopez. Courtesy of Air University, Maxwell Air Force Base, Alabama.

299 Photograph by Specialist Keith D. Henning, U.S. Army.

300 Photograph by Master Corporal Yves Genus. Courtesy of Department of National Defence, Ottawa.

302 Courtesy of Department of National Defence, Ottawa.

304 Photograph by Captain Adam Thomson. Courtesy of Department of National Defence, Ottawa.

306 Photograph by Master Corporal Angela Abbey. Courtesy of Department of National Defence, Ottawa.

310 Photograph by Corporal Mathieu St-Amour. Courtesy of Department of National Defence, Ottawa.

INDEX

U.S. Presidential Unit Citation, 243, 351

Victoria Crosses, 52–53, 56, 67, 69, 73, 81, 95, 109, 113, 140, 148, 159–60, 168, 215, 226, 298

voyageurs and, 4, 18, 40, *41*, 42, *43*

War Measures Act (1914), 85–87, 270

Washington Treaty (1921), 133

White Paper on Defence, 268

Canadian Armed Forces (CAF), 269–79, 281–85, *286*, 287, *291*, 292–93, *294*, 295, *296*, *297*, 298, *299*, *300*, 301, *302*, 303–5, *306*, 307–20

assistance in Ukraine of, 312

Brown v. the Canadian Armed Forces and, 285

budget cuts under Brian Mulroney of, 274

budget cuts under Jean Chrétien of, 275–76

budget cuts under Justin Trudeau of, 314

budget cuts under Stephen Harper of, 313–14

budget increases under Pierre Trudeau of, 272

Canadian Forces Administrative Orders (CFAO) 49-14 and 49-15, 284

"civilianization" of, 271–72, 317

combat missions against ISIS of, 312

Covid-19 and, 312, 314, 319

diversification in, 283–85, *286*, 287, 313, 318

LGBTQ2S+, 285, *286*, 287

"Strong, Secure, and Engaged," 313

women, 283–85, 318

end of Canadian involvement in Afghanistan, 309, 311

extension of Canadian role in Afghanistan, 304–5

future roles of, 318–20

involvement in mission in former Yugoslavia, 276–78

Kanehsatà:ke Resistance ("Oka Crisis") and, 274, *275*

Mobile Command of, 269

recent activities of, 312

recent activities in Middle East of, 312, 318

reforms under Maurice Baril of, 282–83

reinstatement of royal designations in, 313

scandals in, 282, 312–13, 318

Service Women in Non-Traditional Environments and Roles (SWINTER), 285

sexually hostile culture, 312–13, 318

See also Canadian Army

Canadian Army, 5–6, 56, 140, 233–34, 239. 248, 266, 268–69, 279

Canadian Forces Reorganization Act (1968), 269

Non-Permanent Militia (NPM), 24–25, 38, 44, 130, 315–16

Permanent Force, 23–24, 29–30, 38–39, 44, 52, 57–59, 68, 130–31, 136, 239, 315–16

reduction under Pierre Trudeau of, 269

renamed Mobile Command as part of Canadian Armed Forces, 269

unification of services, 268–69

See also Canadian Armed Forces (CAF)

Canadian Military Formations

1 Air Division, 255

I Canadian Corps, 184, 198, 203–5, 228–29, 241, 246, 257

1 (RCAF) Squadron, 163, *164*